D1234416

Behind the Big House

HUMANITIES AND PUBLIC LIFE

A Collaboration with the University of Iowa Obermann Center for Advanced Studies

Teresa Mangum and Anne Valk, series editors

Behind the Big House

Reconciling Slavery, Race, and Heritage in the U.S. South

Jodi Skipper

University
of Iowa Press
Iowa City

University of Iowa Press, Iowa City 52242
Copyright © 2022 by the University of Iowa Press
www.uipress.uiowa.edu

Printed in the United States of America

Design by Omega Clay

Printed on acid-free paper

Library of Congress Cataloging-in-Publication Data
Names: Skipper, Jodi, author.
Title: Behind the Big House: Reconciling Slavery, Race, and Heritage in
    the U.S. South / Jodi Skipper.
Other titles: Reconciling Slavery, Race, and Heritage in the U.S. South
Description: Iowa City: University of Iowa Press, [2022] | Series:
    Humanities and Public Life | Includes bibliographical references and
    index.
Identifiers: LCCN 2021028040 (print) | LCCN 2021028041 (ebook) | ISBN
    9781609388171 (paperback) | ISBN 9781609388188 (ebook)
Subjects: LCSH: Historic sites—Mississippi—Educational aspects. | African
    Americans—Mississippi—History—Study and teaching. |
    Plantations—Mississippi—History—Study and teaching. |
    Slavery—Mississippi—History—Study and teaching. | Behind the Big
    House (Program) | Heritage tourism—Mississippi. | Skipper, Jodi. |
    University of Mississippi—Faculty—Biography. | Mississippi—Race
    relations. | Holly Springs (Miss.)
Classification: LCC F34.S655 2022 (print) | LCC F341 (ebook) | DDC
    305.8009762—dc23/eng/20211007
LC record available at https://lccn.loc.gov/2021028040
LC ebook record available at https://lccn.loc.gov/2021028041

Photos on pages 63, 66, 71, and 123 were taken by the author.
Sankofa bird illustration used in book © Reynolds/stock.adobe.com

For those whose names we don't yet know and whose stories are yet to be told
For David, who is now among the ancestors

Contents

Foreword   by Anne Valk and Teresa Mangum

In November 2020, more than 70 percent of voters in Mississippi approved a redesign of the state's flag. The new flag featured a magnolia blossom and retired the state's long-contentious flag with a Confederate battle flag forming its canton. The 2020 vote represented a surprising reversal. Even though African American residents make up about 40 percent of Mississippi's population, a higher proportion than any other state in the country, the white majority had roundly opposed previous attempts to change the flag, a symbol closely associated with white supremacy. This white majority has also pushed the state to the political right, supporting a conservative agenda on social and economic issues. In fact, the flag decision came at the same time that white voters in the state overwhelmingly supported the reelection of Donald Trump, whose campaign hinged on overt race-baiting and insinuations that reassured white voters of his commitment to policies that would ensure white supremacy if not a white majority. Thus, the overwhelming support for changing the flag seemed out of step with the prevalent politics in Mississippi, except for the fact that the 2020 election took place during a jarring year of social and political unrest.

Activists across the country rallied to protest real and symbolic violence against African Americans. Throughout a brutal summer, crowds denounced cops (and those acting in their name) who abused and even killed African American citizens without provocation and with little accountability. Like protesters in Charlottesville, Virginia, three summers earlier, anti-racist activists in 2020 connected present-day violence with public commemorations of slavery. Toppling monuments to Confederate leaders and slaveholders, activists linked historical narratives that honored such men as heroes to contemporary acts, including police violence. Protesters argued that these cultural images were a daily, visible manifestation of systemic racism and the dehumanization of African Americans. Symbols matter. And symbols that glorify white supremacy and those who fought to maintain it do more than assert a singular understanding of the past. They also convey public values in the present. In the case of a state flag—or monuments, street names, and names of buildings at a public university—those symbols are backed by the power of the state.

Jodi Skipper's new book, *Behind the Big House: Reconciling Slavery, Race, and Heritage in the U.S. South*, helps contextualize the Mississippi electorate's decision about the flag. Blending theory and history, pedagogy and personal experience, the book reminds us that when members of a community decide to recast local history in new ways and for new purposes, they can also lay the groundwork for changes on a larger scale. Skipper assesses efforts by southerners, including herself, to transform how the region presents its history and celebrates its cultural heritage.

Looking at heritage tourism in Mississippi, Skipper discusses two specific initiatives in which she participated. An annual series of tours, the Behind the Big House program, offers visitors access to private homes with outbuildings where enslaved people used to live. These tours make visible the important presence of enslaved people in the operations of white families and the essential contributions that these enslaved workers made to white wealth. The second initiative, Gracing the Table, organizes public conversations that are intended to encourage racial reconciliation. The programs ground dialogue about present-day inequalities in a shared exploration of history. Going beyond the symbolism of the flag, these projects aim to transform historical narratives and create more complicated and inclusive understandings of the past that can reshape the present and the future. Skipper describes her own support for these programs and the ways that she has involved students and others from the University of Mississippi who contribute to and learn from these initiatives.

Moving from the personal to the political and from the emotional to the intellectual, Skipper seeks to understand the factors that cause individuals to get involved in public history and racial reconciliation efforts. She also confronts the limitations of such initiatives to generate cultural change. In fact, part of the power of the book is that while Skipper never avoids the personal and political difficulties that she and other cultural workers encounter, *Behind the Big House* is imbued with optimism about the benefits that such efforts can bring participants. In particular, Skipper highlights the positive effects for African American southerners who had always felt excluded from the histories promoted by historic sites and heritage programs. White Americans open to more honest accounts of their local history also benefit from greater awareness of, as well as accountability for, their intersectional identities and genealogies.

At the same time, Skipper's optimism is tempered by her critical assessment of the larger impact of these efforts to restore suppressed histories. As she shows, historical narratives are stubborn, more easily added to than overturned. Efforts, such as Behind the Big House and Gracing the Table, introduce more inclusive histories and offer individuals a chance to connect to the past in a more realistic way. But these efforts are often unable to shift popular understandings of history, and such work is often plagued by insufficient funds and the struggle to reach beyond a core group of volunteers and participants. In the realm of heritage tourism, these challenges are compounded by politics and economics. Too often, white Americans are perceived as the most desirable customer market and African Americans, if they are represented at all, appear as service workers whose labor sustains the hotels and restaurants that make tourism possible. Behind the Big House tours ask visitors to look beyond elegant china and furnishings, lush gardens and grounds to the enslaved people on whose labor that world relied. These tours make visible not only the stories of those enslaved people but the continued, silent violence represented by their absence. Restoring that past is one step toward addressing present-day inequities. And the hard yet compassionate conversations that take place at Gracing the Table events offer one possible path not only to reconciliation but to change.

We are very pleased to add *Behind the Big House* to the Humanities and Public Life series. Like the authors of other books in the series, Skipper brings a multidisciplinary approach to her public scholarship. Her approach links community members with her students in courses in historical archaeology, African American studies, and southern studies. Her work offers hope that local communities and higher education can draw upon the humanities to respond to the political urgency of the current moment when inequalities and injustices have been amplified after more than a year of COVID-19, unemployment, and violence.

Skipper also offers a timely examination of some of the crises and challenges facing higher education. Speaking bravely from her position as a tenured scholar of color at Mississippi's flagship public university, she lays bare both the opportunities and the costs for scholars involved with publicly engaged projects. She details how the investment of time, expertise, and labor in community history and publicly engaged scholarly projects can lead to meaningful work and community connections that can sustain scholars throughout their careers. But she also points to many contradictions between universities' professed values and the institutional policies and structures that shape the professional advancement of faculty, staff, and students.

Public historians, publicly engaged scholars and teachers, higher education administrators, and others with an interest in creating more just institutions will benefit from Skipper's many insights into the joys and struggles involved in projects like Behind the Big House and Gracing the Table. As America's structural inequalities continue to be laid bare, we hope that more people will feel called to undertake this work and to join Skipper in honest reflection about the ways that public institutions must change to build a more equitable future.

Acknowledgments

To my Holly Springs support system: I begin by acknowledging Jenifer Eggleston and Chelius Carter, without whom there would be no *Behind the Big House*. Thanks for your bravery and willingness to prioritize what you think is the right thing to do for the whole, rather than what feels good or gets you credit. Thanks to David Person for always seeing the slavery interpretation work in Holly Springs through the lens of what it can be and not what it is. Thanks to Rkhty and Wayne Jones for consistently remembering and honoring our ancestors and to Alisea Williams McLeod for the constant reminder that we have the historical tools to do that. We just need to look for them. Thank you, Deb Davis, for finding us and for blessing us with your energy and spirit. Your support, as a direct descendant, affirms our work. Thanks to Linear and Al Patton for your support and constant encouragement. Thanks to Linda Turner for keeping the program going with a steady stream of students and sustained support that upholds the work that we do. Thanks to Mitch Robinson, who used his time at Strawberry Plains to seal the connections between land and people, past and present. You have a bright future as a southern studies scholar ahead of you.

Gwen Wyatt and Alexa Ashmead are the epitome of what you want in community collaborators: people who love to talk about history and who are open to the beauty that knowing historical truths can bring to the present. I look forward to the work that we can continue to do together. Thanks to Harvey Payne for seeing both the value in historically preserving slave dwellings and their potential as teaching tools. Thanks, also, for being so willing to open your new home in such early stages of repair. Thanks to Michael Lawshea for keeping us on schedule at Burton Place—we know when to begin but ending is always an issue. Thanks to Phillip Knecht for making your research so accessible. It's been invaluable to this book project. And thanks for sharing the photograph that you took of the glass plate image of Walter Place.

To my Oxford support system: I've been privileged to have colleagues who are unselfish with their time, even when they have too much to do. Thanks to Carolyn Freiwald for visiting Holly Springs and never leaving. I didn't expect a colleague to come along and relieve so much of our heavy load, but you did. Thanks to Shennette Garrett-Scott for encouraging your students to participate in Behind the Big House, for showing them how to create our curriculum guide, and for being a full participant in so many of our events. Thanks for continuing to show up. Thanks too to Rhondalyn Peairs for always thinking through why cultural heritage tourism should be a priority in Mississippi and for putting so much energy into proving that and to Beth Kruse for being such a willing participant and accomplice and for reminding me why we, as faculty, need to model public history work for students. Thanks to David Wharton for the enthusiasm that you brought to photographing Burton Place descendants. Coming to you with that request was a big ask but didn't feel like it because you are so passionate about what you do.

To White accomplices Michele Coffey, Jessie Wilkerson, JT Thomas, and Garrett Felber who do anti-racist work at great personal risks. Thank you.

To those who've read parts of or all of this manuscript: Mohan Ambikaipaker, Lisa Aubrey, Chelius Carter, Michele Coffey, Jenifer Eggleston, Maria Franklin, Celeste Henery, Jeff Jackson, Rkhty and Wayne Jones, Lidia Marte, and Amy McDowell. Thanks for your time, and thanks for your candor. A special thanks to Celeste Henery for helping me think through what it means to put practice on paper.

Thanks to the Whiting Foundation for valuing public humanists and their work and for putting the necessary resources behind that support, and thanks to Teresa Mangum and Annie Valk for creating an academic series that allows our voices to be heard.

Special thanks to Jim Moore and the Marshall County Historical Museum and Gus Smith III for sharing photographs from his grandmother Chesley Thorne Smith's collection.

Special thanks to John Douglas for graciously giving me the space and support to do this work. You make things a lot easier.

Finally, to my University of Mississippi Sistah Doctors: Deirdre Cooper Owens, Barbara Combs, Latoya Brooks-Key, Willa Johnson, Al Steele, Mikki Harris, Zandria Robinson, and Michèle Alexandre. Many of you have left but, because of all of you, I feel a little less lonely.

Introduction

I am a researcher, educator, and native of the U.S. South who understands that working in the region presents unique challenges to academics of color who often have little awareness of the particularities that dominate their local research and teaching places. In this book, I think through both the ways that place affects the activist academic's engagement in research practices and collaborative relationships and the academic risks and challenges that arise in the merging of scholarship and activism. I share my experiences as someone who identifies as Black, who grew up in the South, and who directly engages the intersection of race and region with historical memory.

Two experiences frame this narrative: my role as a faculty member at the University of Mississippi and my work with individuals and institutions seeking to challenge Confederate ideologies on the Mississippi landscape. At a time when debates about Confederate imagery on the U.S. landscape and the roles of historic plantations as potential sites of resistance are the most visible they have been at any time in U.S. history, we must examine the realities of academics of color who through their teaching and research continuously confront White southern nostalgia and its major effects on their lives. It is also imperative that we understand the lived experiences of those scholars from their perspectives as universities attempt to understand issues in faculty equity and draw on the expertise of Black, Indigenous, and other people of color to offer support in this moment when the impacts of racist policing and surveillance seem to be more visible to White publics.

I began to feel those impacts as soon as I arrived in Oxford, Mississippi, in 2011. That same year, a publication by Florida State University researchers, who found that exposure to images of the Confederate flag increases the expression of negative attitudes toward African Americans among Whites, helped frame an argument in the *State of Louisiana v. Felton D.*

Dorsey case for appeal in Caddo Parish.[1] In 2009 Dorsey, a Black man, had been convicted and sentenced to death for the murder of a White firefighter, Joe Prock, during a home invasion in 2006. His jury consisted of eleven White people and one Black peer in a parish with a population that was nearly 50 percent Black. The prosecution struck one Black man, Carl Staples, from the jury because he expressed discomfort about serving in the presence of the flag of the Confederacy outside the courthouse. The flag flew on a Confederate monument featuring a Confederate soldier and the busts of Generals Lee and Jackson, Beauregard and Allen.[2] In 2011, on appeal, Dorsey argued that the flag memorial introduced race as a factor in the case, reminding "all persons who approach the courthouse of an era when lynching and enslavement of blacks was permitted by law."[3] The Louisiana Supreme Court upheld the death penalty sentence, stating that Dorsey "failed to raise an objection regarding the confederate flag memorial in the district court" and that he "also failed to show the memorial creates an environment giving rise to a constitutionally significant and unacceptable risk that one or more of the jurors in his case acted with discriminatory intent in returning his or her verdict."[4]

Dorsey's legal team might not have been able to prove that the memorial's presence intimidated Black jurors from serving and provoked White jurors into finding Black defendants guilty, but the potential impacts of its presence alone were duly noted. In 2011, an American Civil Liberties Union amicus curiae brief in support of a new trial for Dorsey concluded that "prominently displayed in front of the Caddo Parish courthouse, the Confederate flag represents for many people, and particularly for African-Americans, public entrenchment of racism in the parish's judicial system and an endorsement of historical efforts to deny African-Americans equality under the law. The flag, as a public symbol of racial bias, poses an intolerable risk that capital punishment cannot be fairly administered within the courthouse walls."[5]

I heard about the Dorsey case shortly after I accepted a joint appointment in the Department of Sociology and Anthropology and the Center for the Study of Southern Culture at the University of Mississippi, a university highly publicized for its Confederate symbolism located in the only U.S. state, at the time, with a flag incorporating a battle flag of the Confederacy. I grew up in southern Louisiana and continued my education in Florida and Texas while periodically working in North Carolina, South Carolina, Mississippi, and Georgia. I was no stranger to the South, yet this blatant affirmation of the Confederacy by way of a prominent and seemingly ubiquitous public symbol caused me to reflect on and rethink my many years of living, researching, and teaching in the South. I was elated when someone argued that public symbols of a racist White southern heritage are directly related to structural racial biases, often in states whose senses of racial injustice caused local and state governments to raise the flags in the first place, but I quickly became aware of what this could mean on a larger level for academics of color like me living and working in the U.S. South.

On the university campus, I often drove by Rebel Drive and Confederate Drive and walked by a monument to Confederate soldiers fronting the historic campus circle. In the city of Oxford, I drove by a similar Confederate monument in Oxford Square. All were daily reminders of which histories were sanctioned as important. Those reminders of the university's southern heritage caused me to reflect on what these symbols meant to me, my students, colleagues, and the numerous faculty and staff who encounter these images each day. The impact of these symbols depends not solely on what they look like but on the meanings given to them by those who positioned them and those who encounter them. They represent many years of ancestral descendant knowledge that perpetuates a deceptive and dangerous Lost Cause southern mythology. It was not uncommon to see a five-foot Mississippi state flag in the shape of the state on the university's fraternity row, flanked by similarly large Greek letters above the slogan "This Is Dixie." On a good day, my return home included several displays of Confederate battle flag car plates, a display of the state flag, and at least one thirty-something White male wearing a battle flag bandanna standing in front of Southland Body and Paint Shop. If the ACLU's argument on Dorsey's behalf carried any weight, then I had to wonder what these images were doing to me. At the least, I recognized that this landscape contributed to a hostile living environment, doubly oppressing as a supplement to academic life, a "relentlessly individual and individualizing process" that did not offer many safe emotional spaces.[6]

I am a public anthropologist trained by activist scholars at the University of Texas at Austin. I had done and was prepared to continue to do activist research, but I was not prepared for the commitment required to do this work without any expectation that my surroundings would change. The arguments made in the Dorsey case were not going to immediately change my environment. Through service and teaching, I attempted to work with others on campus interested in changing the university's culture, steeped as it is in Confederate tradition. The stress of this environment took a toll on my emotional and physical health.

I ultimately found like-minded individuals in a nearby city, Holly Springs, who were working to incorporate narratives of enslaved persons into a historically antebellum landscape. They developed a slave-dwelling tour called Behind the Big House to do that work. That experience offered a more nurturing environment for me. However, I became a better activist but a less tenurable academic. During that time, several Black women, three of whom were close friends, left the university. Their experiences, along with mine, led to gradual changes in the university's faculty diversity initiatives that most of them did not get to benefit from. To survive, I looked to relationships with the people with whom I collaborated in Holly Springs as benchmarks for success, rather than to the tenure and promotion guidelines. I also sought counsel from other social science activists as well as publicly engaged historians at other institutions.

One of my goals in this book is to help other activist scholars of color negotiate the nuances of place, the academic public sphere, and its ambiguous systems of reward, recognition, and evaluation. My theoretical task is to raise different sets of questions for those interested in doing this kind of work. By directly speaking to a failed integration of teaching, research, and service as a crisis in academia, I strive not to give others answers but to model another way of being. My theory is support and not architecture. This book is also structured to reflect that integration. My teaching, research, and service experiences are not segregated in chapters but dispersed in sections and narratives throughout the text. I didn't separate them as I worked, and the book is designed to show that.

As I've matured as an academic, I've become more interested in process and, for me, scholarship has gone in a different direction. My theoretical claim is also a methodological claim. My work was driven by process, not by theory. I collaborated on a project that I did not develop with a research design. It was not planned as an academic project. I wanted to support a community doing the work that I saw as filling a gap in Mississippi heritage tourism—slavery on a landscape infused with essentialized White, antebellum, and Confederate histories. My method was to support and learn from community members. My theory is the retrospective learning from this experience.

My Writing Process

Although I've spent a lot of time thinking about how my lived experiences have shaped my perspectives as an academic, until now I have not attempted to put my thoughts into written form. I decided to use autoethnography, a method of writing that uses "tenets of autobiography and ethnography . . . to describe and systematically analyze (graphy) personal experience (auto) in order to understand cultural experience (ethno)," to show how my lived experiences have shaped my perspectives as an academic.[7]

In 2012, I began working as a scholar-in-collaboration with the Behind the Big House program developers and supporters. This book is also about my relationships with them, making it a community autoethnography, which uses "the personal experience of researchers-in-collaboration to illustrate how a community manifests particular social/cultural issues."[8] The particular sociocultural issue here is the representation of Black slavery in the present. The community is a network of people in North Mississippi prioritizing the lives of enslaved people in historic site representations, those "grassroots preservationists" whom Brent Leggs, executive director of the National Trust for Historic Preservation's African American Cultural Heritage Action Fund, described as "the heart of the preservation movement."[9]

For the purposes of this book, I chose not to interview those whom ethnomusicologist Kathryn Radishofski refers to as tourism industry superintendents, "those inhabiting a position of leadership via a managerial, proprietary, or organizational role."[10] Although some Behind the Big House program developers and collaborators manage or are part of official historic preservation entities, their designated historic preservation work does not require them to do social justice or equity work. They choose to do such work on their own.

In *Autoethnography as Method*, Heewon Chang suggests exercises to help writers collect, evaluate, and organize their data. For me, this includes incorporating the influences of life mentors, "used broadly to include anyone . . . from whom I have learned new knowledge, skills, principles, wisdom, or perspectives, that have made an impact on" my life.[11] They are too many to name, so I have been selective about those most significant in my journey to understand and interpret representations of slavery in the present. I mention them throughout the text. The book's first chapter is named in honor of my cousin Geneva, whom I remember as the first person to introduce me to the idea of an African diaspora. That introduction helped generate my sense of curiosity in Black studies.

Autoethnography pioneers Carolyn Ellis, Tony Adams, and Arthur Bochner suggest that "autoethnographers must not only use their methodological tools and research literature to analyze experience, but also must consider ways others may experience similar epiphanies" that might require "interviewing cultural members."[12] In this text, instead of "cultural members," I use "supportive networks" to refer to individuals and institutions that have contributed to the development and/or sustainability of the Behind the Big House program. I have worked with several of these individuals since 2012 yet did not start to interview them until the real beginning of writing this book in 2019. Together, we have had much phone, email, and face-to-face contact. Through those experiences, I have heard bits and pieces of their life stories and have inductively tried to reason why they might have come to do the work that they do. I did not want to ask too many questions and risk being too invasive. Our work together was less about understanding the details of their individual lives than it was about respecting where moments in our lives intersected. This is very much unlike anthropological research. For me, this was not research but work. I wrote articles, largely to satisfy department tenure requirements, and through that process I deductively began with a general theory, then worked my way down to a conclusion based on my personal interactions. My choice to use autoethnography as a method of gathering information and writing caused me to rethink that process.

If I were to understand the impact of my personal experiences on the work that I do, then it seemed only fair to understand the personal experiences of those I was collaborating with. I hoped to learn something different about them in the interview setting than I had when we were working together. Carolyn Ellis, Christine Kiesinger, and Lisa Tillmann-Healy describe these as "interactive interviews" designed to offer an "in-depth and intimate understanding of people's experiences with emotionally charged and sensitive topics."[13] For all individuals in the program's supportive network, these emotionally charged and sensitive topics are race and racism and their relationship to southern heritage. Gender, race, class, and regional identities influence and differentiate their experiences.

"Interactive interviewing involves the sharing of personal and social *experiences of both* respondents and researchers, who tell (and sometimes write) their stories in the context of a developing relationship . . . where listening to and asking questions about another's plight lead to greater understanding of one's own."[14] My interviewees and I had, for over seven years, participated in shared activities and had an already formed relationship. Thinking about their learning experiences around race, over time, helped me better understand my own. My work in writing this book is also designed to put their retrospective learning and their theories on the same platform with those of academics.

Although part memoir, this is not a tell-all book. I have become friends with others in the supportive network, which complicates my relational ethics. I value these ties and, as a result, filter any personal information that I think may compromise my relationships with them or their relationships with others. Those readers who want to know more should consult the sources in note 15, where others have considered how "ethical issues affiliated with friendship become an important part of the research process and product."[15]

I also chose autoethnography to encourage "readers to reflect critically upon their own life experience, their constructions of self, and their interactions with others within sociohistorical contexts."[16] This is a political call to those in public and private historic preservation practice to think about how strongly their life experiences affect their abilities to represent historical actors and ancestors in the present. What is your personal and political investment? Is it economic, personal heritage, guilt, shame, love, or something else? It is also a political call for academics to think not only about the impact of their life experiences but about how academic structures might limit the value of their work. Are you too constrained by disciplinary expectations to tell your truth or to be truthful to those with whom you work? Do you rush your process and thus end up with a product that you are not proud of? Do you pretend that your work has no effect on the present, so that you do not have to deal with personal guilt or accountability? Through your silence, are you doing more harm than good? I have watched folks struggle with all these issues. I have struggled with several, and I hope that this approach might lighten burdens, just a bit. I have found that sometimes it helps to just feel less lonely.

Because I am an academic and a public humanities scholar, this autoethnography weaves story and theory, hopefully in a way that is accessible to most. This is what "good autoethnography" should do.[17] For this reason, I disproportionately rely on *The Mississippi Encyclopedia* online entries as citations for those unfamiliar with particular historical events, places, and persons. It is my hope that referring to the online source will allow a more fluid read for those who might not find journal article or book-length sources accessible or practical. The encyclopedia entries also suggest further reading for those who want it. A print copy, published in 2017, is available from the University Press of Mississippi. Full disclosure: I am on the encyclopedia's advisory board and see this as an opportunity to champion a resource that I believe in.

Chapter Outline

Behind the Big House is not just my story but a narrative of how what I have come to learn and understand about academic practice looks like on the ground. This includes "comparing and contrasting [my] personal experience against existing research."[18] I've found that there's no way to handle the complexity of representing slavery by coming at it with one disciplinary or theoretical claim. There are too many blind spots. My narrative considers the needs of a growing number of professional and lay communities addressing slavery and its impacts through interpretations of local historic sites while speaking across disciplines and institutional settings. It guides the reader through eight years of my research and practice as a Behind the Big House scholar-in-collaboration. I worked as a program docent; am a member of Gracing the Table, a racial reconciliation group in Holly Springs; and helped preserve material culture through archaeological excavations at the Hugh Craft House, one of the slave-dwelling sites in Holly Springs.

Chapter 1 roots readers in the time from my early childhood socialization through higher education to give contexts to how and why I came to do the work that I do in the way that I do it. It's my attempt to frame my academic subjectivity before getting to my academic career.

In chapter 2, I set up the state heritage tourism structure within which I work, as an educator, to help readers understand the significance of the

Behind the Big House program as a site of intervention. I also contextualize heritage tourism in Mississippi by considering the history of garden clubs, pilgrimages, and the state's antebellum landscape. This chapter specifically addresses more recent attempts to represent Black heritage through blues and civil rights movement sites as responses to silences on that landscape, contemporary gaps in representations of sites of slavery, and my efforts to promote return migration tourism for Black Mississippians.

Chapter 3 details the Behind the Big House program's development from the perspectives of its founders and others in the supportive network whom I have come to know. It includes the incorporation of the Behind the Big House program into my heritage tourism and African diaspora courses for other public humanists who might be interested in developing experiential and community service-learning components in their courses. This chapter also discusses the challenges to capacity building as well as where I had success developing social relationships among willing people whom I describe in the chapter as acting "without permission."

Chapter 4 examines my role as a member of Gracing the Table, a program inspired by Behind the Big House to encourage White and Black Holly Springs residents to face the impacts of slavery in the present. I address this program's work by analyzing what it is about our individual and shared life experiences that brought us to racial reconciliation work. As with others in my supportive network, I never asked why they were doing the work. That was much less important than the fact that they were doing it. I never thought much about why until this writing process. This chapter, more than any other, explores the why of historic preservation as a form of racial reconciliation work. I begin the chapter by introducing first the organization and then each individual group member through personal narratives of how and why they came to do racial reconciliation work and reconcile race in their personal lives.

In the final chapter, I consider the challenges of being a public scholar, specifically when academic values did not align with mine as a community-engaged scholar. For much of my career as a junior scholar, I was unable to effectively advocate for my public scholarship. This chapter is for those with similar struggles, those with the ability to transform academic practice, and those members of communities supporting and seeking to collaborate with such scholars.

I conclude the book by reflecting on how my work intersected with the

2020 Movement for Black Lives with a piece that I call "What to Throw Away and What to Keep." I finished the first draft of this book a week after George Floyd was murdered. At that time, the Mississippi state flag still had its Confederate battle flag emblem. Calls for it to change began shortly after. A lot seemed to change but, in many ways, I felt the same about the state of race in this country. I felt the same about my place in academia. I wasn't sure how to write about that. I'm still not sure, but I hope that my concluding piece will capture both some of what I felt as I watched the news and what I see as the implications for those who seek to interpret historical Black lives in the present. I'm sure that much more will happen in between the moment that I first began to jot down those thoughts and the time that this book is published. It's one of the unknowns of ethnographic writing. It's also the moment at which I've chosen to end this book, December 2020, assuming that some things will change and that much will stay the same.

Finally, in my writing, I prefer to capitalize both Black and White as racial designations. That has been my personal practice for several years, but it now also aligns with the National Association of Black Journalists, which has said that White should be capitalized. The capitalization is designed not to equate the experiences of Black and White people but to acknowledge their racialization, both significant although asymmetrical. This book is not only about centering the experiences of Black people, historic and contemporary, but about centering the experiences of White people who recognize that their racial identity (through ancestry and experience) affects the lives of Black people. To me, keeping White lowercase shifts the focus away from that racialization, affirming whiteness as the norm as well as reinforcing its invisibility. It is my hope that my intentional capitalization of White will invite others to reflect on how whiteness has historically influenced and continues to influence the lives of people of color as well as the lives of people racialized as White. It is also my hope that the narratives of my White collaborators can demonstrate how understanding that racialization can serve as a catalyst for racial repair.

Behind the Big House

Thank You, Cousin Geneva!

I am a Black woman and a southerner who has lived or worked in nine southern states. I grew up in Lafayette, Louisiana, from the late 1970s to the early 1990s nurtured by a supportive Black Creole community living with the vestiges of slavery, apartheid segregation, and the internalized racism stemming from the historical White male possession of Black female bodies who produced lighter bodies, and lighter bodies, sometimes socialized to think of themselves as superior to darker bodies. Still, I knew that I mattered to that loving-hating Black Creole community. I also felt like I didn't matter in a White supremacist community, in which those who were not Cajun (meaning White) had no history. After eight years of working intimately with a group of people in North Mississippi, representing the experiences of enslaved people who didn't seem to matter in interpretations at historic sites, I was compelled to critically think about how my identity as a descendant of countless enslaved people and my experiences as a Black woman, as a U.S. southerner, and as an activist anthropologist could influence how I do academic work in ways that make that work accessible to racially diverse communities. That reflection begins with understanding my early racial formation tied to Louisiana Cajun and Creole identities.

I knew that "the Cajun ('White') identity" was "privileged and promoted at the expense of" my Black Creole identity.[1] I experienced a time of Cajun revival, which began around my birth. I watched it flourish, and I felt excluded. I was confused and angered by what seemed to be this privileged place in society. I despised being underrepresented. At the same time, I experienced a counternarrative of Creole zydeco festivals, restaurants, newsletters, and grassroots organizations designed to make those like me more visible. At the time, this collection of events and perspectives didn't have a name; it just was. It's something that scholars like Alexandra Giancarlo have now studied and named a cultural Creole renaissance. I did not know that it was intentional.

I struggled through elementary school narratives of Belizaire the Cajun, Clovis the Cajun Crawfish, and French yule logs at Christmastime. I felt too dark to be a teacher's pet or to carry the Virgin Mary's crown during church celebrations. The latter seemed reserved for light-skinned Creole kids. Being the exceptionally smart kid of uneducated parents did not help. Still, I was nurtured by a supportive community of adult relatives and friends who understood the value of supplementary education. Ms. Rose invited me over for arts and crafts projects. Cousin Janet took me to the public library club with her kids, and Cousin Geneva introduced me to an African diaspora.

I was in a French immersion program in my local public school when our bilingual teacher, Cynthia Dupuis, had us volunteer at the burgeoning Festival International de Louisiane, an "international music and arts festival . . . with a special emphasis on the connection between Acadiana and the Francophone world."[2] Although I don't recall what I did as a volunteer, I do remember the U.S. flag–inspired short sets that my friend Kim Auzenne and I wore. I guess that I thought it appropriate to represent the U.S. at an international festival.

My mom's first cousin, Geneva, seemed to have something else in mind. What I remember most is the phone call that she made to my mom one night during the festival. Through my mom's intermittent responses, I vaguely understood an invitation for my sister and me to come to her house to visit—did she say Tahitians? With excitement, I relayed that message to my sister, also eager about the opportunity to engage folks from another country, something we rarely did.

When we arrived at Cousin Geneva's house, I realized that her invited guests were not Tahitians but Haitians, people I had never heard of who were, surprisingly, Black. My excitement waned. I don't recall if I was less excited because they were Black and, therefore, not something new or because they were too much like me and thus victims of my internalized racism. Geneva introduced us to two young women along with a sprightly gray-haired woman from a place called Martinique. They all began to sing beautifully in Creole variations of French. What Cousin Geneva knew is that Black was bigger than my small world, and that I should know that.

What she also knew was that there was an African diaspora of Black bodies, disconnected by a vicious slave trade, longing to be reconnected. What she knew is that the French festival would be accessible to them but that she, as a "standard" French-speaking Black woman, could make them most comfortable. Cousin Geneva introduced me to an African diaspora and, unknowingly, in that moment, I began to love myself and wanted those like me to do the same.

For the next several years, however, I continued to struggle. My new-found love for myself and for others like me meant holding those unlike me, White people, accountable and keeping them distant. I was geographically segregated from them, growing up in a post-1960s White flight neighborhood on what was then (and still is) the Black side of town. I was emotionally segregated from them in my high school with its 51:49 percent Black:White ratio. I had my last White friend in the third grade, when we seemed to become more racially cliquish, and I had no White friends in high school.

I was an angry Black woman who articulated that rage through Texas gangster rap. I was too ignorant to recognize its misogyny. Those women were not me, but the racism the lyricists expressed was my experience. I carried that experience through high school and then to Grambling State University, a historically Black institution in the northern part of the state. I had never felt like I quite belonged in Lafayette. I was too dark in skin shade, too activist, and too sick of what seemed to be too few collective responses to blatant racism. I was reluctant to change, so I left after what I choose to remember as an experimental summer session at what was then the University of Southwestern Louisiana, a historically White institution in the city.[3] I had poor experiences in my courses, one English and one history. The English professor trashed my work as "overly cryptic," and I spent countless minutes debating the history professor about whether or not Thomas Jefferson had fathered Sally Hemings's children. The professor thought that it was not only unlikely but impossible. "What if I tried to make you related to Louis XIV?" he sarcastically asked. I, on the other hand, didn't find that possible connection illogical, because I was raised with a disproportionately large number of Black people with blond hair and blue eyes. Five out of the seven Black students enrolled in that history class dropped. I defiantly stayed but had no interest in continuing my education at a historically White institution.

Discovering History as a Discipline

I found some sense of security at Grambling State University in northern Louisiana. There I was not too dark, and there were plenty of other students on the front lines making their grievances known to the administration and to the rest of the world. I didn't feel like I had to fight. I could also express a sense of self, centered on my blackness, one that I didn't have to repeatedly question. On the other hand, I was too Catholic and too country compared to the nearly 40 percent out-of-state student population, many from large urban centers outside the South. It was 1994, and many of us across U.S. regions had a cultural college experience against the backdrop of a new postapartheid era in South Africa, the widely televised O. J. Simpson trial, the impact of the Five-Percent Nation's influence on hip-hop culture and music, and *A Different World*, a television series based on a fictional historically Black college.[4] Grambling also had an Afrocentric bookstore, Black to Basics, which gave me access to "third eye" books on African and African American history and culture.[5] I so relate to how Ta-Nehisi Coates features Howard University as a contradiction to his middle and high school experiences in West Baltimore.[6]

In high school my friends and I, all Black, worked hard to make grades that would give us the best opportunities, but we were nevertheless largely excluded from institutional recognition. I received the first scholarship award letter my senior year, but the scholarship awards were not announced until a White student got one. I don't know if that was intentional, but it felt that way. My best friend in high school had the highest GPA in the school but was not the class valedictorian. A White student, the class salutatorian, was placed at the head of the class at our graduation after school administrators decided that well-roundedness, not GPAs, determined that status. I vowed to boycott graduation but walked because my friend did. She felt that she would get her just due in life; I felt like we had to fight for it. I loved my people in Lafayette, people like my friend, but I hated how institutions like my high school excluded me.

At Grambling, I began as a broadcast journalism major but shifted my major to history after an instructor recognized an interest in the subject that I did not know I had, even with the time I spent at Black to Basics. Through class-instructed research projects, I began to examine texts on Louisiana Creoles of color, eventually coming across Robert Maguire's research on postplantation societies in Louisiana, where he did his PhD work.[7] I contacted Bob, who sent me an envelope filled with research manuscripts. This was not the Cane River Creole community in Natchitoches Parish, with which I had become most familiar through the available literature, but rather a community of familiar names, places, and descriptions in St. Martin Parish, my family's ancestral community. I was amazed to see descriptions of *my* people in academic writing.

Around the same time, I watched an interesting documentary on the architecture of slave dwellings and the ingenuity of the enslaved persons who built them. By that time, I was familiar with archival and secondary research on historical communities but less so with the potential of material culture to help me understand Black lives. I recall a segment of the documentary showing the significance of chimneys formed of wood and mud on the most modest slave cabins, which were often susceptible to tumbling down or catching fire. That was important because they could easily be knocked down and replaced if they caught fire. This was around the time that John Michael Vlach's *Back of the Big House: The Architecture of Plantation Slavery* was published. The program might have been a spotlight on that. I just don't remember. The architectural creativity seemed so simple yet so complicated. I wanted to know more.

At the time, I was influenced by Afrocentric perspectives on Egyptology and thought that classical archaeology would be a good fit for graduate study. That changed, after watching the documentary, and I began looking into plantation archaeology programs. I knew no archaeologists and was ignorant about how to find one, so I did a rudimentary internet search that showed several plantation archaeology projects related to faculty at Florida State University. I applied to their M.A. in anthropology program in 1998 and was accepted.

Managing Cultural Resources

I became a student of Rochelle Marrinan's, whose focus was Spanish mission archaeology, but she gave me the flexibility to examine a later antebellum-era occupation of the O'Connell Spanish mission site near Tallahassee as my thesis research. Through historical documents and material culture, I was able to examine the history of a slave-owning family and some members of their enslaved community. I simultaneously worked as a curatorial assistant and archaeological technician at the Southeast Archeological Center, a National Park Service entity, conducting research that included slave plantation sites in Georgia and Florida and one Civil War site in Mississippi. My work with the Park Service also included cowriting a Cultural Resource Management plan for prehistoric and historic sites at the Timucuan Ecological and Historic Preserve in Jacksonville, Florida. This wealth of experience as a graduate student gave me less-restricted access to how archaeological research intersects with historic preservation management at local, state, and national sites.

Through Cultural Resource Management projects, archaeologists help federal and state agencies identify and evaluate archaeological and historic sites, protect them from disturbance and destruction, and assist with investigating and recording those that cannot be saved. This work, performed in compliance with state and federal laws, offered me diverse training in collections management and excavation techniques. What I did not have was the ability to explain and understand the institutional dynamics at work when a Black park ranger in Florida chastised colleagues for not being sensitive about the need to have people of color in their marketing materials or when a White Mississippi park manager flippantly asked us to "help him find the slaves." As a Black woman and a southerner, I clearly understood why I felt uncomfortable when a Georgia news journalist used my photo to represent an entire excavation of slave dwellings and when I ate with colleagues at a restaurant in Corinth, Mississippi, with Confederate battle flags on the walls and ceiling. I always ordered what at least one White colleague did to lessen the chances of my meal being tampered with. I swore that I would never go back to North Mississippi. I also clearly understood why I was so relieved to have a White male colleague sensitive enough to understand that not every bathroom along the route from Jacksonville to Tallahassee was safe for me to use. He once apologized for not asking if I felt safe before parking the car in a random convenience store lot. I appreciated his gesture.

Representing the Past

As a doctoral student at the University of Texas at Austin, I expanded my Cultural Resource Management experience by working with private environmental firms to help conduct archaeological testing throughout

Texas. My experience in Texas, from 2002 to 2010, was quite different from my experience in Florida in that those doing historical archaeology in Texas were influenced by public archaeology and public history practice as well as by cultural representations in museum studies. Archaeologists like Maria Franklin focused on how modern communities and individuals affected and are affected by archaeology and on the necessary role that archaeologists should play in considering and being reflexive about that. This reflexive approach "acknowledges and accommodates subjectivity, emotionality, and the researcher's influence on research, rather than hiding from these matters or assuming they don't exist."[8] Later, as my dissertation adviser, Maria helped me develop a dissertation project that did all those things.

I was also influenced by an academic wealth of African diaspora cultural anthropologists, who supplemented the structured four-fields approach to anthropology that I learned at Florida State with one that made me think more about who I was in a broader African diaspora. I was not essentially a Black woman but a racialized and gendered body to be interrogated repeatedly. Blackness was not a given, and neither was womanhood. That understanding permeated how I think about myself as well as how I think about myself in relation to others. Those identities are also cultural and political choices, which have effects on how I see others and how I am seen. That was and still is not traditional archaeological training. More traditional archaeological approaches "promote an erasure of the body from the process and product of research," especially when the researched community is distanced from identifiable descendants.[9] That training makes it easier to ignore the human impacts of the research.

Other Texas faculty like Pauline "Polly" Turner Strong and Martha Norkunas introduced me to the politics of representation and museum studies. In one graduate course, Polly asked that students collaborate on an exhibition in which we would determine a common theme and create displays around that theme. Our theme was titled "DISORIENTATION: Exploring Technologies of Proximity and Distance." I did not keep notes that would capture the meanings behind that exhibit but remember that collaborative effort as one of the best bonding experiences I have had in a classroom. I connected with the other students and became invested in our success.

Inspired by Atlanta's *Without Sanctuary: Lynching Photography in America* exhibition, I wanted exhibit visitors to feel the impact of witnessing lynchings by hanging actual photographs of lynchings from the ceiling. I do not recall Polly's specific critique of my proposal, but it might have been some academic version of catching more flies with honey than vinegar. I shifted to a display of a wooden chair draped with a baby girl's dress to represent the 1918 lynching of Mary Turner, a thirty-three-year-old Black woman lynched after she objected to her husband's lynching. One member of the Georgia mob "cut her stomach open and her unborn child dropped to the ground where it was reportedly stomped on and crushed by a member of the mob."[10] She was murdered because she dared to hold a White lynch mob accountable. The wooden chair and dress represented the spaces that Turner and her child would never occupy.

Polly's class was about representation. I chose Turner because she was a lynched Black woman carrying a lynched child, two demographics underrepresented in America's historical lynching memory. That collaborative class experience taught me that representations of the past do not have to be literal or explicit to have a powerful effect. In addition, Martha Norkunas offered students opportunities to do community-based historic preservation work with state-supported funding. She created the Project in Interpreting the Texas Past, through which I helped develop educational posters on the Civilian Conservation Corps in Texas.

Also through Martha, I became a scholar-in-residence at the Women's Museum in Dallas. At that point in my graduate career, I was ABD, "all but dissertation," having met all the requirements for a PhD except the dissertation. I was brought in to help the museum staff connect to girls in the working-class communities surrounding the museum, especially those considered Black and Latinx. The museum staff struggled to understand that it was possible to connect to those communities only if the museum itself were culturally and logistically accessible to them. At the time, the staff seemed to be more interested in connecting to already established exclusive women's groups that might provide funding and prestige to the struggling institution. The staff also seemed more interested in having an assistant help with that goal instead of someone to help them think through underrepresented group accessibility. Unenthusiastic about this agenda, I left the museum six months into my one-year appointment and began working with Sistas in the Light, a Black women's grassroots program centered on the health and well-being of girls, and with a summer camp of young Katrina evacuees living in an apartment community in South Dallas. The latter left New Orleans after the deadly 2005 hurricane's storm surge overwhelmed the city's levee system. After working with those two groups, I wrote three interpretive programs predominantly targeting youths of color. I then developed curriculum guides for the education of underrepresented youth populations visiting Texas museums, something I hoped the Women's Museum might use one day but did not think they were ready to do so at the time.

That failed collaboration with the Women's Museum influenced the institutions I chose to work with and how I worked with them for the next several years. The staff members I met prior to my appointment seemed to say all the right things about connecting to underrepresented youths, yet they didn't show that commitment in practice. It took me six months to come to that realization. I recall a good friend advising me to "get the hell out of there" as soon as possible. Her life experiences had led her to be skeptical of the things that people in institutions say and more aware of what they do. I wanted that collaboration and thought they could be convinced if I just showed them that more accessible community engagements were possible. In the end, they just weren't ready for that. I subsequently learned to give more weight to institutional deeds than words. I would also come to value collaborations with individuals and institutions already involved in some form of community engagement. I later came to work with such people in Dallas who were just in need of some additional human resources support. I have learned that those voluntarily engaging communities are more likely to be serious about continuing their work than those who have to be convinced to do diversity work in the first place.

In Texas, I was also influenced by archaeologists in private practice in Austin, like Fred McGhee, who persistently pursued community archaeology initiatives. When I met Fred, he had been hired as a community liaison between the Houston Independent School District, which owned a sixteen-acre tract of land to be excavated, and embattled members of the former Freedmen's Town community, some of whose property had been annexed for the district's expansion. A Black archaeologist, president of his own archaeological firm, and community activist, Fred submitted a culturally sensitive research proposal to the district that requested local community collaboration at the onset and throughout the excavation project, citing the African Burial Ground project in New York City as a model of what not to do. Fred wanted to have a Black archaeologist as project manager to show the community that this was a diverse effort. I agreed to comanage that project.

For the first time, I felt the unease of being an archaeologist, essentially caught between a city institution and aggrieved citizens, several of whom were Black. My blackness didn't make them any less angry, and my role as an archaeologist working on behalf of the city of Houston made me the enemy. I learned what that ambiguity could mean for people of color with good intentions who are working on behalf of institutions whose intentions were often motivated by profit. Fred experienced and understood those politics on the ground in ways that I didn't. Although I had always felt like I was on the side of underrepresented communities, I now knew how tenuous such a position could be. It was much easier to imagine myself that way when I was a graduate student living in an academic world. Operating as a professional with a career was another matter. I will share much of that experience through the rest of this book.

Lessons Learned and Next Steps

Grambling taught me how to be comfortable enough with my blackness to advocate for it. I didn't learn that as a child growing up in Louisiana. My parents protected me by segregating me. That's what they knew how to do. Those Black women in my family and community with more cultural capital, like Cousin Geneva, understood the value of supplementary education and the necessity of taking me outside the boundaries of my segregated community. After high school graduation, I was somewhat prepared to live outside those boundaries, but not completely. I went to a historically Black university as a haven from the inequity that I felt at institutions like my high school and what was then the University of Southwestern Louisiana. I did not know this at the time, but I needed the experience at Grambling to shore me up before getting out into the real world. One of my history instructors there, Lawrence Garner, always warned us about what was beyond the four walls of Grambling. He clearly knew what he was helping prepare me for at a time when I didn't. That groundwork was necessary to my survival at Florida State.

While at Florida State, I was able to get behind the scenes looks at how historic site owners and managers determined site significance and how they chose to represent historical narratives in the present. In Texas, I learned to draw connections between archaeological theory and the cultural representations of subordinated groups and to communicate sophisticated concepts—for example, regarding theories of race and enslavement—clearly. My experience as an archaeologist exposed me to the intersections of material culture, cultural representations, heritage, and bureaucracy and how they related to larger economies. My decision to become an academic caused me to consider how I could feasibly teach what I had observed and learned to students interested in comparable issues. This book project is also about teaching my experience.

This chapter communicated that experience before I began living in Mississippi. The next one begins with the Mississippi that I encountered when I arrived in 2011. By then I was interested not only in public archaeology and public history but in the decisions that institutions make about what and whose stories are made accessible to publics at historic sites. Although I had vowed never to go back to Mississippi, I wanted to understand more about the politics of representing southern history in the present and thought that the interdisciplinary nature of the southern studies program in Mississippi, combined with a joint appointment in anthropology, might be a good way to do this.

I came to understand that those politics often emerged in the field of tourism, something with which I was much less familiar. Many of the resulting decisions reflected what institutions perceived to be their tourist audiences. I unknowingly arrived at a time when state officials were thinking about how to sell Black heritage amid perceptions of the state as historically hostile to African Americans. As counternarratives, Mississippi tourism would come to center blues—without a critique of the Jim Crow conditions that gave birth to this music—and male and to a lesser extent female civil rights movement heroes recognized through what Owen Dwyer and Derek Alderman describe as the Won Cause battle for civil rights—without a critique of ongoing civil rights issues in the state.[11] Both could be consumed by tourist audiences without dealing with complications or contradictions. I was interested in complicating those narratives but more interested in what I saw as a major gap in them: slavery tourism.

Slavery tourism involves promoting sites connected to the development and propagation of Black slavery, usually through the transatlantic slave trade, for consumption by a tourist public. Mississippi had a history of interpreting its antebellum period through a Lost Cause mythology that positions post–Civil War White southerners as losing the war but fighting for the right cause. The acknowledgment of slavery as the root of that cause isn't part of that narrative. The Behind the Big House program filled that gap in Mississippi. I briefly introduce the program in the next chapter as a counternarrative to the Lost Cause narrative in Holly Springs.

Heritage Tourism in Mississippi

In 2019 Unite Mississippi, "a Flowood-based nonprofit that focuses on racial and social reconciliation among Mississippi's Christians," encouraged then Governor Phil Bryant to declare the month of April the Month of Unity. According to a video on the organization's website, Unite Mississippi was developed through the common interests of "several pastors and community leaders" wanting to address "systemic issues" in the state's cities through prayer. They were planning a Night of Unity event, a revival dedicated to uniting all Mississippians. Governor Bryant was listed among its sponsors and donors. One event leader called the April 27 event "a 21st century Billy Graham crusade on steroids," and its executive director touted it as one not to be missed, yet somehow I had missed it.[1]

The event was held at the Mississippi Veterans Memorial Stadium in Jackson. I live in Oxford in the North Mississippi Hill Country. Depending on where you are in Oxford, you are a little over a two-hour drive north of Jackson and a little over a one-hour drive south of Memphis. Oxonians, technically in the mid-South region, get Memphis news stations on television. During the course of my daily life, I would not have seen television advertisements for this event. I also do not attend a church, so I might have missed church advertisements for it.

The paradox that the event for *all* Mississippians was a Christian-centered effort was not the oddest one in a conservative Christian state. Most illogical to me was the fact that Governor Bryant proclaimed a month of unity in a month previously designated Confederate Heritage Month. The Night of Unity was just two days before the state-observed Confederate Memorial Day, a particularly divisive honor in the state with the disproportionately highest Black population. An article in the *Jackson Free Press*

Map of southern states showing Oxford, Mississippi.
Map created by Gerry Krieg.

highlighted this hypocrisy with accusations from Democratic state representatives like Jeramey Anderson, who called Bryant's proclamation "hollow," ineffective, and one in a long line of the governor's failures to "unify the people of Mississippi," including his opposition to "changing the state flag to remove its Confederate imagery." That state flag was first introduced in 1894, at the height of Jim Crow lawmaking in Mississippi. Although "more than 60 percent of Mississippi voters rejected a new flag design that did not include the Confederate battle flag" in 2001, efforts to change the flag ramped up after the 2015 murders of nine Black residents in Charleston, South Carolina, and led to protests and calls for the removal of Confederate iconography from public spaces across the nation.[2]

Bryant issued a proclamation declaring April Confederate Heritage Month the following year. A year later, in 2017, he declared April 24 Confederate Memorial Day, proclaiming that it was "important for all Americans to reflect upon our nation's past, to gain insight from our mistakes and successes, and to come to a full understanding that the lessons learned yesterday and today will carry us through tomorrow if we carefully and earnestly strive to understand and appreciate our heritage and our opportunities that lie before us."[3] Bryant's proclamation was not an attempt to reconcile the state's history with slavery. It strategically masked the westward expansion of slavery as the root cause of the Civil War and, even more irresponsibly, made a call for *us* to reflect, understand, and learn without a template for doing so. What Bryant correctly did was to proclaim Confederate *Heritage* Month instead of Confederate History Month. I say that with an understanding of history as an always incomplete chronicling of facts and heritage as "that from the past which groups consider important to remember and re-member" in the present.[4] Bryant made that decision for all Mississippians.

The Confederate Heritage Month proclamation explicitly asked that *we* recognize those who served in the Confederacy. *We* were asked to do some state-sanctioned memory work, work that by its very nature forgets and silences millions of enslaved people in the process. This is complicated when, for many, heritage "is most often associated with positive achievements." If we hope to claim the best of those who came before us, also supposing that that says a lot about who we are, then what about "the negative, brutal, violent and destructive" sides of humanity?[5] What allows us to do, and then to justify doing, the worst things to others? What do we do with that history?

We often choose to be selective and to forget, as Governor Bryant did. Although those acts might seem banal, they are structural, affective, and potentially dangerous. Christine Buzinde and Carla Almeida Santos remind us that that which we "choose to remember, overlook, obliterate, erase, and/or silence is influenced [by] and influences [our] social order and the socio-political relations that govern [our] existence."[6] Bryant's 2016 proclamation, amid backlash, said a lot about whom the head of the state's government chose to remember and forget. It said that those who lived in this state during the Civil War, outside of those who served in the Confederacy, did not matter then and, by default, neither do their descendants.

By February 2019, Mississippi "lawmakers [had] filed more than a dozen bills to redesign the flag" just that year, but all died before consideration by the House and Senate committees.[7] It would again take widely publicized murders of Black people to increase protests and calls to change the flag. On May 25, 2020, George Perry Floyd, Jr., a forty-six-year-old Black man, was killed by police in Minneapolis, Minnesota, generating massive public demonstrations against systemic inequities in U.S. policing. Floyd's public death shortly followed the death of Ahmaud Marquez Arbery, a twenty-five-year-old Black man who was pursued and fatally shot by White men while jogging near Brunswick in Glynn County, Georgia, on February 23, and the fatal shooting of Breonna Shaquelle Taylor, a twenty-six-year-old Black woman, after officers forced entry into her apartment in Louisville, Kentucky, on March 13. Those deaths, which were among many publicly recorded instances of White people policing Black bodies, culminated in public pressure to change the state flag. By June 2020, a bipartisan group of Mississippi lawmakers was working to do just that. Governor Bryant's successor, Tate Reeves, had up to this point refused to take a stand on the flag issue but then signed a bill to change the flag. On November 3, 2020, Mississippi voters chose a new state flag, designed after the old flag was removed and a Commission to Redesign the Mississippi State Flag was formed.

Although Governor Reeves acknowledged "the need to commit the 1894 flag to history, and find a banner that is a better emblem for all Mississippi," he doubly recognized the "people of goodwill who are not happy to see this flag change. They fear a chain reaction of events erasing our history—a history that is no doubt complicated and imperfect. I understand those concerns and am determined to protect Mississippi from that dangerous outcome."[8] Bryant's *us* had become Reeves's *our*. Changing the flag was only a symbol, and Reeves made a systemic pledge to keep things the same. He kept that promise.

In November 2020, Reeves released his balanced budget recommendation for the 2022 fiscal year, which included the creation of a Patriotic Education Fund on its list of key priorities. Reeves proposed a $3 million investment, from capital expense funds, through which "schools and non-profits should be able to apply to fund teaching that educates the next generation in the incredible accomplishments of the American Way." That "American Way" is one that doesn't indoctrinate young children with "far-left socialist teachings that emphasize America's shortcomings over the exceptional achievements" and "uniquely American values" like capitalism and democracy. Reeves then ironically prioritized "Supporting Quality K–12 Education" in the next section of the report.[9] One of my southern studies colleagues, Ralph Eubanks, connects Reeves's actions to the state's late nineteenth-century attempts to reject inclusive histories in Mississippi public education, culminating in students who know little to nothing about the Civil War in a state steeped in Confederate ideology. In this curriculum, the civil rights movement was limited to Martin Luther King's "I Have a Dream" speech, glaringly omitting "the Mississippi State Sovereignty Commission, Mississippi's civil rights–era spy agency, despite broad public access to those archives," and glossing over the murder of Emmett Till in a state seeking to remedy its shameful past by representing the civil rights movement as Dwyer and Alderman's Won Cause.[10]

I understand what my colleague was talking about all too well. I began to see those gaps clearly shortly after arriving in Mississippi. What I also noticed is that public counternarratives to "whitewashed" histories, largely evident in blues and civil rights tourism narratives, ignored or minimized the impact of slavery, which was particularly ironic in what some would argue is the most Confederacy-nostalgic state in the United States. My efforts to teach a class on southern heritage tourism were and continue to be influenced by all those issues.

What's Missing in Mississippi? Teaching Tourism

When I arrived in Mississippi in 2011, I was largely ignorant of historic preservation work there, outside of my time with the National Park Service working at the Corinth Battlefield Unit in Corinth and visiting the Melrose Estate in Natchez. I quickly became familiar with efforts to remember blues and civil rights movement individuals, institutions, and sites, but the footprint of slavery was mostly an ephemeral one, briefly mentioned within the context of Jim Crow–era blues and the civil rights movement. Slavery is largely ignored in Mississippi state tourism development. While subsequent historical phases, such as Jim Crow (through blues tourism) and the civil rights movement (through civil rights tourism), receive some attention, some narratives in the former, especially blues tourism, are still sanitized. Although many communities are historically rooted in the state's economic dependency on cotton and the legacy of slavery, tourism promoters neglect "to fully embrace and critique the important role Mississippi played in benefiting from the institution."[11]

In the fall of 2011, my first semester at the University of Mississippi, I began teaching a graduate course on heritage tourism in the U.S. South. I proposed the class as a multidisciplinary seminar for students who wished to employ theoretical and practical approaches to examining the movements of heritage site tourists within southern regional spaces. The director of the Center for the Study of Southern Culture seemed excited about the idea but admitted that students likely would not have been attracted to such a class five to ten years prior. Tourism was a relatively new field of interest in southern studies, an interdisciplinary study of the U.S. South. My primary interest in tourism centered on southern U.S. plantations and heritage dialogues around enslavement. There were no core faculty or graduate students in southern studies with comparable interests. Most students were interested in blues tourism, which aligned with other faculty interests.

Mississippi offered the first bachelor's degree in southern studies in the United States and has the only master's degree program in the subject. Graduate students in this program have a broad range of theoretical interests with diverse methodologies, including oral history, photography, and filmmaking. This means that an instructor can have a classroom composed of twenty graduate students, each of whom has a different interest with different methodological practices.

Although I came to the university familiar with historic preservation literature by way of my work as a historical archaeologist, that work had not yet intersected with the anthropology of tourism. Early anthropologists were generally interested in non-Western communities and considered tourism a Western phenomenon. Tourism scholarship in the social sciences slowly developed in the 1970s and in anthropology in the 1980s.[12] Developments in anthropological tourism theories occurred over the next few decades, but it's still underrepresented in anthropological study.[13] I now had the task of combining a relatively new focus in two fields, anthropology and southern studies, into a class curriculum. The diversity of students' interests also meant that I had to frame the topic to give them some common ground from which to work.

I drew on what I learned at the University of Texas—public history from Martha Norkunas, public archaeology from Maria Franklin, cultural representations in museum studies from Polly Strong, and Cultural Resource Management practice from working with folks like Fred McGhee—to establish course goals. I asked my students to be familiar with theories and debates and terminology regarding the representation, commodification, and authenticity of the past; consider the differences between history and heritage; examine the contested political nature of heritage projects and analyze the ideological and symbolic content of some notable heritage sites; and explore how heritage reflects contemporary notions of authenticity, reality, and social identities by critically scrutinizing case studies. I thought about the southern landscape, as I understood it at the time, and selected readings split into the broader themes of politics of the past, authenticity, tourism management, preservation, the Civil War sesquicentennial, the tourist experience, dark and disaster tourism, and festivals and events tourism. I tried to include as many types of tourism within those themes as was practical.

My review of tourism journals revealed social scientific examinations of authenticity as a concept in tourism research, so I tried to pattern what seemed to be relevant for students to know. According to Dallen Timothy and Stephen Boyd, "in addition to its scholarly importance, authenticity is an important buzzword in the [tourism] industry as well, to which the multitude of tourism-related agencies, organisations and businesses using the term in their marketing campaigns, slogans and itineraries bears witness. . . . Some observers have argued that people travel in a constant search for authentic experiences and genuine places."[14] That marketing practice was evident in the state of Mississippi when I first began teaching the heritage tourism class. Although the state's tourism agency, Visit Mississippi, did not use the buzzword "authenticity" in its 2011 advertising campaign, its new slogan, "Find Your True South in Mississippi," was evidence of the agency's attempt to respond to tourists' perceived desires for authentic experiences, drawing on "Mississippi's reputation as the most southern state in the nation and the mother of southern culture."[15] The slogan "Find Your True South" is a generous interpretation of historian James Cobb's widely known claim that the Mississippi Delta is "the most southern place on earth" in its display of gross inequities of wealth, White supremacy, and reactionary politics.[16] Visit Mississippi's promotional videos describe the state as "authentic and sincere," filled with opportunities for visitors to find their "true" selves through Mississippi music, literature, sports, food, gaming, and history.[17] The state was marketed as the most authentically southern experience one could have. It was my hope that students could make theoretical connections to what we saw on the ground.

I also asked students to think through concepts that more specifically related to studies of tourism in the South, like those of Jennifer Eichstedt and Stephen Small, some of the first scholars to theoretically frame southern plantation tourism experiences, primarily focusing on the plantation museum industry in Virginia, Georgia, and Louisiana. Their primary representational and discursive strategies for categorizing how slavery is represented in southern plantation museums are symbolic annihilation and erasure; trivialization and deflection, including those sites in which slavery and African Americans are mentioned but mainly through mechanisms, phrasing, and images that minimize and distort them; segregation and marginalization of knowledge through sites that include information about enslaved people but present it largely through separate tours and displays that visitors can choose to see or ignore; relative incorporation in which topics of enslavement and those who were enslaved are discussed throughout the tour; and in-between sites, which are still quite conflicted in their representations of enslavement and enslavers, incorporating more information than many sites but doing so in a way that still valorizes whiteness and diminishes the experience of slavery.[18]

With such resources, I had sound theoretical structures for the students to think through, but I had to be more creative about getting them to understand tourism as method. To incorporate some tourism methodology, I used a Historic Site Evaluation project model that Martha Norkunas assigned in her Cultural Representations of the Past course (see appendix A). One of her class goals was to interpret the Civilian Conservation Corps' role in developing Bastrop State Park in Bastrop, Texas. Norkunas asked that we tour the park, spend time with park staff, and then submit a site evaluation. That experience was so profound for me because I was able to get theoretical context for historic site interpretations, tour a historic site, understand what site management was like, and then help create narratives about that site all in one course. I attempted to replicate parts of it for my first class. At the time, I didn't have one specific site focus for the class as Norkunas did, so I asked students to visit a local site of their choice.

Students also interviewed at least one member of the site's staff. As one example, a student wrote a site evaluation of Elvis Presley's former home, Graceland, and then interviewed Alicia Dean, then media assistant for Elvis Presley Enterprises. The interview component was designed to get students to understand practitioners' perspectives as a complement to their perspectives as tourists.

Overall, I think that the course content of heritage tourism analysis somewhat paid off, but all the theory in the world could not help my students grasp what this kind of work might look like on the ground. I showed a 2001 episode from the *Haunted History* television series, which focused on the Myrtles Plantation in Louisiana, narrated as haunted by a former enslaved woman who unintentionally murdered a few of her owners; Les Blank's 1978 documentary film, *Always for Pleasure*, featuring Black Mardi Gras celebrations in New Orleans; and "Unearthing Secret America," an edition of *PBS Scientific American Frontiers* that showed how slave quarters at Monticello and colonial Williamsburg represented the experiences of enslaved and free people.[19]

Students analyzed tourism as a practice, observed tourism in practice, and interviewed a practitioner, but they didn't have experience with tourism from the interpretive side. So much of our theoretical analysis was about that. I learned historical archaeology and public history by practicing them. I knew that this would likely be the case for my students. They would either get practice through my course or on the job. One of those early students, Patrick Weems, subsequently became executive director of the Emmett Till Memorial Commission, formed in 2006 after a group of Black Tallahatchie County, Mississippi, politicians began conversations about how they could honor Emmett Till, a fourteen-year-old Black boy from Chicago murdered in 1955 by local White men after being falsely accused of assaulting a White woman, Carolyn Bryant, in Money, Mississippi.[20]

At that point, I had not yet heard about the Behind the Big House program, and students like Patrick did not have the benefit of an applied component that would give them the opportunity to work from the practitioner side of tourism. I had general information on slavery tourism, but it was not specific to Mississippi. There were general contexts for blues and civil rights tourism in the state. Those contexts, largely engaging tourism and race, are what I offered to that first class.

Tourism and Race in Mississippi

In 1997, President Bill Clinton made an appeal for multiracial community dialogues and proactive measures for dealing with systemic social divides in the United States through his One America initiative on race. The William Winter Institute for Racial Reconciliation began in 1999 in Oxford as a direct response to Clinton's request, "targeting both the accumulated inheritances of the state's racial conflict and the salient issues governing its contemporary racial divisions."[21]

By the time the Winter Institute was founded, the Mississippi Delta had already become "internationally known as ground zero for all things blues" following regional and statewide efforts to market the state's blues history as a form of economic development.[22] The institute's focus offered state officials, like then Governor Haley Barbour, a two-pronged approach to promoting this economic development initiative through tourism and racial reconciliation. According to sociologist Brian Foster:

> When Haley Barbour became Mississippi's sixty-third governor in 2003, the Delta was in its fifth decade of a development crisis that had created a matrix of problems on top of problems for the region's residents. There was the problem of a polarized and precarious labor market; which intensified the problem of poverty, especially among the region's Black residents; which compounded the problem of a fragile, underfunded public infrastructure; which accelerated the problem of population loss. Barbour saw the problems and offered a solution: reimagine what "development" could look like for the region. To Barbour's eye, the Delta had more than agriculture and manufacturing, two shrinking economic sectors. "The Delta has the blues."[23]

In 2009, Barbour pronounced Mississippi "the real 'Birthplace of America's Music,'" signifying the structural affirmation of the state's blues tourism initiatives.[24] Mississippi's attempts to build its reputation as a pioneer of racial reconciliation work, through organizations like the Winter Institute, eased into blues tourism initiatives with branding clichés like "no black, no white, just the blues," a reconciliatory narrative proposing that Black and White citizens had now come to terms with the past.[25]

Communication scholar Stephen King describes reconciliation as a "byproduct of blues tourism," most evident as "reconciling" or bridging racial divides through "white audiences who express genuine admiration for African American blues musicians and racially diverse blues musical groups, as well as local and national blues organizations that feature a membership noted for its cultural and racial heterogeneity."[26] This is problematic in that it highlights contemporary efforts at cross-racial cooperation and dialogues, even if at surface level, without getting to the roots of the historical atrocities responsible for contemporary racial discord and the resulting trauma, which makes it difficult to achieve a "realer kind of reconciliation," one that speaks truth to power.[27]

"No black, no white, just the blues" was part of the Mississippi, Believe It! public relations campaign to challenge the state's public perception as racist and uneducated through education and information about accomplished Mississippians and Mississippi institutions.[28] Such slogans fail to consider the economic and cultural impacts on the state of antebellum slavery and Jim Crow, as well as contemporary confrontations between Black and White Mississippians met with the challenges of representing shared histories. Blues becomes "an inherently integrating force," one that "involves transforming the death place where African Americans were lynched into the 'birthplace of the blues,' a timeless, mysterious land with a notably downplayed racist history."[29]

In 2013 Debra Devi, rock musician and author of *The Language of the Blues from Alcorub to Zuzu*, wrote a three-part series for the *Huffington Post* titled "Can the Blues Rescue the Mississippi Delta?" Through research for her book, Devi had "discovered that passionate blues fans and entrepreneurs, as well as state and local governments, [were] committing significant time and money to see if blues tourism can make an economic rescue of" the Delta. She asked several tourism planners and promoters, mostly White males, such questions as, "I saw African Americans and whites working together at top administrative levels of museums and tourist sites, yet I've read charges that blues tourism is 'whitewashing' the blues, Southern racism and African American history. How do you respond?"[30]

Devi's respondents included Jim O'Neal, research director for the Mississippi Blues Trail; Matt Marshall, editor-in-chief of *American Blues Scene* magazine; Wesley Smith, executive director for the Greenville and Washington County Convention and Visitors Bureau; and Roger Stolle, documentary filmmaker and owner of the music and book store Cat Head Delta Blues and Folk Art in Clarksdale. O'Neal replied that Blues Trail markers directly address and acknowledge the troubled racial history of Mississippi; he highlighted the markers as signifying a "healing process" between the races and asserted that most of the "whitewashing" of the racial background of the blues has occurred outside of the state of Mississippi. That outsider narrative has been a recurring one for those in Mississippi who seek to distract attention from racism in local communities.[31]

Marshall began his response with the atrocities of Jim Crow in the Delta that made the music what it was and then "whitewashed" this fact by observing that although racial turmoil caused many blues musicians to leave, decades later people are coming back to the Delta to appreciate the music and, therefore, this profitable venture in historic preservation cannot be a bad thing. Smith extended this argument by stating that "what the Delta needs most is more dollars flowing into its economy. The tumultuous past is too complicated to market," but once tourists arrived, "our 'on the ground' presentation should be the truth laid bare for all to see." In other words, to Smith, "whitewashing" history seems to be productive if it is "on the ground" but not when it is marketed through magazine ads or websites. Tourists should face the truth when they get there.[32]

Stolle stressed that the tourism industry had grown significantly during the ten years that he had been in Clarksdale and that interracial progress had been made. He added that although "you'll see more white folks at blues clubs, juke joints and festivals it doesn't mean that you can't still have an authentic, culturally relevant Mississippi blues experience."[33] When I attended the Sunflower River Blues and Gospel Festival in Clarksdale in 2013, I did see more White folks than Black folks. Festivals such as that one largely draw White tourist audiences. Some state blues festivals do attract Black audiences with a fondness for soul blues. Yet they are not the primary target of the blues tourism industry in Mississippi. Black Mississippians also do not seem to be the main economic beneficiaries of the development that blues tourism officials promote.

Between 2014 and 2019, Brian Foster interviewed Black residents of Clarksdale, who told him that "the town's emphasis on blues tourism benefited white elected officials and business owners at the expense of Black music and musicians. Local blues scenes catered to white audiences with little regard for the tastes and interests of Black residents." Clarksdale's tourism industry's targeted audience is still a White outsider who seeks pleasure from nostalgic representations of blues music and its artists, what Stephen King refers to as "the pleasure and leisure principle of tourism." That pleasure is often dependent on silencing the pain of Black Mississippians.[34]

Lynell Thomas describes something similar in New Orleans tourism narratives: a "desire" for consuming blackness, for celebrating and consuming Black culture "without the uncomfortable acknowledgement of an exploitative slave system or its persistent legacy of racial and class inequality," which she presents as the intersecting trope of "disaster." This "racialized consumption is afforded without censure and with the added benefit of absolving whites of guilt and culpability for a racist past or present" and "substitutes for the more abnegating task of sustained antiracist work to create economic, educational, and environmental [racial] parity."[35]

Instead of creating economic equity, the city of New Orleans and the state of Mississippi comparably become economically dependent on exploiting Black creative cultures while silencing the oppressive systems that catalyzed that creativity as a means of survival. Even in a case like New Orleans, where tourism is dependent on accessible Black workers, Black people are systemically segregated from the tourism industry or come to rely on it as a means of low-wage employment. I live and work in a state where entire regions, like the Delta, depend on the savior of heritage tourism, something that I knew would not be a benefit to Black Mississippians without simultaneous anti-racist work.[36] I knew that the economic hierarchy would largely remain the same, with Black people providing the bulk of low-wage labor in the tourist industry. I saw this in other places that relied on tourism for survival, like New Orleans, where some of my family members provided this low-wage labor, and Memphis, where I went at least once a week. I wanted to better understand what these issues looked like throughout the South. Without the anti-racist work necessary to understand and address the institutional racism responsible for these labor relationships, this class structure would remain the same. I wanted my students to be sensitive to these issues.

Each year, I assign a final project for students in my heritage tourism course. The project asks that each student profile tourism in one region in the state. I assign those based on Visit Mississippi's five designated regions: the Capital/River, Coastal, Delta, Hills, and Pines. I ask students to review online and hard copy (if available) marketing and publicity materials for towns and cities in each region and profile tourism in that region based on an assessment of those materials. One student, assigned the Delta region, asked for clarity about the assignment after gathering several hard copy brochures at sites in the Delta. I immediately noticed that the materials' images showed Black Deltians as producers of cultural expressions and not as tourism industry consumers. Consumers were largely middle-aged White women, presumably outsiders. I asked that the student compare those marketing materials to the web marketing of Explore St. Louis, which presents racial diversity in tourism producers and consumers.[37] I asked that the student think about what this might say about whom a place wants to attract and why.

Discrepancies like this indicate that Mississippi's efforts are an attempt not to confront blues music as it relates to racial agonies but to frame it historically as a constructive cultural response to Jim Crow and, ultimately, a safety device in the state's racial reconciliation efforts. After all, who doesn't love the blues?

African Americans, Roots, and Returns to Mississippi

What these discussions largely omit are considerations of the impacts of these representations on Black folks in Mississippi and the potential to attract a burgeoning Black heritage tourist audience. This hinges on state and local failures to recognize that some African Americans' perceptions of the state cause them to consider it a precarious space in which to engage African diasporic lives. Here's one example.

In December 2017, I met Joye Hardiman on a trip to Cameroon organized by scholars and Cameroonian institutions researching Bimbia, the first site of transatlantic enslavement to be located and recognized in the country. Joye had served as executive director of the Evergreen State College campus in Tacoma, Washington, for nearly twenty years and was then interim director of the Washington Center for Improvement in Higher Education. She'd led a very colorful life with travels to Egypt, Ethiopia,

Kenya, Uganda, Mali, the Gambia, Ghana, Senegal, the Ivory Coast, Cameroon, South Africa, India, the Yucatán Peninsula, Trinidad, Brazil, Ecuador, Panama, and Cuba. This was a repeat visit to Cameroon. Relatively late in that ten-day trip, Joye revealed that her ancestors came from Pocahontas, Mississippi, in northern Hinds County near Jackson, and Coldwater in Tate County, Mississippi, part of the Memphis metropolitan area. We had several virtual group meetings prior to the trip, and I didn't recall her mentioning a connection to the state even when I introduced myself as affiliated with the University of Mississippi.

Joye grew up in Buffalo, New York; her parents were both children of Mississippi emigrants. Although she had not been to Mississippi, her grandparents' premigration narratives of the state as oppressive and violent diminished any desire that she might have to go there. The rest of what she knew about the South came from stereotypical popular culture images like Buckwheat and Uncle Remus and newspaper coverage of lynchings and the Ku Klux Klan. The most traumatizing was the *Jet* magazine photo of a young Emmett Till's ravaged body in an open casket. Joye would have been just a few years younger than Till when he was murdered. I tried to convince her to visit the state by touting the African American heritage preservation work that others and I were doing, but to no avail. I wanted her to experience Mississippi for herself.

In August 2018, Joye responded to that invitation. I had not expected her to reconnect with an inquiry about visiting Mississippi, but she had decided that she wanted to get reacquainted with her Mississippi family. I asked her about family names and any past contacts that she'd made. We followed one family connection who still seemed to be living in North Mississippi. During that search, Joye and I corresponded about when might be best for her to visit and what the transportation logistics looked like. She accepted my invitation to stay at my house. She wanted to know if it was possible to get a plane or train or bus from Jackson to Oxford, where I live. It's not an unusual request from first-time visitors, who presume that Oxford is most accessible from Jackson. Most Oxford visitors fly into Memphis, a shorter distance from Oxford than Jackson is.

I soon realized that when Joye proposed an idea, she moved quickly. We settled on a date in November 2018, scheduling around a conference that she had in Jackson. She would take the route from Jackson after all. She

Mississippi counties. Courtesy of the U.S. Census Bureau.

flew into Jackson, and she and her daughter, Soulma, drove to Oxford. I asked a friend and collaborator, Rhondalyn Peairs, to help develop an itinerary for Joye's trip, a balance between her desire to reconnect with family and the goal of gaining a better understanding of Mississippi in general.

Rhondalyn, an Oxford native, was a documentary projects and education coordinator for the Winter Institute when I began working at the university. As a local, Rhondalyn had helped me navigate my way around Oxford and North Mississippi and, through historic preservation connections, around the state. As a Black woman who understood the landscape historically and personally, she had been invaluable to me. I knew that I would be teaching during the time of Joye's visit and needed to limit the regional scope of her visit to places within a relatively short drive from Oxford. Rhondalyn helped expand that scope by offering to tour Joye around Oxford and through North Delta cities like Clarksdale in Coahoma County, once home to many famous blues and R & B artists and musicians, and Mound Bayou, a historically Black city in Bolivar County founded by former slaves.[38] The cities are respectively about an hour and an hour and a half drive from Oxford. Rhondalyn also guided Joye to meet Chandra Williams, executive director at Crossroads Cultural Arts Center in Clarksdale, and set up an informal performance by Guelel Kumba, a musician of West African Fulani heritage whose Unrecorded History of Blues performance broadens blues origin narratives by connecting North Mississippi blues traditions with Fulani music. She also gave Joye and her daughter a truncated version of a Black Oxford tour that she was in the process of developing.

Soulma and Joye are both expressive renaissance women. Soulma, an Xennial, is an outgoing creative with multiple talents, including photography, which came in handy on the Mississippi trip. Soulma seemed to be just as interested in their family ancestry as Joye was. According to Joye, Soulma's more sociable personality allowed her to make connections with family members at a reunion years before. One of those cousins, with whom they reconnected in Tate County, guided them through family photos and took them to family cemeteries.

Joye and Soulma were inundated with sites and experiences over a span of three days. I intended to show them some of the Behind the Big House sites in Holly Springs, but we arrived there after dark, with only a few minutes to take a quick peek at one of the slave-dwelling sites. Joye was so moved by that experience that she offered to return to Holly Springs, with Soulma, in April 2019 to help with the Behind the Big House program. And she did.

What Joye didn't know is that when I met her, I was thinking through the idea of roots tourism, which takes into account "those tourists who travel to a destination, specifically chosen for its connection to ancestry."[39] African Americans are often motivated to go on tours that connect them to perceived ancestral homelands in West Africa related to the transatlantic slave trade; I had met Joye on one of those tours to Cameroon. At that time, one of my anthropology graduate students, Suzanne "Suzy" Davidson, and I were in the process of publishing an article that examines the gap in theoretical discourse on the experiences of African Americans who take trips to sites of slavery in the U.S. The dominant discourse preferences the experiences of African Americans who take trips to places linked to slavery outside the U.S., like Bahia in Brazil or Ghana in West Africa.[40] We argued that certain things had to be in place for African Americans to take roots tours to U.S. sites of slavery. They had to have access to slavery-related sites and acceptance by historic site owners or managers; embodied reunion with enslaved and enslaver ancestors and union with other historic site descendants; and then the acknowledgment of plantation sites as homesteads.[41] They wouldn't simply visit those sites because they were invited to come. They needed to feel accepted, welcomed, and carefully guided. Suzy and I had made an academic case for this, and Joye became an exemplar. She was reluctant to travel to Mississippi but, with thoughtful guidance, she was able to embrace it. She even returned.

On her second visit, she chose to stay in Holly Springs instead of Oxford to place herself and her daughter as close to Behind the Big House as possible. During her visit, I asked her to give a talk on roots tourism as a form of return migration as part of the Center for the Study of Southern Culture's Brown Bag Lunch and Lecture Series. I knew that return migration was my particular academic understanding of Joye's trips to Mississippi, not necessarily how Joye would articulate her experience. She had just gone where her ancestors led her. As a result, I knew that she wouldn't be tied to that frame and I welcomed that. On April 30, in "A Soul Comes Home to Her Mississippi Roots," Joye narrated her life experiences, some of which I've shared in this narrative. She spent the next several days with my collaborators and me in Holly Springs, visiting sites like the Ida B. Wells-Barnett

Joye Hardiman on the back porch of the Butterfly Cottage, Holly Springs.
Photo by Soulma Ayers.

Museum, talking to Behind the Big House participants, and sitting on back porches, just breathing the Mississippi air. I was glad that she returned. I think that it did much good for her. It certainly did for me. I was able to help someone reconnect.

The Potential and Challenge of Heritage Tourism

I often considered Mississippi's potential to attract that burgeoning Black heritage tourist audience, like Joye, and recognized that her inherited family trauma about the state presumed it to be a hostile environment. That meant that I would have to facilitate making that environment accessible to her. The state would have to do similar work if it wanted to attract the growing multi-billion-dollar Black travel market.[42]

In fiscal year 2018, tourism was the fourth-largest private-sector employer in the state and generated more than $6.34 billion in visitor spending.[43] The Mississippi Development Authority's report highlighted Visit Mississippi and Visit Mississippi Gulf Coast as hosts of the 2018 Travel South USA Domestic Showcase, designed to "provide the easiest, most efficient way for tour operators to book business in the Southern states" by bringing tour and bus operators and journalists together for appointments with "state tourism office representatives, destination marketing organizations . . . , hotels, attractions, restaurants, outfitters and travel service providers (advertising media)."[44] The success of this event was partially measured by the number of editorial pieces, online reviews, social media shares, and print impressions that appeared after it, assumedly one outcome of journalists' participation. The report also updated additions to the state's three heritage trail networks, including the Mississippi Blues Trail, the Mississippi Freedom Trail, and the Mississippi Country Music Trail. These are the most visible authorized heritage discourses, what Laurajane Smith describes as a "characteristically professional (and authorizing) discourse of practitioners, policymakers, texts, and practice."[45] The Mississippi Development Authority also partially funds a Mississippi Mound Trail, with thirty-three marked sites listed in 2019.

According to *Remembering Emmett Till* author Dave Tell, the subsequent Mississippi Freedom Trail "was originally proposed as an extension of the Mississippi Blues Trail."[46] In 2011, the Mississippi Development Authority announced that this trail, "created during the fiftieth anniversary of the Freedom Rides," was designed to commemorate the state's civil rights legacy and to educate the public about this part of the state's heritage.[47] The first marker was officially unveiled in memory of Emmett Till. Others were placed at the Medgar Evers House, the Greyhound bus station in Jackson, Fannie Lou Hamer's gravesite in her hometown of Ruleville, and the Mississippi State Penitentiary at Parchman. In 2011, music legend Charlie Pride was honored with a Country Music Trail marker. Outside of that, this trail is largely disconnected from Black lives.

Visit Mississippi connects the Freedom Trail sites to the Mississippi Civil Rights Museum, which opened in Jackson in December 2017. It was a long-stalled project that finally secured $20 million from the state legislature after Governor Barbour spoke in its favor. It is part of a new generation of civil rights museums that Ayisha Jeffries Cisse, vice president for global affairs and international policy at the African American Islamic Institute, stresses as important but not placeholders for the failure to address "the issue of race in America, and until we do, that hydra is going to keep raising its ugly head."[48] In fact, the issue of race overtly reared its head around the museum's opening when Donald Trump attended despite controversy. Several state and federally elected officials boycotted the opening ceremony, "citing what they said was Trump's tendency to stir racial divisions and his questionable record on civil rights issues of importance to ethnic and racial minorities."[49]

It remains uncertain whether these larger efforts to educate diverse publics about the state's heritage can help people have "meaningful conversations about racism that still expresses itself in everything from interactions at a grocery store to the presidential election."[50] It is even more evident in the U.S. state with the highest Black population, the last state to have a Confederate battle flag emblem in its flag, and the state in which its highest public officials are being asked to account for their associations with White supremacist ideologies.[51] These realities are amplified with a seeming neglect of the institution of slavery and its impacts on the state that disallows real interracial reconciliation work as the truths of slavery remain unheard. Such neglect is doubly irresponsible because the "southern antebellum plantation is ground zero in understanding not just African American history but also how the modern tourism industry has tended to disinherit black travelers from their heritage."[52] Unfortunately, most assessments of the U.S. heritage tourism industry do not privilege

African Americans as travelers, and the state of Mississippi fits that model by prioritizing Whites as heritage travelers and tourism consumers. Failing to address slavery remains one of the biggest challenges to open and honest discussions about race. It was the weight of that specific challenge that I felt when I came to Mississippi.

Since 2011, I have watched Confederate Drive on the Mississippi campus become Chapel Lane; the development of the University of Mississippi Slavery Research Group (discussed in more detail in chapter 5); students, faculty, and staff successfully push for the removal of the state flag at most public institutions; and a resurgence of calls to change the flag statewide. These have all influenced how I have come to understand history, heritage, and tourism in Mississippi, but none of them had the most impact on me. It was my introduction to the Behind the Big House program in Holly Springs that accomplished that.

The same semester that I began teaching the heritage tourism course, I learned that a recent contact, Joseph "Joe" McGill, Jr., a National Trust for Historic Preservation program coordinator and Civil War reenactor, was staying overnight in slave cabins in Holly Springs, about a thirty-minute drive from Oxford. I had met him in 2010 in Anderson, in South Carolina's Upper Piedmont region, before he spent the night there in former slave cabins. Preservation South Carolina, a nonprofit state preservation organization, was trying to bring attention to the cabins' need for historic preservation amid the threat of developers who were planning to turn them into single-room rental homes. Founder of the Slave Cabin (now Slave Dwelling) Project, Joe had been spending the night in slave cabins to draw attention to their need for historic preservation and to help publicize current historic preservation efforts. I heard about his activities on the radio, contacted him, and asked if we could meet. Since then, we had kept in touch. Joe had moved on to other slave cabin sites and was invited to Holly Springs by his friend Jenifer Eggleston and her husband, Chelius Carter, who had decided to start interpreting slave dwellings, including one on their property.

In 2012, Jenifer, a National Park Service grants writer, and Chelius, a restoration architect, piloted the Behind the Big House program after discovering that the detached kitchen on their property, the historic Hugh Craft House, was likely a former slave dwelling. They identified twelve other similar sites in Marshall County and the city of Holly Springs and organized a pilot program through Preserve Marshall County and Holly

Springs, Inc., a local historic preservation institution that Chelius directed. In 2005, Chelius had cofounded (with W. O. "Bill" Fitch) the institution, "envisioned as being an umbrella organization to manage preservation activities within the town and county."[53]

Chelius and Jenifer designed the Behind the Big House program to interpret the lives of enslaved persons through the former slave dwellings that are hidden in plain view. Some structures had been readapted for various uses, making it difficult to recognize their original purposes; they had been suppressed from historical memory, unintentionally or by design. According to Jenifer, "it was clear that a significant part of the historic narrative was missing. While a number of the silent witnesses—the structures directly related to the slaves' accommodations were extant—the stories of the people who lived [in] and used these buildings were largely being forgotten. The personal histories of the 'Big Houses' had been preserved but what of those personal lives 'Behind the Big House'?"[54] She and Chelius developed a slave-dwelling tour meant to supplement the lack of narratives about enslaved populations on the Holly Springs Garden Club's annual pilgrimage tours, an eighty-plus-year-old tradition of showcasing historic antebellum homes. I discuss the Behind the Big House program in detail in chapter 3.

Behind the Big House exists not only because the pilgrimage survives but because the pilgrimage silences. The state of Mississippi's more recent efforts to sell its Black history can't be disentangled from its history of selling White nostalgia, most evident in the pilgrimages that took place in several regions across the state beginning in the early twentieth century. The Holly Springs Pilgrimage is not unique. It's a localized model of the state's largest pilgrimage: the one in Natchez in the southwestern part of the state. The pilgrimage phenomenon is largely outside the scope of this book, but the reasons it exists are integral to understanding the landscape of slavery tourism in Mississippi and how Behind the Big House became its counternarrative.

The Holly Springs Pilgrimage

The garden club's pilgrimage began after five Holly Springs women—Ruth Francisco, Marjorie McCrosky, Nina Craft, Marguerite "Rita" Binion Cochran, and Laura Binion—returned from the Vicksburg and Natchez pilgrimages in 1936. The Natchez Garden Club began its official pilgrimage in 1932 after homeowners gave Mississippi Garden Club delegates peeks inside their homes after the spring 1931 garden tours. The Mississippi Federation of Garden Clubs state president, Etta Mitchel Henry, praised Natchez's historic mansions, prompting the garden club women to start a pilgrimage tour of homes. In *Remembering Dixie: The Battle to Control Historical Memory in Natchez, Mississippi, 1865–1941*, Susan Falck notes that Henry may have coined the name Natchez Pilgrimage at the close of the garden club convention that year.[55]

Garden clubs, which Falck describes as "hugely popular" in Mississippi by the 1930s, were among many early twentieth-century women's clubs nationwide, in this case with the goal of home and city beautification projects.[56] All but one of the attendees from Holly Springs, Laura Binion, were charter members of the Holly Springs club. On the car ride home, the four club members agreed to push for the inauguration of a pilgrimage. Because 1936 was also the city's centennial, the women decided that Holly Springs too should have a house tour in conjunction with other centennial celebrations that year. Although they were confident about the pilgrimage idea, Marguerite Cochran noted that the all-male Rotary Club was lukewarm about supporting the event and that others were skeptical that the lack of the big estates and rural antebellum landscape so visible on the Natchez tour would restrict Holly Springs from attracting "people like Natchez." Holly Springs was a site of urban slavery, with in-town estates on relatively small plots of land. Still, the pilot pilgrimage was successful, with guests who came from all over the mid-South region, greeted by "a Negro orchestra, hired for the occasion to lend a Deep South atmosphere and stationed on the veranda," playing "Dixie."[57]

Cochran's "Deep South atmosphere" was designed to entice pilgrimage guests in the way that Natchez's natural landscape did, yet the Deep South that she staged was more of a reality at a time when "most of the old social and economic patterns stayed in place." The official Holly Springs Pilgrimage began two years later, in April 1938, becoming Marshall County's "most important tourist attraction," and April continues to be pilgrimage month.[58] Even though the Holly Springs properties lacked the natural rural landscape of some of the homes on the Natchez tour, the Natchez Pilgrimage became its model because the women "thought [Holly Springs] had far more than Vicksburg and compared favorably with Natchez."[59] By

1939, the Holly Springs Pilgrimage included the Confederate Ball, the daily Civil War pageant at Walter Place, "and the nightly singing of negro spirituals from Rust and [Mississippi Industrial] negro colleges there, as well as their presentation of the African American folk drama, 'Heaven Bound.'"[60]

Cultural and historical geographer Steven Hoelscher describes similar scenes in his examination of the Natchez Pilgrimage, with a cultural performance presenting the "'refinement, exclusiveness, and prestige' of white Natchez society as well as 'a series of folk dances and plantation songs . . . rendered by colored entertainers.'" As in Holly Springs, in Natchez "different African-American choirs performed musicals that went by names like 'Straight and Narrow Path,' 'Heaven Bound,' 'The Glory Road,' and 'Negro Spirituals.'" Black citizens were included, yet "the logic of southern white memory contained very little room for [their] experiences . . . not surprising, of course, for remembrance always implies forgetting, especially when the political stakes are so high."[61]

Walter Place during the 1936 centennial. Chesley Thorne Smith Collection, courtesy of the Marshall County Historical Museum.

The pilgrimage characterizes what historian Charles Reagan Wilson identifies as a "southern civil religion," materializing out of White southerners' "spiritual and psychological need ... to reaffirm their identity" with romantic and nostalgic yet mythic representations of southern plantation life after their defeat in the Civil War.[62] Susan Falck describes the Natchez Pilgrimage founders as being on "a passionate quest to remember a neatly packaged white selective telling of the past that honored the longstanding moonlight and magnolias version of the narrative, while erasing dark, troubling memories of slavery."[63] In this case, the pilgrimage tourism industry meets at "the nexus of authenticity, myth, and public memory" in the same way that Stephen King proposes the blues tourism industry does.[64]

I am unclear about the specific reasons for the use of the term "pilgrimage" in the garden tour contexts, so I rely on the notion of secular pilgrimage in tourism anthropology to understand what these pilgrimage journeys may mean in the context of some White southerners' "ceremonious exaltation of [a] mythic past as the collective yearning to inhabit it . . . amid runaway social change: the Great Depression, World War II, and later the Cold War and the classical civil rights Movement."[65] Nostalgia for the South's loss in the Civil War and for life before the war, including slavery, may have generated a need for "travel to, and communion with, a site that embodies" those values.[66] Southerners were not the only pilgrimage visitors, especially in Natchez where garden club promoters strategically marketed the events nationally, yet Holly Springs seemed to mainly attract midsoutherners, people Marguerite Cochran noted as being "from Memphis, from the Delta, from the hills, from the prairies, from Tennessee, [and] from Arkansas."[67] For them, Holly Springs was a more accessible drive than the garden club pilgrimages in cities farther south such as Aberdeen, Laurel, Woodville, Hattiesburg, Vicksburg, Greenwood, Carrolton, Jackson, Meridian, Columbus, Leland, Greenville, and Natchez.[68] All existed by 1940, when newspapers like the Washington, D.C., *Evening Star* were dedicating entire pages to "Garden News," with the pilgrimages from around the South advertised, including the one in Holly Springs.[69]

Holly Springs's 1936 centennial and its featured home tours had revived Marshall County's social and cultural life, following the adverse effects of a three-month drought, crop failure, and the Great Depression, from which the state did not begin to recover until that year.[70] Through the events that Cochran proposed to the Rotary Club—a tour of historic homes, historical skits, a jousting tournament, the Confederate Ball, and a pilgrimage to Hill Crest Cemetery—descendants of Holly Springs's White settlers celebrated Marshall County's one hundred years of existence. None of them was likely alive when the county was settled, but they connected to those ancestors through oral family narratives, which their descendants preserved in writing, institutional archives, family letters, and academic theses.[71] It is logical to think that many of these recollections were shared during the planning and presentation of these events.

That same year, the Works Progress Administration's Historical Research Project began in Mississippi. As part of the Federal Writers' Project, Holly Springs native Netty Fant Thompson interviewed some of the former enslaved living in Marshall County. Thompson, a photographer, writer, and trained artist, was a descendant of the county's White settler families. She interviewed William Edward Black, Ernest Branon, Lizzie Fant Brown, Belle Caruthers, Josephine Cox, Rena Crawford, Sally Foltz, Violet Ford, John Gilstrap, Callie Gray, Laura Jane Jackson, Emma Johnson, Aaron Jones, Abe Kelly, Liza McGhee, John Archie Moseley, and Alice Shaw. I don't know if anyone asked them how they felt about a descendant of the planter class interviewing them, or if they had personal relationships with Thompson that might have affected the interviews in other ways.

It is logical to think that Thompson and other planter descendants might have spoken fondly of their ancestors' former slaves, even some of those mentioned, as they reminisced during the centennial events. I think it's less likely that they talked of the memories of those who stood among "Mississippi's former slaves [who] spoke so bluntly about harsh conditions and cruel treatment that state [Federal Writers' Project] officials, apparently offended by such candor, chose to violate [Works Progress Administration] guidelines and not forward their narratives to the Library of Congress in Washington." Thousands of those pages "were discovered in the Mississippi Department of Archives and History in the 1970s."[72] Henry Walton's first statement recalled his former mistress whipping his mother to death with a cowhide. Lizzie Fant Brown recalled her master whipping her and blistering her because she lied about leaving the henhouse door open. Callie Johnson had scars on her body from the overseer's beatings. Alice Shaw's job was to fan flies off the table while "the white folks [ate]" and "to tote the dishes to the kitchen." Her mistress cracked her on the head if she dropped one. Liza McGhee told Thompson, "I remember some things about old slave days, but I don't want to say nothing that will get me in bondage again. I am too old now to be a slave. I couldn't stand it."[73] In 1936, the year of the centennial and the pilot pilgrimage, she still felt threatened by the possibility of being enslaved again.

Belle Garland Myers Caruthers stressed to Thompson that she wanted her full name included in the narrative. She boldly shared that her master struck her with his muddy boot after he caught her studying a Blue-Backed Speller. She was one of the most candid interviewees, referring to the overseer as "common white trash," adding that "if the niggers didn't get to the field by daylight, he would beat them." She also talked about her fear of slave patrol punishments. When asked how she felt about Abraham Lincoln, she replied that "the negroes never heard of Lincoln till after the War, but if the white people had listened to him and freed their slaves, there wouldn't have been a war." She spoke directly to Thompson, stressing that all the presidents who had been assassinated were Republicans. Caruthers's master was a clerk in the Marshall County courthouse and would not allow her a license to marry. It seems that Thompson ended the interview by asking Caruthers what she felt about the institution of slavery itself, to which she replied, "Give me liberty or give me death."[74]

The candor of those interviewed reflects a level of bravery that might have shocked some of those White centennial descendants who thought of them fondly or who remembered slavery with a sense of paternalism. Such is evident in Ann Fant Rozell's written recollections of settler log house construction in the late 1830s. In 1917, she wrote, "By spring there was a good size piece of land cut and ready for log rolling. For miles around the males—black and white—were invited to a log rolling which consisted of a big dinner and a jolly time."[75]

Even seen through White lenses, these narratives are complicated. They show the embeddedness of slavery in the minds of those who lived and witnessed it as children, even as Marshall County celebrated its founding with a "Deep South atmosphere." Though unstated, that atmosphere reeked of slavery. Regardless of individual or institutional motives for developing and continuing the pilgrimage, one thing is clear. The institution of slavery is what made both the development of Marshall County and Holly Springs and the success of the pilgrimage possible.

Holly Springs

Holly Springs was founded in 1836 by White settlers benefiting from lands available just after the Chickasaw Cession. By the 1850s, it was a seat of one of the wealthiest counties in the state of Mississippi. Slavery made that possible. Part of Holly Springs's contemporary built environment still reflects that wealth through estates, historically interpreted during the pilgrimage and now during the Behind the Big House program.

The hilly terrain and rocky soil found in Holly Springs dominated the topography of northern Mississippi, which initially proved less suitable for the establishment of large cotton plantations than the southwestern part of the state. However, many of the Hill Country's early White settlers hoped to enter the planter class by capitalizing on the cultivation of the region's yellow loam soil with the use of enslaved labor once the Chickasaws responded to pressure to cede their lands to the U.S. government.[76] The Treaty of Pontotoc Creek, ratified on March 1, 1833, "led to at least three major developments: (1) widespread Chickasaw movement out of Mississippi, (2), rapid purchases of northwestern Mississippi public land by speculators, and (3) new migration into the area by whites and their slaves."[77] In February 1836, the Mississippi legislature divided the Chickasaw Cession into ten counties, including Marshall County. It became an antebellum cultural and economic hub in northern Mississippi, largely developed by the recent White settlers whose cotton plantations depended on Black slave labor. By 1837, the county "held the largest white population in the state, having grown in one year from under four thousand to 13,498 (8,274 whites, 5,224 slaves). The population of Holly Springs was counted at 1,544, the third-largest town in Mississippi, only Natchez and Vicksburg exceeding it."[78]

Holly Springs developed as a support system for rural farms and plantations in Marshall County, affording "facilities for moving the agricultural crops to market and for importing farm and plantation supplies."[79] By 1850, Marshall County had nearly 30,000 residents, nearly half of them enslaved, and "it led the state in the production of cotton and of almost every other agricultural product."[80] The Mississippi Central Railroad, which ran through Holly Springs, increased the city's affluence. Although one of the largest antebellum towns in the state, in 1860 Holly Springs had a population of less than 3,000 persons, compared to 38,000, 40,000, and

169,000 in Richmond, Charleston, and New Orleans, respectively. It was a site of small-town urban slavery, the most ambiguous amid contemporary understandings of the rural plantation–large city binary. The antebellum owners of these in-town estates were prosperous, yet the contemporary landscape masks the reality that their prosperity was inextricably tied to slavery.

It is that built environment that Chelius Carter and Jenifer Eggleston hoped to represent more critically. I spent so much time critiquing Mississippi tourism efforts for not including slavery in their interpretations that I knew I had to get involved to help them in some way. I just wasn't sure how. By the time I heard about Behind the Big House, it was too late to introduce my tourism class to the program. The class was over, but it wasn't too late to collaborate with Chelius and Jenifer. Through the Center for the Study of Southern Culture, I was able to contract with the Gilder Lehrman Institute of American History in New York as part of a one-week summer workshop for teachers. The institute was interested in developing longer-lasting partnerships with institutions like the center and creating different approaches to the content and structure of its workshops. Teachers came from all over the country to a central location. In these workshops, teachers were assigned readings ahead of time and expected to come to the site prepared to discuss them.

I proposed a Race and Tourism in the Modern South workshop designed to help teachers explore historical and current issues encompassing tourism development in the southern U.S. There is particular attention given to how representations of various racial groups are confronted and conflicted in historic site development. It was my hope that teachers would have opportunities not only to discuss these issues but to visit a local historic site and engage site managers.

In May 2012, I contacted Jenifer by email to ask permission for the workshop participants to visit at least one of the historic sites in Holly Springs. I emphasized the significance of teachers having the privilege of hearing about cultural representations at historic sites from a management perspective. The next day, Jenifer replied affirmatively. I had missed their pilot program, so she and Chelius offered a repeat tour "with a discussion about how these sites were included on [the] annual [pilgrimage] tour of homes for the first time and what the plans/hopes [were] for the future of documenting, researching, and including the slave outbuildings and narratives." They offered to open the main houses and the slave quarters and expand on "how these buildings functioned together and how the histories of them are really one history that needs further interpretation and expansion."[81]

Together we coordinated a day of events, which began at the Holly Springs Tourism office followed by a windshield tour of related sites. We concluded with on-site tours of the Hugh Craft property, owned by Chelius and Jenifer, and Burton Place, owned by David Person, another private homeowner interested in showcasing the slave dwelling on his property in addition to the main or "big house" in which he resided part-time. We toured the two houses, which included discussions of how enslaved persons' accommodations related functionally and socially to the "big house." The homeowners also surprised us with a small reception at David's home. The event even warranted a local news article, and several of the teachers and I were interviewed.

My second opportunity to teach the heritage tourism course, in spring 2013, prioritized the incorporation of an applied project. This class of five students was much smaller than the previous class, which made the applied component more practical. This time around, Chelius and Jenifer visited the class to discuss the politics of the Behind the Big House program, including its relationship to the garden club and other local institutions not convinced of the necessity of interpreting slave dwellings. Chelius and Jenifer also requested help with documentary and archival research. Unfortunately, this was a weak point among students in the southern studies graduate course because they lacked backgrounds in historical research. In addition, students were to interview tourism officials in Holly Springs to get a better sense of its political climate. The pinnacle of the course was the students' opportunities to work as program docents.

The 2013 Behind the Big House tour was held at the same time as the pilgrimage but was a separate program. It had its own maps and docents, including a few local volunteers. Chelius and Jenifer served as managers of the site. There was a $25 fee for the pilgrimage. Behind the Big House was free of charge, a stipulation of its Mississippi Humanities Council grant. The tour was organized so that each docent had the opportunity to work at more than one property. I worked at the Hugh Craft House and Burton Place in addition to McCarroll Place, another former slave dwelling readapted for reuse as an antique store in the early twentieth century.

As I write this, I am preparing for my eighth year of collaboration with Behind the Big House. The reason that I continue to collaborate is the ongoing commitment of Jenifer, Chelius, and a few others who give voices to historic sites as silent witnesses. I had hoped that by now their work would have had more institutional impact on slavery interpretations in the state. I find some comfort in the likelihood that the impact on individuals can't be quantified. Unexpectedly, Behind the Big House did lead to a similar program in Arkansas, also called Behind the Big House.[82] In 2015, fellow public archaeologist Jodi Barnes, then president-elect of Preserve Arkansas, the Historic Preservation Alliance of Arkansas, visited the program in Holly Springs and began a comparable program in Arkansas the next year.

The Arkansas program focuses on one main interpretation site in the state per year. It is a partnership among Preserve Arkansas, managers of each chosen historic site, and the state's Black History Commission. Barnes developed the Arkansas program and has helped shape it since its beginnings. I hoped that others in Mississippi would have picked up the challenge as Arkansas did. I continued to work with Chelius and Jenifer because Behind the Big House had not yet become the replicable state model that they had envisioned. That work still needs to be done. This book is less about what didn't get done than it is about the people and personalities that it took to make the progress that has begun. What happened in Holly Springs is rare.

In Holly Springs, there are local citizens who explicitly recognize that all histories should matter, but that they do not. These individuals did not wait on a proclamation from the state governor, a federal mandate, or social pressure to do the right thing. They did not need an academic historian to tell them that "history is about seamless relationships that cannot be parsed . . . it must encompass all people."[83] The history of the enslaved cannot be separated from the history of those who enslaved them or from the history of those who inherited a hierarchy rooted in a centuries-old system of free labor. It still affects everyone.

I interviewed Chelius and Jenifer in 2019 after seven years of working with them. I wanted to better understand how they came to do the work they do, so that I could share that knowledge with people interested in doing comparable work. Instead, I found it difficult to get them to think about why they do something that, to them, just seems to be the right thing to do. It was also challenging to draw individual experiences from the couple, who see their work as a partnership. What the interview does offer is a clearer picture of what grassroots heritage activism can look like, in all its complexity, without a binary that assumes a right or a wrong way to do this work. I hope, at the least, that it causes those too quick to critique it to rethink those critiques and those too anxious to engage in it to pause. The next chapter begins with my interview with Chelius and Jenifer. It's the story of how they came to develop Behind the Big House as well as their hopes and motives, beginning with Chelius's purchase of the Hugh Craft House, a historic "big house" with an adjacent slave dwelling. It also lays out my role as a scholar-in-collaboration—service-learning and teaching—and introduces the others in their supportive network who help make the Behind the Big House collaboration work.

The Behind the Big House Program

In December 2019, just after the Christmas holiday, I touched base with Chelius to see if he and Jenifer would be available for an interview. We agreed to meet and I was given a heads-up that their kids would be in tow. This meetup was long overdue, and it was rare. Chelius and Jenifer were hardly in Holly Springs at the same time. They live in Virginia most of the time, with Chelius traveling to Holly Springs as needed. Since I have known them, they have lived full-time in Holly Springs, part-time in Holly Springs, and then full-time in the state of Virginia, balancing parenthood and jobs in between Holly Springs preservation duties. Behind the Big House, although almost logistically impractical for them, seems to still be a passion of theirs.

Sometimes I wonder why. I barely understood what kept me motivated and never asked the folks with whom I worked. I hoped that interviewing them would offer a deeper understanding. When I first started to think about writing this book, I really wanted people to appreciate what it means to sustain a grassroots level of preservation work, because one of the hardest things about doing this work is sustaining it. I know this through my personal experience. I also know that most people without that experience do not or cannot understand. This was evident in colleagues who asked me for insights into some of their community-engaged aspirations and added how much fun it might be. For me, it is rarely fun—fulfilling at times but rarely fun. Most times, I just nodded, knowing that I could not verbalize how complicated this all was and still is. Without seeming impolite, I couldn't begin to express the level of commitment that had to be made.

I suggested that I meet Chelius and Jenifer in Holly Springs to keep them from having to travel to Oxford with their kids. Rhondalyn Peairs also wanted to come along to surprise Jenifer. When I met Rhondalyn, she worked for the Winter Institute, consulting with Chelius and Jenifer on their program development. She became the unofficial tour guide for the teachers in my Gilder Lehrman workshop, and her suggestions helped my graduate students to be more reflective about how they do cultural heritage work, especially in a state with which she is more familiar. Rhondalyn represented an institutional affirmation of the work they hoped to do, particularly against the backdrop of a reluctant local community. To me, she represented the local knowledge and experience that I didn't have and badly needed to better understand the place where I worked. She gave clarity to what I didn't understand about Mississippi tourism at local levels and about the people involved. I was observant but still blind to some of the nuances, like local family and community histories and structured racial norms. Rhondalyn sustained a relationship with Chelius and Jenifer and with me even after her tenure with the Winter Institute ended. Neither of us had seen Jenifer in years. We met them at the Hugh Craft House, their home in Holly Springs and the orientation site for the Behind the Big House program.

Chelius bought the house in 2002, after first coming to Holly Springs in the 1990s to work on the restoration and stabilization of the old St. Joseph's Church, now the Yellow Fever Martyrs Church and Museum.[1] He lived in Memphis at the time. He remembered seeing the Hugh Craft House but never imagined owning it. That changed after he decided to settle in Holly Springs, a place where he "could possibly have an effect on the historic preservation community."[2]

The Hugh Craft Property

The property is named after Hugh Craft, who came to Holly Springs in 1839 from Milledgeville, Georgia, as an agent for the American Land Company. Chelius describes Craft as "a land speculator and purveyor of many things," adding that "in one 1820s Milledgeville advertisement, he offered 'Pickled York River Oyster!'" He also sold decorative ironwork like the fence that surrounds the Hugh Craft property, which Chelius imagines was a marketing gimmick. Hugh Craft lost everything in the economic Panic of 1837, what Chelius describes as the "dot-com bubble" of its day.[3] Overspeculating in land prices caused banks, landowners, and land agents like Craft to lose all they owned. The opening of new lands in North Mississippi gave him an opportunity to remake himself.

The Craft family home was completed in the early 1850s "as Marshall County entered its most prosperous and architecturally significant decade," evidenced by the construction of "big houses" or main residences such as the Hugh Craft House on South Memphis Street near the town square.[4] Craft's mother-in-law, Chloe Collier, purchased the lot from Sam McCorkle, a land speculator from Tennessee, in 1842. She then transferred the property to her daughter Elizabeth Collier Craft, Hugh Craft's third wife (Craft was twice widowed), in 1850. Collier's frame cottage was then dismantled, and the present structure was completed in 1851. Craft's surveying and land speculation became quite successful, and he built a small office, no longer extant, on the current property's east side. He also came to own much of the lot across the street from the present property (now a private parking lot), where he had barns, a horse lot, and vegetable gardens.

The Hugh Craft property is most notable as the headquarters for Union Colonel Robert C. Murphy, commander of the 8th Wisconsin "Old Abe" Infantry Regiment, during Confederate General Earl Van Dorn's raid on Holly Springs's supply depot.[5] On December 20, 1862, Union soldiers sought cover as the Confederates advanced toward the town. Hugh Craft had suffered a disabling stroke in 1860 and remained an invalid until his death in 1867. It was his infirm state that persuaded Colonel Murphy to allow the Crafts to remain in their home. During Van Dorn's raid, the Hugh Craft House was one of the Confederacy's targets, and while Colonel Murphy was probably captured near the Holly Springs rail depot, one of his staff officers, Captain William J. Dawes, was captured by some of Van Dorn's men in the entry hall stairwell of the main house.

According to Chelius, during his 2009 rehabilitation work, a leaden musket ball was found in one of the interior walls of the entry hall. A Craft descendant related that as a young boy, before the 1930s, he could see several pockmarks in the east and north exterior stucco walls from rifle and musket balls fired during the raid. Craft family members occupied the main house for 141 years. It was subsequently purchased by two other owners and then by Chelius in 2002.

When Chelius was thinking about purchasing the property, he wondered about the storage shed on it and was told that it might have been slave quarters. He wasn't sure. Then he wondered why there was a ladder stair going up to the attic space. That didn't make sense to him if it was just a shed. As he gave a tour in 2018, he said,

> In an earlier life, I used to do telephone work, telephone installation repair. I was very used to walking around the attics and feeling around rafters and ceiling joists covered in insulation to make sure I was stepping on the joists and not stepping into the ceiling and falling into the floor below. And the upstairs here was all covered in insulation so I sort of reverted to my telephone man habits of feeling around and thought, "Hmmm . . . solid floor. I said why would there be a solid floor in the attic up here? And then it occurred to me, oh, this is where *they* slept [my italics]. And that's when it began to dawn on me that this humble, rudimentary slave quarters and its kitchen were far more significant culturally than the main house, that it really deserved to be called out for recognition for what it was.[6]

Chelius thinks that the kitchen/quarters might pre-date the main house and might have been built for the frame cottage that Collier would have built for herself earlier on the property. Unlike the main house, which is clad in stucco, the kitchen/quarters structure is board and batten, leading Chelius to believe that Collier's cottage would have better matched the slave dwelling in building materials than the Craft House does. This matching of main house–slave dwelling construction materials is not a consistent pattern for similar urban structures, but it does reflect a pattern of other sites in Holly Springs, like Burton Place, and other places in the U.S. South.

The Craft House slave dwelling has three rooms on its main floor: two separate rooms and a kitchen. "All three main-floor rooms employ fireplaces in a central chimney set parallel with the front and rear walls."[7] Only one room has direct access to the main house and seems to have been the private quarters for an enslaved house servant, possibly a butler or a maid. The other separate room has access to a door that opens onto the property's front yard and direct access to the kitchen. The kitchen door leads outside and directly to the main house. The kitchen includes a ladder stair to the upstairs loft. Because enslaved children made up the majority of the nine people enslaved on the property, in both the 1850 and 1860 slave census schedules, Chelius suspects that they slept in that loft.

The room with direct access to the kitchen is interpreted as the cook's quarters.[8] The cook could practically go from her private quarters to the kitchen to prepare meals and then directly into the main house to deliver those meals. The cook's quarters and the other room now have a doorway in between them but were historically closed off from each other as private residences. The people who lived in them did not have easy access to each other, but they both had easy access to the main residence. The allocation of space and access reflects the building's multiple purposes as private sleeping quarters, a working kitchen, and a dependent unit for those in the main house. The structure prioritizes enslaved persons' access to White owners and not to each other, outside of the cook's access to children who might have slept in the loft.

The slave dwelling is only a few steps from the main house. For slave owners, the placement of urban slave quarters was about having visual authority over enslaved persons' movements.[9] It was also about enslaved people having direct access to servicing their owners while having limited access to the main house. Shortly after its construction in 1851, the main house had a slaves' circulation stairwell that created segregated access from the slave quarters to the main house, on its south side, and gave access from the main house cellar to its roof. Chelius observed this during rehabilitation work on the main house done in 2009. There is also an upstairs window on the west side of the main house that used to be a door; hence there was an exterior stairway that enslaved persons used that was removed at some unknown date, as its window appears to be from the early twentieth century.[10]

The structure also includes a cellar with a fireplace. There was an exterior stairwell to the cellar that appears to have been a secondary smoking room, due to the wrought iron meat hooks still in place, as well as the unmistakable odor of cured ham that still lingers on a hot and humid day.[11] It seems that persons would have occupied the kitchen/quarters at least to 1900, when the census lists forty-year-old Lillie Wright as a cook and twenty-year-old Mary Garrison as a chambermaid. Both were Black women. The late nineteenth-century newspapers glued to the walls in both rooms might have been placed there as insulation.

"How Much Truth Do They Want to Hear?"

When Chelius first moved onto the property, he had a few conversations with other homeowners with slave dwellings on their properties. Some were intrigued, others in denial, but there were no specific conversations about interpretation. Chelius, a restoration architect, intended to use the slave dwelling as his architecture studio, but he knew that the space had something more to offer. To him, its significance was more important than that of the main house, but he wasn't sure what to do about it. His future wife, Jenifer, would have an answer.

Chelius and Jenifer met when she served as the National Park Service's primary grants manager for the Hurricanes Katrina and Rita Recovery Grant Programs at the federal level, and he managed the state-level arm of the programs for the Mississippi Department of Archives and History. Jenifer visited Holly Springs in 2007, when the two were dating, and moved there in 2008. She first attended the town's pilgrimage in 2009. As a historic preservationist, she was intrigued by the idea of walking through the old houses, describing herself as the type of person to "seek out a house tour," but was surprised by what she saw as "a stuck relic of the past," with no histories—Black or White—being adequately represented.[12] She didn't expect a National Park Service–grade tour, but she did expect a more historically grounded one. She does admit that the garden club, with its all-volunteer effort, does not have a corps of people able to develop a narrative-based history, outside of the descriptions of interior furnishings narrated by a group of young girls with distributed scripts.[13]

Jenifer had thought a lot about Preserve Marshall County and Holly Springs's role as a historic preservation institution and felt that it had restricted its potential by not moving its "preservation work beyond just bricks and mortar."[14] Early on, the organization acquired the Chalmers Institute, an antebellum building that had housed Mississippi's first legislatively recognized university. Preserving that building had been and still is the organization's primary role.

With her master's degree in regional planning, Jenifer understood that one of the biggest challenges for preservationists is communicating preservation's value to different stakeholders. She considers the major stewardship question to be, Why should people care about it? "You've got to preserve more than just the stuff. You've got to preserve the stories that go with those things. If you're going to come back to Holly Springs in a hundred years when we're all long gone, who's going to still care and why? What is going to be still standing, cared for, and thought about? And you're not going to get there still holding on to stories that are not relevant or were never even true to begin with."[15] Since her first visit in 2007, she had been astounded by the number of extant slave dwellings, then puzzled by the lack of mention in citywide tourism efforts, especially the pilgrimage. She suggested that, through Preserve Marshall County, she and Chelius develop a program working together with those homeowners who seemed interested in the sites' histories of enslavement. It was one way to get locals to connect to and invest in the preservation of those spaces.

Jenifer got in touch with her friend Joe McGill, Jr., who had started his Slave Cabin (now Slave Dwelling) Project in 2010, to ask if he was interested in collaborating. Joe suggested they seek grant funding from the Mississippi Humanities Council to operate the program, based on his success securing South Carolina Humanities funds for his project. Jenifer did a Google search for owners of private properties with comparable programs, not "the Monticellos, Mt. Vernons, and Williamsburgs" that "rebooted pieces of their story" to include narratives of slavery. She had no luck and consulted Joe, who told her that their program would be the first community-wide program that he knew of. That made things a little more complicated but not impossible. Chelius and Jenifer, both White, also felt that the story of slavery in Holly Springs should be told but that it was not necessarily theirs to tell—meaning that they should not be the faces of interpretation. "We were going to have to have scholarly African American interpreters, historians, and contributors involved in this or it wasn't going to be successful."[16]

Chelius consulted property owners with whom he had had architectural discussions about their slave-dwelling sites and assessed who might be willing to open their properties for a slave-dwelling tour. That first year, 2012, he and Jenifer envisioned a partnership with the Ida B. Wells-Barnett Museum, a Black history site that seemed to be a good fit.[17] It is likely that the famous educator, journalist, and women's and civil rights activist was born on the property where the museum is located. Chelius and Jenifer also decided to hold their program at the same time as the pilgrimage, with the assumption that their narrative would complement the pilgrimage's "with a merging stream of more accurate history."[18]

They realized that garden club members might not receive their offer as the gift they perceived it to be and struggled with how to present their program as a necessary option. Chelius describes their approach as "the soft shell of a shotgun wedding." They'd already decided not to ask permission with an understanding that they had just as much right as anyone else to develop this program and present it when they best saw fit. They pitched it as a way to expand the pilgrimage's audience. They put two houses on the tour, their Craft House and Burton Place, which was on the pilgrimage for the seventh time since 2006. Chelius describes this initial attempt as a "scratchy" partnership with the garden club.[19] They made the best of it, negotiating Montrose, the club's home base, as the host location for their program's opening reception. The club invited Joe McGill and Rhondalyn Peairs to speak at the reception and waived pilgrimage fees for the speakers.

Chelius had contacted the Winter Institute, asking for support for their new program, and Rhondalyn was sent to address those needs. She remembers the institute's director getting the call. Rhondalyn, who had been working with the Oren Dunn City Museum in Tupelo, headed to Holly Springs on her way back to Oxford. At that point, she had been away from Oxford for sixteen years and North Mississippi for five. When she met Chelius at his home for the first time, she admitted that she really didn't think about Holly Springs's pilgrimage and wished that all pilgrimages would just die out. The mainstream hoopskirts narrative was just too difficult for her as a Black Mississippi woman. She came into the meeting not trusting people who say that they want to interpret enslavement. She wanted to know if Chelius was really about truth telling.

This was not the first time that Rhondalyn had faced community struggles to represent pasts in the present. Her travels through the Winter Institute had revealed a thread of grassroots efforts seeking to interpret histories at several civil rights sites. I personally observed the amount of effort she put into locating resources and thinking through issues of profitability and sustainability at smaller museums and cultural sites, which had so much potential to bring in tourists from other states. As a result, in 2012 she developed and hosted Making History Last: Tips and Tools for Ensuring the Success of Your Cultural Site, Museum, or Historical Landmark, a training workshop for community preservationists engaged in historic and cultural preservation projects around the state. Both Chelius and Jenifer participated.

Rhondalyn is one of the most consistently candid people I know. Still, she wondered what she would say at the reception, asking Chelius, "Carter, how much truth do they want to hear?"[20] She had never been in any of the "big houses" and "never desired to do so."[21] She knew that she was not going to mince words and that her role was to tell the truth. She just didn't know how that pilgrimage crowd would respond. Rhondalyn shared some of her presentation notes with me; her words in April 2012 capture the intention of the Behind the Big House program:

> My purview at the [Winter] Institute includes educational concerns and outreach to schools, museums, and efforts that promote local, community tourism. I am also involved in oral history and documentation projects including the training, planning, and community support of said projects throughout the state of Mississippi. Consequently, I have had four work-related community engagements scheduled for this week. On Tuesday evening, the Institute, along with the UM School of Law and others, sponsored a panel discussion on the Trayvon Martin case which is presently being fiercely litigated in the media. Last night I journeyed to Tallahatchie County to take part in a Museum, Marketing, and Tourism Meeting concerning the Emmett Till National Historic site at the Courthouse in Sumner, Mississippi, where, in September 1955, Roy Bryant and J. W. Milam were found not guilty of the brutal murder of Emmett Till that took place only the month before. I also found out during the meeting with a small, excited gasp that George Zimmerman had been arrested for 2nd degree murder in the Martin case. Tomorrow, I will journey to Meridian to educate East Mississippi parents and community members about the uses of oral history in their local school curriculum at a Parents' Leadership Institute held by Parents for Public Schools.
>
> Because I am a certified educator, historian, and one familiar with archives, libraries, and museums, the other three engagements would be old hat. Of the four, I contemplated this last presentation and venue the most. Why, you may ask? Was it the location? No. After all I was born and raised in neighboring Lafayette County, and my mother is a Rustite and a Methodist. I came through Holly Springs as a child not just en route to Memphis for shopping or the airport, but to attend events at Rust College or Asbury United Methodist Church, a historic cornerstone church and congregation in the history of Methodism and specifically black Methodism in the state

of Mississippi. This event required that I ponder my relationship to the big house.

Even as a child I had always been curious about history and identity, both personal and public. Who I was and where I fit. As a Southerner, I had a keen sense of place and developed a passion for the stories the elders told that didn't ever make it into my history textbooks at school. The family history that had been passed down for over a century called me to go on a twenty-year personal pilgrimage that continues to this day and indeed has led me to this place. All history is cyclical.

You see, as a native Mississippian in my thirties, I had never been to a pilgrimage of antebellum homes. I had never been welcomed into any of the homes on North or South Lamar in Oxford or Salem Avenue in Holly Springs and that had been OK. Candidly, I have always had a bit of trepidation about the nostalgic feelings the stately plantation homes stir in others and the ambiguous feelings they arouse in me. The first profession I entertained as a youth was one in architecture because I loved buildings, not just the edifices themselves, but the history they often represented and symbolized. For me and many others, the grandeur and majesty of these homes are tempered, maybe even tainted, with the sordid history of slavery, inequality, and Jim Crow. I had not gone to a pilgrimage or sought entry into their genteel porticos simply because they didn't seem to reflect or represent me. They didn't tell my story. I knew that people of African descent had labored at many of these properties both during enslavement and afterward, but they were rarely mentioned and there was almost no evidence of their existence. They often built the houses, cooked, cleaned, and reared the children, but I could find no trace of them "on the place." I went in search of them. I went back to the plantation.

The history books told me they were chattel—something to be owned and used at whim—that they had been miserable both in Africa and the Americas, that they were illiterate and unintelligent due to lack of opportunity, lack of aptitude or capacity for learning, and because of legal and social systems that kept them so. Furthermore, these sources informed me that their original cultures had been primitive at best and their past had been rife with degradation. Slavery had been good for them as a Christianizing and socializing element. But was that the whole story or did the traditional narrative of our shared past have gaps that we as Southerners, as Americans as human beings are duty and honor bound to span? Who will speak for them—the enslaved human beings who dwelled behind the big house and on whose backs a whole way of life and prosperity of a region and nation largely depended and were built? Why are they relegated to the margins of our memories and traditional narrative?

My first intimate encounter with a big house was an ironic one. In 1992, I entered Tougaloo College, a historically black college founded by the American Missionary Association, an outgrowth of the Amistad Defense Committee, on the grounds of the old [John W.] Boddie plantation in Madison County in the year 1869. It had been off the beaten path and therefore not burned by Union soldiers. The grand home still sits on top of the hill with its tall cupola facing Jackson so that his fiancée could see her hometown. Like her affections and the engagement, the plantation folded during the war.

The slave pen was always said to be behind the mansion in a place I passed by every day, yet there was no physical trace of the enslaved human beings who dwelled on the Boddie place. Their legacy, however, lived and lives on in that place, giving students and visitors alike a tangible link to the past and constant motivation for the future. Their stories are ever present and paramount. They mattered in their own right. While there are few written records of enslaved persons beyond the nameless entries in the slave schedules, the moderate canon of slave narratives published since the 1830s, and the Works Progress Administration interviews of surviving ex-slaves in the 1930s, oral traditions and the rare and extant dwellings of the enslaved must be preserved to supplement the written record and document those who once dwelled within. Yes, as Mr. McGill so aptly says, "These Places Matter."

While I do not have a PhD, I do have a passion for the oral narrative, what some would call oral art, storytelling, oral histories, testimony, or truth telling, and its ability to shed light, pass on, and give a face and clear dimensions to history, my chosen field. Oral narrative in its broadest sense and oral histories especially expose all who hear them to the complex realities of historic as well as present-day contexts in which we live and by which our lives are shaped. And in this way, they teach community members, students, and researchers about matters affecting their shared history. Often, we shirk and shy away from those parts of our shared history that are complex . . . complicated or that we view as difficult or divisive, hoping that if we ignore it, it will just go away. This is particularly true when unearthing or evaluating history that reveals unfairness, inequity, hatred, pain, violence, and more honest images of ourselves and our communities that make us realize that as Mississippians, as Southerners, indeed as Americans, we fall short of our aspired-to ideals. In our race for what legal scholar Patricia Williams has termed "premature community" we relegate the unpleasant bits to the margins of our memory and traditional narrative. I concur with Lee Anne Bell, Professor and Director of Education at Barnard College at Columbia University, that premature community impedes the progress we make on difficult issues by blocking awareness and knowledge, reinforcing the status quo and traditional narratives, and preventing us from taking steps to remedy the very real inequalities that persist in our narratives specifically and throughout our society more broadly.

Chelius and Jenifer feel that the garden club members were caught off guard the first year and that now their participation was probably less reluctant but also more aware—they were less willing to commit to a second year once they realized the magnitude of collaborating with another program. This was compounded by misunderstandings about financial commitments, with Behind the Big House being a not-for-profit event and the pilgrimage being a fundraiser for the upkeep of Montrose. Chelius and Jenifer saw Behind the Big House as a complementary gift to the pilgrimage with the economic benefits of a broader pilgrimage audience and a more inclusive narrative, one in line with future directions in historic site interpretations. To them, it was an opportunity for the pilgrimage "to be on the leading edge of something different from all other pilgrimages in the South."[22] The garden club seemed to see any contributions to Behind the Big House, including expanded marketing and reception costs, as an additional financial burden. The fact that the club's leadership changed each year only made a sustainable commitment to Behind the Big House less practical. Some leaders might be less committed or more disinterested than others. Even with a successful attempt at integrating the two programs (discussed in chapter 4), they never became cohesive.

The first program year, Chelius and Jenifer did a reconnaissance survey of extant slave-dwelling sites in order to create a comprehensive site map. They developed historic site narratives through archival research and family oral histories. They also looked at slave census schedule data for demographic information on enslaved people at each property in 1850 and 1860 and created display panels including that information. They had access to family narratives of slave owners from the Craft House and McCarroll Place. Chesley Thorne Smith, who was raised in the Craft House, took a series of photographs as a young girl.[23] One of those photos is of a Black man, "Uncle Tom," and his wife, who returned to the property in 1924 to visit her grandmother. Smith described them as "once slaves of the family."[24]

Additionally, Chelius and Jenifer received help from locals like native Marshall Countian Willie Mallory. In 2008, Mallory published a book on Strawberry Church, built by former slaves from the Ebenezer "Eben" Nelms Davis plantation at Strawberry Plains.[25] Davis completed the construction of a large brick manor house in 1851 with slave labor. This mansion is now part of the Strawberry Plains Audubon Center's nature and historic preserve. Mallory, a member of the church whose maternal family has deep roots in it, pulled the Works Progress Administration narratives for Marshall County and shared what he had with Chelius and Jenifer. Jenifer supplemented that repertoire with other narratives that were more accessible through the Library of Congress by the time they started program planning. That year, 2012, local performing artist Alex Mercedes did what they describe as a wonderful job at program orientations. They were disproportionately dependent on Joe McGill to combine what he knew about slave-dwelling sites in general with their collated information into narratives accessible to audiences. In addition to guiding tourists, Joe spoke about his project during the opening reception at Montrose and spent a night each in the dwellings at the Hugh Craft House and Burton Place, still an essential component of his Slave Dwelling Project model. He also gave a lecture on the Slave Dwelling Project to a small group at the local historically Black Rust College as part of Chelius's and Jenifer's efforts to prioritize community education in historic preservation.[26]

I asked Chelius and Jenifer about verbal visitor responses from that first year. The main feedback came from Black visitors who said that "they were aware of this pilgrimage tour all their lives and for the most part it held nothing for them. Here is a history they could own." Chelius and Jenifer also received positive feedback from some of the crossovers who had thought the pilgrimage would be like all the others and who came to Behind the Behind House after seeing advertisements for it. At the reception, Jenifer remembered some segments of the "typical garden club attendees" saying how proud they were of the more inclusive narrative. One commented that the reception was the most representative social event they had seen in the town.[27]

In 2013, the program expanded to seven sites: the Hugh Craft House, Burton Place, the Magnolias, Polk Place, Featherston Place, McCarroll Place, and the plantation office at Strawberry Plains.[28] That was the first year I included students in my heritage tourism course as docents. According to Chelius, my offer of student docents encouraged the program's expansion. I shifted the class from the fall to the spring semester to accommodate the program's spring schedule. In addition to some of the texts studied in the previous class, I included anthropologist Antoinette Jackson's *Speaking for the Enslaved: Heritage Interpretation at Antebellum Plantation Sites* to give students more contexts for the cultural representations of antebellum slave sites. I also invited Joe McGill to give a public talk on his Slave Dwelling Project at the university. I arranged a special lunch with him to give students in the course personal time with someone involved with interpretations of slavery on a national scale. He also gave a presentation on the Slave Dwelling Project to students in my African diaspora course. That year, I also began my tradition of having students take the Behind the Big House tour before working as docents and then write an evaluation of that tour. This included preliminary site visits to the Craft House, Burton Place, and the Magnolias.

In its second year, Behind the Big House had a brochure with site descriptions and maps funded by the Mississippi Humanities Council. Yet that was not enough to ensure that visitors saw all available sites. Most of the program traffic went to the Craft House, positioned right across from the public library, also the pilgrimage ticket office, then to Burton Place a couple of blocks away, and then to the Magnolias, an 1853 property owned by Genevieve and Frank Busby, just another couple of blocks down from Burton Place. The Craft House's location across from the library gave the impression that the house was the first stop on the pilgrimage tour. Most visitors toured the house, as well as the two others, even when we told them that this was not part of the pilgrimage tour. Others opted out and went on to garden club properties. Other properties, like McCarroll Place, were in different parts of the city, and it was difficult to direct visitors to them. I recall one McCarroll Place student volunteer writing that her only site visitors were squirrels and birds that year. McCarroll Place was too

The Magnolias with the former slave dwelling at left.

inconvenient a trip for pilgrimage tourists coming to the Behind the Big House program only by default.[29]

In 2013, Behind the Big House also had the benefit of securing school partnerships through a local woman, Linda Turner. One Preserve Marshall County board member had tried to get Holly Springs schools involved but had no luck. Turner, an African American woman, had attended several Preserve Marshall County events and, according to Chelius, quietly observed, "watching from a distance to see if we were really doing this."[30] She offered to help bring students in after hearing of the program's struggle to do so. She began facilitating local school groups the next year, bringing in hundreds of students per year, mainly from the Marshall County School District. There have also been a few schools from the private sector that come on their own accord. Each year, the program structure is determined by the number of homeowner participants and student volunteers as well as school district schedules. The only constant variable has been that the program takes place at the same time as the pilgrimage.

In 2014, Chelius and Jenifer limited the program to the three sites in closest proximity to each other: the Craft House, Burton Place, and the Magnolias. Even with the added volunteer base, they felt like the program was spread too thin. When the school group visits started in 2013, there was not an efficient way to get the students from site to site without more volunteers to give orientations and to make bus and foot traffic easier. Chelius and Jenifer also felt that some of the sites needed more research for the narratives.

Since then, the program has continued to be limited to one to three of those sites. It would be ideal to have all the identified sites on the tour, but this is impossible to manage with a small volunteer base. Jenifer and Chelius hope that Behind the Big House and the pilgrimage could someday still be a fully integrated program, with those sites on the pilgrimage presenting themselves as sites of slavery. At the least, their temporary collaboration with the garden club helped them set themselves around a tour structure already in place. And although some of the partnerships they imagined at the beginning of the program did not take hold or sustain themselves, their partnership with Linda Turner and the local schools has remained steady. Their partnership with me has also. According to Jenifer, the University of Mississippi's name gave a legitimacy to the program and the student volunteer base provided "sustained energy."[31]

I began this chapter by admitting that I barely understood what kept me motivated to collaborate with Chelius and Jenifer and others in Holly Springs. I'm still not sure but I think that the program continues to offer something to me in addition to the reward of helping others. We shared a common interest: more equitable representation of African American pasts in the present. Yet working with them was reciprocal in its ability to allow me to connect to a network of people outside the university who were doing the vindicationist work that I thought was necessary to reinsert Black lives onto the state's memorial landscape. It had the added benefit of offering students the opportunity to connect to that network.

I began involving graduate students and then broadened the opportunity to undergraduate students in my African diaspora course. Those new to anthropology could get a chance to be participant-observers, and those interested in African American studies, with which the class is cross-listed, could be introduced to a public history project in a local community, an opportunity that might not otherwise be accessible to Black students on campus.[32] In turn, my students became the program's primary volunteer base.

In November 2013, I invited my bioarchaeology colleague, Carolyn Freiwald, to an event at Strawberry Plains cohosted by members of Gracing the Table, a group that works toward racial reconciliation by planning events that facilitate interracial discussions (further discussed in chapter 4). The Strawberry Plains event included a wagon tour of the preserve and visits to the old sharecropper house sites and the slave-sharecropper cemetery. One of the group's cofounders, David Person, also a Behind the Big House program homeowner, invited me to the event, and I invited Carolyn and our anthropology grad students. Although Carolyn's major area of concentration is pre-Columbian Mayan culture, we had a shared interest in Mississippi history. She had attended Behind the Big House earlier that year and in 2014 added students in her courses to the project through excavations at the Hugh Craft House. Her interest in local history shifted to an ongoing commitment to the program.

My work with Carolyn was a response to tourists' requests for more artifacts on display during the program and comments like "who doesn't like to see an excavation going on?"[33] Our larger goals were to offer students applied historical archaeology experiences and identify features associated with culinary practices of the time as well as other household activities. Carolyn and I began excavations at the Hugh Craft House with a crew of graduate and undergraduate students in the university's anthropology program as well as some Rust College students working with Alisea Williams McLeod, then chair of humanities at Rust and a Gracing the Table cofounder. Restoration work on the foundation of the 1850s "big house" and the detached slave dwelling revealed evidence of antebellum ceramics, mostly whitewares, and other artifacts. Our goal was to get a sense of foodways patterns and practices on the property and share that information with tourist audiences. We excavated the areas between the "big house" and the detached kitchen/quarters and cellar. Our excavations revealed that white-tailed deer, turkeys, pigs, and cows had been consumed.

As part of the 2015 Behind the Big House program, students in my historical archaeology course began participating in the excavation and managed an on-site artifact display. By that year, we had students from

Anthropology students Martha Grace Mize (left) and Robert Waren presenting archaeology displays to guests at the Hugh Craft House in 2017.

Carolyn's seminars on biological anthropology and archaeozoology and my heritage tourism and African diaspora courses as part of the program's volunteer base. Behind the Big House became a collaborative partnership with university faculty and students with a community service-learning component.

Collaborative Partnerships and Community Service-Learning

In 2013, I started to give students in my African diaspora course options to participate in the Behind the Big House program as an alternative to a class research project. The course offers an anthropological perspective on the cultural movements of Africans and their descendants through ethnography, linguistics, human genetics, and archaeology. In 2017, I cowrote a book chapter, "Public History, Diversity, and Higher Education: Three Case Studies on the African American Past," that chronicles my attempt to diversify the Behind the Big House volunteer base by incorporating African diaspora course students, many of whom were African American.[34] I engaged the public history argument that some African American students are ostracized from the field due to societal and familial pressures to major in fields that are more lucrative. I don't disagree and saw this short-term, volunteer community service-learning experience as an opportunity to get them to engage in public history practice, recognizing that a required service-learning project could raise "serious pedagogical issues" with students juggling class work and jobs.[35] Students who had an interest and could commit approximately eight hours of time chose to participate. Graduate students generally offer four hours of service as guides, undergraduate students two hours. The eight-hour commitment included travel to and from Holly Springs for the first site visit and the actual program. I provided transportation for those who did not want to drive or did not have access to transportation, at times with a university van sponsored by the Center for the Study of Southern Culture.

According to Tania Mitchell, "because service-learning as a pedagogy and practice varies greatly across educators and institutions, it is difficult to create a definition that elicits consensus amongst practitioners," yet I find her definition of community service-learning as "community service action tied to learning goals and ongoing reflection about the experience" to be succinct and relevant to describing Behind the Big House as a component of my coursework. Mitchell adds that "the learning in service-learning results from the connections students make between their community experiences and course themes.... Through their community service, students become active learners, bringing skills and information from community work and integrating them with the theory and curriculum of the classroom to produce new knowledge. At the same time, students' classroom learning informs their service in the community."[36]

I ask African diaspora and heritage tourism students to participate in a Holly Springs site visit prior to working with the program. As a class requirement, each student submits a written evaluation of the site visit, usually some variation of visits to the Hugh Craft House, Burton Place, and the Magnolias. Each student then chooses a site at which to work, based on their availabilities, and are given talking points for that site. Their roles as guides include counting the number of visitors, interpreting what is known about each property, answering visitor questions, and asking that each visitor fill out a survey. They then submit a written evaluation of their experiences as guides. I cue the students with a series of questions to guide them in their evaluations but stress that they are not limited to those questions. Otherwise, it can become difficult for undergraduate students to think through how to frame their experiences.

For the African diaspora course, the community service action of interpreting slavery is tied to course learning goals and ongoing reflection about the experiences. The learning goals for the course are to assess important cultural developments stemming from the transatlantic slave trade and major issues structuring cultural ideologies in the African diaspora, discuss the diversity of experiences of African diasporic groups regarding different sociohistorical contexts, demonstrate how marginalized populations actively participated in the creation of American cultural practices and social institutions, and construct an effective research project about an African diasporic cultural group, issue, or region. I present one student's experience as a case in point.

This student, as with many others, was an African American Mississippi native visiting a slave-dwelling site for the first time. In March 2017, she toured the Hugh Craft House, Burton Place, and the Magnolias in an over two-hour site visit. In her evaluation of the site visit, she commented that she was familiar with popular culture representations of slavery, largely "confined to big plantations and fields of cotton," and that the "tour met my expectations by helping me to understand what life was like for those slaves that lived in a small town in northern Mississippi and how that differed from bigger plantations." She also reflected on how the slave dwelling's proximity to the "big house" emphasized "how heavily these owners relied on their slaves to get through daily life." She mentioned their reliance on enslaved people for food preparation, a significant part of the narratives at the Hugh Craft House and Burton Place. (The Magnolias is the most heavily renovated site of the three, and its historical kitchen is no longer visible.) She made connections to specific course topics, something that I cue, and related what she saw to our class discussion on hegemonic processes and the structures of enslaved communities and their social and labor roles. She concluded that the site visit "basically embodied what we had been talking about in class, but we were able to get up close and personal."

By that year, I had given more structure to the undergraduate course experience by asking the students not only to write a Behind the Big House site visit evaluation and postservice evaluation but also to engage several specific themes related to the program: culinary justice, reconciliation tourism, and "whitewashing" the past. The first, culinary justice, was made possible by the introduction of Afro-culinary historian and chef Michael Twitty to the program.

Chelius met Twitty at Joe McGill's first Slave Dwelling Project conference in Savannah, Georgia, in September 2014. Jenifer and Chelius were scheduled to present a paper at the conference that year, and because she was unable to make it, I filled in. I had heard of Twitty through "An Open Letter to Paula Deen," his candid, scathing, and necessary critique of the "culinary injustice where some [White] Southerners take credit for things that enslaved Africans and their descendants played key roles in innovating."[37] This is a cultural appropriation of Black foodways. I don't think that I knew much more about Michael Twitty then, but Chelius and Jenifer clearly did. They'd been tracking him for a while, and Joe's conference gave them the opportunity to make an in-person connection.

Chelius spoke with Michael briefly and asked if he'd be going down to Mississippi anytime soon. Michael was the Southern Foodways Alliance Smith Fellow that year—the Southern Foodways Alliance is part of the Center for the Study of Southern Culture—and was planning a trip to Oxford in October of the next year. "The program, underwritten by a gift from Pam and Brook Smith, celebrates individuals whose work promises a positive impact on the southern region and its foodways."[38] Chelius was living in Virginia part-time then, and Michael, living in the D.C. area, said that if Chelius could give him a ride to Oxford, he could stop in Holly Springs, check out the program site, and meet the folks involved. They indeed got to know each other on the thousand-mile drive to Holly Springs. Chelius took Michael through the Behind the Big House program sites and took him down to Annie's Home Cooking, a soul food restaurant owned by Annie R. Moffitt Lucas. He also met prominent local officials and other local historic preservationists and, subsequently, he committed to participating in the program in April 2015.

I took Michael's visit as an opportunity to share his knowledge with folks in Oxford. I had done this in the past with Joe McGill, who gave a public talk at the university in 2013, my first year collaborating with Behind the Big House. Joe also gave in-class talks to my African diaspora course students. This aligned with Behind the Big House's education component, in which Chelius and Jenifer see the significance of sharing participant knowledge with educational institutions. With help from the center and the Southern Foodways Alliance, I organized a talk that April, which Michael titled "The Evolution of African Foodways in the Most Southern Place on Earth: Colonial and Antebellum Mississippi."

I think that this level of collaboration and reciprocity is the program's strength. That year, Behind the Big House was held from April 7 to 11. Michael committed to giving tours and cooking demonstrations on those days. His talk on the Mississippi campus the night of April 8 was a bonus. The center provided a lecture room, the Southern Foodways Alliance provided dinner and a stipend for Michael's talk, and Preserve Marshall County housed Michael and arranged his travel to Mississippi. My role was to coordinate the collaborators. That meant communicating with all parties and making sure that Michael got to Oxford and to dinner. It also meant advertising the event to ensure that as many people on campus got to hear Michael as possible. Michael's ability to make a wealth of information accessible to diverse audiences is a strength that most don't have. It worked that night on campus and works with the breadth of audiences at Behind the Big House from student to family groups.

Michael's addition to the program became an invaluable one and an experience that most of my students don't seem to forget. I took advantage of their enthusiasm for him and added culinary justice as a theme to help them make connections between their experiences and the course themes. I always include a discussion of African diaspora food in the course content, linking African contributions to foods in the Americas, including U.S. soul foods. Twitty's on-site food prep and discussions reinforce what they learn in the class, and then the final research project theme, culinary justice, gets them to think more about the contemporary impacts of institutional racism and who gets the privilege of marketing and selling African diasporic food traditions.

As part of the final research project for those who participated in the 2017 Behind the Big House program, I gave them a list of five required read-

Chef and southern studies graduate student Kevin Mitchell (left) assisting Michael Twitty with food prep at the Hugh Craft House in 2017.

ings all related to the course's three themes, including Michael Twitty's "An Open Letter to Paula Deen" and a 2016 blog post by Joe McGill titled "We Grew Up Together." The student introduced earlier in this section engaged some of the themes by sharing personal observations:

> I got the opportunity to watch Michael Twitty cook using methods that are said to "disseminate the real history of our enslaved Ancestors" by practicing similar techniques to what the enslaved Africans used during the 1800s in his cooking demonstrations. . . . Culinary injustice, according to Michael W. Twitty, is when "Southerners take credit for things that enslaved Africans and their descendants played key roles in innovating." In Twitty's "An Open Letter to Paula Deen," he stresses the subliminal injustices that often times are ignored due to the commonality of it. "Gentrification in our cities, the lack of attention to Southern food deserts often inhabited by the non-elites that aren't spoken about, the ignorance and ignoring of voices

beyond a few token Black cooks/chefs or being called on to speak to our issues as an afterthought is what gets me mad. In the world of Southern food, we are lacking a diversity of voices and that does not just mean Black people—or Black perspectives!" . . . Twitty makes a statement that broadcasts the social conflicts embedded in culinary injustice. "Visitors come from all over to marvel at the architecture and wallpaper and windowpanes but forget the fact that many of those houses were built by enslaved African Americans or that the food that those plantations were renowned for came from Black men and Black women truly slaving away in the detached kitchens." . . . The repression of how enslaved African Americans ultimately shaped and defined southern cuisine has always been a topic of little discussion and refute. Twitty's post ultimately encompasses the alarming contradiction on how much of Paula Deen's success wouldn't have been possible if not for the innovations of "niggers," whose roots have traces back to West and Central Africa, paving the way.

In this one short-term service-learning experience, this student was also able to get a slave-dwelling site tour and serve as a tour guide at Burton Place, where she spent much time speaking to tourists about the detached kitchen. She said that one of those tourists said, "We are standing on the shoulders of our ancestors and their voices and sacrifices should be acknowledged and honored." She also watched brickmaking demonstrations (discussed in chapter 4), about which she wrote:

The laborious work of the enslaved Africans was really encapsulated on my visit as a volunteer. While there I got the opportunity to expand my knowledge by listening to a man talk about how the men, and in some cases children, worked vigorously to build the houses from ground up. He told the stories of how people perceive enslaved Africans to be "dumb and worthless" when in actuality the work involved in their everyday life entailed a lot of information and close precision to their tasks. Often times if they weren't, then their lives were at risk. For instance, when making the bricks used to construct the houses, if they didn't drain enough water out of the mud, the excess water would escape and result in an explosion.

She also watched Michael Twitty give antebellum cooking demonstrations and wrote, "I was able to get an understanding of just how important cooking was for both the slaves and the slave owners. Also, I could see some of the tools that were used by the slaves at Burton Place and in Michael Twitty's demonstration." She introduced those thoughts with these words: "Patrick Manning states how cuisine was one area in which Africa and the Americas gained from the exchange of the two regions and how many of the West African methods of cooking survived and became influential in the Americas." (Manning's *The African Diaspora: A History through Culture* was one of the assigned course texts for that year.) Behind the Big House was also a gateway for the student to enter into conversations about race with her family members. She said that, without this experience, she "most likely wouldn't have taken the time to talk with older relatives like her maternal grandmother who grew up in rural Marshall County." I had no idea that she had such a personal connection to Marshall County until I read her paper.

Elaine Bennett describes the service-learning model as "'discipline-based service-learning,' in which students perform service in the community and reflect on or analyze their experience using course content." Student participation also showed signs of Bennett's "'problem-based service-learning,' in which students and their instructor take on a consultant role in conducting research for the community partner, collecting and/or analyzing data, and offering recommendations or developing products for a particular problem identified by a partner organization."[39] Here are a couple of examples.

In 2014, first-year graduate student Lauren Holt put together a booklet that Chelius and Jenifer could give to Holly Springs school groups coming through the tour. Lauren was not in the heritage tourism course but in my southern studies graduate seminar in fall 2013. I introduced those students to my work in Holly Springs. Lauren offered to help with the project. I suggested that she attend a Behind the Big House volunteer information session. She did that and recognized the need for informational texts for school groups.

Lauren's mother was an elementary school librarian who also taught kindergarten and second-grade students. Her mother was working to make her school's Thanksgiving presentation more accurate with inclusive representations, so Lauren suggested to Chelius and me that her mother might have some ideas about how to do something similar with the history of slavery. After volunteering her mother's help, Lauren unexpectedly became in charge of putting together the booklet, working mainly from guidelines from Chelius and Jenifer, program information panels, and a high school textbook on Mississippi history. Her mom took on a more limited role of assessing her text for appropriate reading levels. She also asked if I could do a quick edit, which I did. Lauren also volunteered as a docent for four of the five program days in 2014, leading pilgrimage guests and local school groups. In all, some 450 students from Marshall and Benton County schools came through the program during a three-day period that year.

Chelius and Jenifer also expressed a need for additional research. To assist with their research needs, I solicited help from History Department colleagues who might have students with antebellum history and public history interests. Deirdre Cooper Owens, then on the history faculty, recommended a doctoral student, Justin Rogers, to help with locating photographs, Works Progress Administration interviews, census records, and so on for sites associated with Holly Springs and Marshall County slave history. Justin's doctoral research on the cultural and social evolution of religion and spirituality in the North Mississippi Hill Country, including enslaved Black communities, made him a natural fit. This welcome gift from the History Department allowed Justin to work with Preserve Marshall County as a part-time research assistant. Justin was especially helpful with offering broader contexts to slavery in North Mississippi.

I certainly faced "the sporadic nature of engaging college students," what Erica Yamamura and Kent Koth consider to be "a significant challenge of many campus community engagement efforts," yet at this point the students that Carolyn Freiwald and I recruit remain the bulk of the program's volunteer base.[40] I did hope that as my partnership with Chelius and Jenifer grew, so would their volunteer base. That has not been the case. My collaboration continues to sustain the program, along with a committed core of willing participants who've kept it going every April since 2012.

Other Partnerships and Outcomes

The Mississippi Humanities Council has consistently financially supported Behind the Big House, largely with hopes that it would come to some resolution with the garden club. There was a brief collaboration in 2015, but that was not sustained (discussed in chapter 4). Humanities Council directors have also offered to financially assist others in the state who might want to replicate the Behind the Big House model; this is precisely what Chelius and Jenifer stated as their early goal. That also has not happened yet.

Chelius and Jenifer have maintained their partnerships with Joe McGill and Michael Twitty. Twitty remained committed to the program even while writing and promoting his book, *The Cooking Gene: A Journey through African American Culinary History in the Old South*. His celebrity also brought in folks specifically coming to see him, as did Joe's. Joe's followers travel from locations around the country to share an overnight stay with him in former slave quarters. Most stick it out. Others have left in the middle of the night. Either way, Joe is committed to making his work accessible to anyone who wants to participate. That work has extended to overnight stays at Rowan Oak, a property most known as author William Faulkner's home but also the former antebellum Sheegog Estate, home to at least seven enslaved people. Joe's first sleepover at Rowan Oak, organized through the University of Mississippi Slavery Research Group (discussed in detail in chapter 5), was in October 2017.

Chelius and Jenifer describe Michael and Joe as partners they can't do without. "The only way to improve Michael Twitty or Joseph McGill is to replicate them. You can't improve what they do."[41] There aren't many people who do what they do. Periodically, Chelius and Jenifer kindly say the same thing about my contribution to the program.

I asked Chelius and Jenifer what Behind the Big House would look like to them in an ideal world. Much of their response centered on building a sustainable network of local resources, such as a local corps of docents instead of my students. In addition to Joe and Michael, the program is able to rely on two local men, Wayne Jones and Dale DeBerry, who talk about and demonstrate antebellum brickmaking, and Tammy Gibson, an entrepreneur from Chicago who enacts the role of an enslaved laundress.

Tammy has probably exhibited the most passion about African American history that I've ever seen. As the Sankofa Travelher, she considers that "her mission is to raise awareness, impact youth and preserve pride in African American culture through her personal journey."[42] Tammy, who has a B.A. in African American studies, describes her work as travel history. She visits national parks, historic landmarks, museums, historic markers, cemeteries, and former slave plantations to honor African American ancestors. She then shares that knowledge through exhibits, blogs, public presentations, and living history demonstrations. Tammy's Facebook page reads as a Today in Black History timeline, not just in its writing but in her experiences. She's been to sites associated with every individual, institution, or event that she publicly presents, a pretty amazing feat.

It should have been no surprise that her first time sleeping at the Craft House slave dwelling, in 2016, was her fourth stay at a Slave Dwelling Project site, but it was. I am constantly amazed by the number of people who travel great distances to spend a night with Joe and who have the economic and emotional resources to do so. Reflecting on that night, Tammy wrote that "the feelings and emotions I was getting through the night made it very uncomfortable for me to sleep. The temperature was about 30 degrees and I can't imagine how the enslaved endured trying to sleep. I had on two pairs of socks and two layers of pants and I was still cold."[43]

Tammy traveled from Chicago that year. Another couple from Missouri was scheduled to sleep over as well but left in the middle of the night. According to Joe, his "skepticism about the couple staying throughout the night began to emerge as the young lady was afraid of cats and bugs. That skepticism came to pass as the couple left the dwelling at 3:00 am without saying goodbye. Although it was unseasonably cold, Tammy and I toughed it out until 5:00 am."[44]

In 2018, Tammy visited the program for a third year, this time volunteering to share the experience of an enslaved person in the role of a laundress. She did the same the next year. That year, Preserve Marshall County was able to offer her an honorarium for her work, thanks to the generosity of a Mississippi Hills National Heritage Area grant. In an ideal world, Chelius and Jenifer would have many more folks like Tammy, who wrote, "I do these travels to learn about the enslaved because, if I don't do it, who will."[45]

Personal Reflections

In 2017, I was awarded one of eight Whiting Foundation Public Engagement Fellowships to help expand the Behind the Big House program model to other parts of the state. Prior to applying for the fellowship, I consulted with Chelius and Jenifer about what kind of project might be most helpful to their long-term goals. After some discussion, we agreed that creating a series of public programs that address the nuts and bolts of interpreting slavery or designing and implementing a series of professional development workshops on interpreting slavery for local historic site communities would be most helpful. That nascent idea morphed into a Best Practices for Interpreting Slavery workshop and corresponding website, behindthebighouse.org, that serves as a how-to guide for local communities interested in creating their own slavery interpretation programs.[46]

The workshop and website were the capacity-building pieces that Chelius and Jenifer had touted since the program's beginning. They had always envisioned the program as a template, not unique to Holly Springs but suitable for "any town, community, historic site that recognizes the need for retooling their historical narrative to one that is more accurate, complete, more inclusive . . . with the political will to do it."[47]

Chelius also hopes to secure funding to restore the fireplace in the slave-dwelling kitchen to its original purpose so that Michael Twitty can demonstrate cooking techniques in the original kitchen. The fireplace was sealed by a previous owner. Chelius made funding attempts for this restoration, with no luck so far. He thinks that the program's status—occurring only once a year without a full-time staff—is one possible barrier to large grants. They have had success with small grants from state or regional entities like the Mississippi Humanities Council, the Mississippi Hills National Heritage Area, and the Mississippi Development Authority, which gave promotional funds for five years. Getting funds to restore private properties is a more difficult task.

It is unclear to me why sustaining local support has been a challenge. I think that the reason can be found in a combination of several factors, in particular the dominance of the pilgrimage as Holly Springs's main tourism narrative, the project's inherent call to deal with a difficult heritage in a racially fractured community, and the problems that so-called outsiders like Chelius and Jenifer encounter in trying to penetrate a relatively insular society.[48] Chelius and Jenifer, although residents of Holly Springs, are not from there. Neither am I. I think that it's harder for those whose ancestors were enslavers or were enslaved in an area to reconcile that history in a public or even a private way. It's even rarer to witness homeowners narrating slavery on properties where their ancestors enslaved others.

Chelius is a southerner with ancestors rooted in the Confederacy. His grandmother was in the United Daughters of the Confederacy. He doesn't hide this history. He accepts it for what it is. I think that's what allows him to do this kind of work. I think that he's reconciled history in a way that doesn't tempt him to choose sides. I think that is the case for me and for others with whom I work. Otherwise, whiteness or blackness or something else wouldn't allow us to see historical actors with equity. That doesn't mean that we don't understand that some folks haven't been silenced and need to be equalized in the present. That means that we are not only able to recognize that challenge but can seek to remedy it. Chelius can still respect and love his grandmother, knowing that his personal experience with her doesn't make her actions acceptable and doesn't prevent him from prioritizing Black lives in the present. To work with him, I didn't have to know the details of how he came to do that; I just had to know that, somehow, he had.

On a personal level, I had to reconcile my negative experiences with White people, especially during childhood, to be as fair as possible in how I think about people historically. I had to be able to value their ancestors just as much as mine. A retired teacher from Jackson once told me that you can't teach what you haven't reconciled. I think that the same goes for doing historic preservation work. You can't represent what you haven't personally resolved, and for many Americans race is that unresolved issue. I think that the same goes for certain members of the garden club and others in Holly Springs who haven't reconciled their families' pasts with their nostalgia for them in the present. Somehow, making Black lives matter in the present troubles their personal family histories. This would mean recognizing that their ancestors' actions, although not their fault, still have real impacts. I see the work that Chelius and Jenifer do as a form of reparation, although they don't articulate it that way. I think that this could be the case for others in Holly Springs if they were ready and willing to accept it.

Chelius periodically mentions his desire to see the University of Mississippi take on the program, possibly by an entity like the Center for the Study of Southern Culture. He sees potential benefits to the Craft House being an institutional property with a fixed presence, an on-site lab for the study of slavery in North Mississippi. I tend to try not to discourage that notion, although I don't think that it's very likely to happen. Mississippi's faculty are in the early stages of structuring historic preservation work at institutional levels. Up to this point, most attempts at historic preservation work have been responsive, not proactive, or individual attempts like mine. I have no confidence that the institution, as it stands, can or would take on such an effort.

At times, I try to revise Chelius's notion of a collaboration with the university into a collaboration with Jodi Skipper and Carolyn Freiwald. That revision never seems to stick. I know that the collaboration is dependent on the commitment of two faculty members, with some university support, rather than that of a university institution. I wrote chapter 5 to give some clarity to these circumstances for my sake and the sake of others in comparable positions. University administrators often misunderstand the significance and logistics of this work and rarely understand how to value it. That doesn't matter to my supportive network. To them, it only matters that I show up.

I think that the legitimacy that the university affiliation offers is an even more desirable one, especially when Chelius and Jenifer "can no longer sustain" holding the property. At the time of the interview, they were planning to sell and had "no control over what happens to it when they sell it."[49] An insensitive new owner might mean the property's destruction. Joe McGill often reminds us of the vulnerability of slave-dwelling sites, which could be demolished due to neglect, lack of owner awareness or concern about their significance, or what owners might perceive as undue pressure to historically interpret the slave histories of such sites. He often repeats a cautionary tale of one site owner, not in Mississippi, who felt pressure from local historic preservationists to restore the property to its original condition. The owner demolished the property rather than yield to such pressure. Joe now advises those who want to save slave-dwelling properties to acknowledge the legitimacy of the pressure that such owners might face and seek a reasonable compromise, rather than risk losing a property.

Anyone who owns a historic property can tell you that renovating and restoring those properties take time and money, privileges that most don't have, including Chelius and Jenifer. Those circumstances plague other homeowners who seek to tell more complicated histories or secure the viability of their homes with little to no financial incentive at the local, state, or national level. They are largely on their own. Chelius and Jenifer have been the victims of several break-ins to the detached kitchen/quarters, proving that the slave dwelling is not only vulnerable to neglect as a place considered less architecturally significant than the "big house" but is also vulnerable without full-time care. I'm saddened by the fact that Chelius and Jenifer could leave Holly Springs permanently, at any time, and that their slave dwelling could become even more vulnerable. At the same time, I'm amazed at how long they have been able to sustain the program under such difficult circumstances.

I'm also sure that this work has been exhausting for them, with failed efforts to convince other locals of these sites' significance and the endless travel between Virginia and Holly Springs. I know this firsthand, because I'm also tired. I'm able to sustain my work there because they continue to show up. I'm not sure that I would have much incentive otherwise, outside of the realization that many of my ancestors didn't have the privilege of giving up. I'm embarrassed to say that that realization is not always enough to keep me going.

After I interviewed Chelius and Jenifer, I asked Rhondalyn Peairs if she had anything to add. She confirmed Chelius's version of their first meeting and then went on to talk about how rare the couple is. Rhondalyn, who rarely makes a point in a straight line, compared Chelius and Jenifer to the people you like even more than your own family members, the cousin's wife that you like more than your actual cousin. Her comment mimicked *In Living Color*'s Benita Butrell, who gossips about everyone in the neighborhood but dares anyone to say anything bad about her neighbor Miss Jenkins.[50] Rhondalyn said about Chelius and Jenifer:

> Y'all didn't have to do any of this. But you chose to do that. Ain't nobody
> perfect, but you better not say nothing about Jenifer and Chelius, because
> they've actually put the energy, the work, the time, the money, into getting
> things done. You might not agree with everything they say but, until you're
> going to take their place and do it as well, then there is nothing for you to
> say. I never thought that a national model could be developed, of this type,
> in my own home territory."[51]

Rhondalyn's comment was not only a laudatory one but a response to those who have critiqued or who might critique their work without offering a better option. We both agreed that Chelius and Jenifer are our Misses Jenkinses.

Part of my attraction to Chelius and Jenifer is the fact that they created this program without asking anyone's permission. It contradicts all my sensibilities as a public anthropologist trained to ask local community permission and to share authority, a process that could lengthen or obstruct the work but that promotes long-term community buy-in. The point is that having all or almost all on board should strengthen an initiative. What I do know is that efforts to get most or all folks on board often mean that the project doesn't happen. I think that Chelius and Jenifer would still be in the process of negotiating with individuals and institutions if they hadn't chosen to prioritize what they thought was the right thing to do, rather than wait for consensus from others in the historic preservation community. I struggle with that reality in my work, the reality that negotiations might go on and on with no concrete movement toward goals in the foreseeable future.

I also value the fact that Chelius and Jenifer didn't have to do this. They are two middle-aged White people who aren't wealthy. There's no economic incentive for them. And as White people, they get no praise for doing this. As a matter of fact, a backlash of negative critiques was more common in a city in which both Black and White residents have either enabled or signed on to the pilgrimage through silence or indifference or have been "compelled by economic necessity to conform to these tourist performances that distorted and trivialized black history and culture."[52] As with the blues tourism industry, as Stephen King writes in *I'm Feeling the Blues Right Now: Blues Tourism and the Mississippi Delta*, in pilgrimages

> mythic representations, while not historically accurate, are often uncritically accepted by indigenous populations and consumers as unquestioned truths. The stability and perpetuation of myth often rest on issues of power and control, for it is the cultural producer, among other agents of institutionalized culture, who manages, controls, and communicates a privileged narrative that is inevitably associated with a larger collective understanding of the past and present.[53]

Black residents might critique Holly Springs's pilgrimage in private while recognizing its economic contributions, ignore it completely, or sign on to it especially if it comes with economic benefits to them. Others just might be indifferent. I think that these are conflicts that Black communities throughout the South face, when White cultural producers control economic power. As I mentioned in chapter 1, in my hometown of Lafayette, White Cajuns communicate a privileged narrative that has been publicly accepted for years now. I'm sure that some folks across racial demographics have come to accept the narrative as one tied to economics, even though it's rooted in a racist practice. A few have contested it.

In early 2019, I saw a Facebook post publicizing a conference titled Representing Enslavement in Public: Louisiana's Past in the Present. I noticed that Ian Beamish, a slavery historian at the University of Louisiana at Lafayette whom I had met at a public history conference in Jackson, was the organizer. The conference, hosted by the Department of History, Geography, and Philosophy and the Guilbeau Center for Public History, was "designed to bring together experts and practitioners in the public history of enslavement in Louisiana," too often "twisted or erased in service of comfort and tourist dollars."[54] The conference largely focused on efforts in southern Louisiana to make narratives of enslavement more visible. My personal experience in Lafayette struggled to reconcile the existence of this conference, a public attempt to critique the state's simultaneous silencing of Black oppression, with White Cajun joy and economic survival. I was intrigued enough to attend and was fascinated by the conference's diversity of artists, museum professionals, academic historians, other public historians, and community organizers.

One of those attendees, a Lafayette resident, Takuna Maulana EL Shabazz, gave me a copy of his book *"Black I Am!" Cajun/Creole I Am Not!* His Afrocentric Black nationalist appeal transcends a Cajun/Creole–White/ Black binary with a critique of Cajun cultural pride as Black cultural genocide and Black creolist movements as elitist attempts by those whose families have benefited from ancestral multiracial relationships, mainly between White men and enslaved Black women, to negotiate a multiracial Black identity. He chronicles the history of local overt resistance, beginning with a group of community social activists in southwestern Louisiana called the Un-Cajun Committee, catalyzed by the University of Southwestern Louisiana's (now the University of Louisiana at Lafayette) move "to change its school mascot from Bulldog to Ragin' Cajun," disregarding African contributions to the region's settlement and using the Cajun cultural frame as part of a neocolonialist project to "maintain and support White Supremacy!"[55] I find it hard to believe that I knew this as a child, when the Un-Cajun Committee and others contested the new mascot. At some point in my life, I began to understand what EL Shabazz writes to be true. At some point in my life, I had come to expect that White supremacy and economics, often inextricable, had come to mean the inability or unwillingness of White people to do the right thing.

Chelius and Jenifer are rare as private historic property owners with historic preservation backgrounds. The private part gives them a certain amount of flexibility to do this work without permission, and their historic preservation backgrounds give them a select skill set. Yet I rarely see people willing to take such a social risk—to do what they perceive to be right even if it is unpopular. Their whiteness did not bar them from the difficulties that come with centering a Black narrative in a city with a historically White narrative tradition. They received little credit for their work at a local level.

Even national credit is limited. At times, folks know about the program but don't associate the two with its founding. Jenifer was once at a meeting in D.C., "something for the Park Service," she said, in which Senator Thad Cochran's staff asked everyone to go around the room and introduce themselves. When she said that she lived part-time in Holly Springs, a staff member asked if she knew anything about the Behind the Big House program.[56] That meeting came on the heels of Humanities Advocacy Day, in which Mississippi Humanities Council staff and I (with university colleagues) separately raved about the program to legislators. The perceived bigness of the program masks its founding by two ordinary people.

Maybe their politics of anonymity is intentional. This makes sense for program developers who see their program's success through its replicability. That goal, by default, would require their identities to be less significant. Still, by now, Chelius and Jenifer had expected other Mississippi individuals and institutions to have adopted this model. That would ease some of their burden. The Arkansas program has been the most successful adaptation, with some interest from individuals and institutions in other places.[57] Other Mississippi versions of the program are nonexistent.

Even if their politics of anonymity is intentional, my politics is one of naming. Even though I've been reluctant to write this book, I am motivated by the possibility that Behind the Big House may be forgotten or may be remembered without their contributions and the contributions of others discussed later in this text. My intention is to minimize if not eliminate the chances of that happening.

Reconciling Race

On July 9, 2015, the *Holly Springs South Reporter* published a
"Letter to the Editor" from Gracing the Table. The letter, signed by
David Person, one of the group's cofounders, was a condemnation
of the murders at Mother Emanuel Church in Charleston as well
as a call for Holly Springs's residents to support removal of the
Mississippi state flag from the grounds of public institutions. The
murderer's image with a Confederate battle flag in his left hand
and a semiautomatic weapon in his right hand illustrated the
flag's presence as a powerful symbol in these hate-filled crimes
and intensified calls for rethinking U.S. gun legislation and the
contemporary veneration of the flag. Just weeks after the murders,
Brittany "Bree" Newsome removed a Confederate battle flag from
the South Carolina State House grounds near the South Carolina
Soldiers Monument, where in 2000 it replaced a larger Confederate battle flag that began flying over the state capitol building in
1962.[1] David's letter was prompted by Newsome's actions as well as
by efforts to remove these flags around the state. A response by
J. R. Dunworth, an attorney in Holly Springs, immediately followed the letter. I already knew what it would say and, at that
moment, I wouldn't read it.

At that time, I had been a member of Gracing the Table for
three years, doing what I could to bring attention to the impacts
of slavery, including symbols of Confederate nostalgia, on the
Holly Springs community. I assumed that Dunworth's letter would
be a scathing rebuttal of our letter. Not until four years later, as I
write this book, did I feel emotionally healthy enough to read his
response without driving myself crazy.

Dunworth summed up calls for the flag's removal as misguided
leftist attempts to race-bait. After all, according to him, African
Americans were overall happy with race relations, based on a

2008 poll he did not identify. He insinuated that this attitude toward the flag had emerged only during Obama's administration, that somehow Obama's election had fanned the flames. Why would liberals, winning at that moment, worsen race relations by complaining? At the same time, he argued that the Left was composed of sore losers who could not accept Mississippians' 2001 vote to keep their flag as is. He made moral equivalency arguments about Reverend Al Sharpton and the Ku Klux Klan (a small group, according to him, by the way) all being racists. After all, South Carolina's governor and two of its senators were of color (my term, not his); Black people fought for the Confederacy; and the flag was ultimately about heritage, not about hate.

It was all so typical and so expected, but I knew that reading it would still hurt. I didn't read it at first because, if I had, then I would have felt a need to respond. I had learned not only to pick and choose battles wisely but to fight them as part of a community. Thinking through a Gracing the Table group response to Dunworth would take time and energy but, at the least, ease the burden of an individual effort. A written response would only risk an open-ended cycle of misunderstanding. This might mean that our public response would be followed by another public response from him or someone else restating his beliefs. Although we knew that some Holly Springs residents read what we wrote and seemed to appreciate it, we weren't sure how productive a public exchange would be. So much of our work had been through intimate in-person group discussions. We wrote that piece as a public call to action. We didn't want a public fight. As a group, we decided to respond through our work.

Gracing the Table

When David Person and Alisea Williams McLeod cofounded Gracing the Table in 2012, their goal was to provide a space for Marshall County residents to have candid, facilitated communications about race. They wanted to transform race relations in Holly Springs through understanding, not grandstanding, and then action. It's been a worthwhile struggle; for me, it has been made possible only by the commitments of a few people who ended up in the same place at the same time with similar goals. I worked with them—Alisea Williams McLeod, David Person, Rkhty Jones, and Wayne Jones—for seven years before I asked them how we came to take similar journeys. This is my attempt to present our journeys over time; it is meant as a model not for racial reconciliation work but for how to keep going.

By the time our "Letter to the Editor" was published, Gracing the Table had been active for about three years. It began after David and Alisea, who was then chair of humanities at Rust College, witnessed interracial conversations at a Behind the Big House event. Alisea, who works across the boundaries of her literature discipline to engage in public history projects, had taken her students on the first Behind the Big House tour. They expressed so much enthusiasm that she felt that the dialogue and communication should continue. Alisea and David, along with some of her students, organized Gracing the Table.

The group broadly modeled itself after the South African Truth and Reconciliation Commission and, more specifically, after Coming to the Table, an organization started at Eastern Mennonite University in Harrisonburg, Virginia, by Black and White descendants of ancestors linked by slave–slave owner relationships who wanted to create a model for racial healing in the United States.[2] Alisea met David during the 2012 pilgrimage, the same year that his property was on the first Behind the Big House tour. That summer, she let David know that Coming to the Table was having an informational webinar. They participated in that and decided that "we can do this in Holly Springs."[3] That's how Gracing the Table was born. The group's motto became Community Healing through Communication. Its four basic tenets are uncovering history, making connections, working toward healing, and taking action.

Prior to joining Gracing the Table, my understanding of racial reconciliation groups came from what I generally knew about the Winter Institute's work across the state or the work of colleagues and students who had assessed racial reconciliation and tourism efforts in the state. I found that many of these efforts evolved as a result of economic development initiatives, sometimes based on tourism, and resulted in inadequate mediative processes between unhealed White and Black communities. To me, Gracing the Table's proactive method served as a more sustainable bridge between historic preservation initiatives and racial reconciliation than methods that approached racial reconciliation as a secondary or tertiary goal after economic development.[4] It was not a response to historic preservation projects entangled with community efforts to interpret racially sensitive sites but, rather, a desire to help the larger Holly Springs community think through how representing its history could be more considerate of the emotional needs of contemporary communities. It was developed to facilitate ongoing and sustainable conversations, irrespective of historic preservation efforts.

Behind the Big House made Gracing the Table's work possible by providing a space in which it could facilitate one of its major principles: uncovering history. Chelius and Jenifer developed Behind the Big House with sensitivity and inclusiveness as a primary goal, stating that Preserve Marshall County would like to have more participation from the African American community and recognizing that it would "take time to develop that spectrum of support and interest" and "credibility in the community at large." Chelius cited a "long-term goal to build more community and less polarization through a shared history." His 2012 Behind the Big House project director's report added that "the program's impact upon the community will be a long-term objective towards . . . recognizing [how] this shared history can provide a stronger, more unified footing upon which a stronger sense of community can develop."[5]

Gracing the Table's founders understood the effects of slavery in the present as being innately tied to the Behind the Big House program goals. They understood that therapeutic work was necessary to represent difficult histories and heritages in local communities. I wanted to know more about the people willing to do this beyond what I knew or assumed about their lives. I was most interested in how and why they came to Holly Springs and what it was about their life paths that caused them to pursue racial reconciliation work. I also wanted to better understand what about our life paths was alike or different. We all do this work from different angles; the group is where you meet, with each of us coming from different points of exploration.

I experienced Gracing the Table but wasn't very reflexive about it. I didn't journal or take notes as I did the work—I depended on my interviewees' memories to supplement my own. I assumed that our familiar relationships could make these interviews more of a conversation. That was certainly my hope. I came in with a different set of questions for each person, questions that might get at some of the things I wanted to understand, with a lot of room for whatever else they wanted to share. Their responses are narrated in the order that I recall meeting with them.

David Person

I don't remember exactly when or how I met David Person, but I believe it was during the Gilder Lehrman teachers' visit in 2012. That was my first visit to Holly Springs. I also don't remember my first impression of him, but it must've been like the first impressions of many others: somehow, he's too good to be true.

A South Texas native, David became part of the Holly Springs community after retiring there in 2002. He'd been coming to Holly Springs from Goliad, Texas, since he was a kid to visit his mother's relatives. In Texas, David was influenced by Goliad's historical significance in the Texas Revolution as well as by his father's interest in African American history in Goliad County, specifically, African American cemeteries. David isn't sure where his dad's interest came from but recalls that African Americans were part of his father's constituency as a judge. His dad was also multilingual, speaking variants of Texas's European settler languages. David became interested in the amalgamation of Spanish and African cultures and the German, Czech, and Polish cultures that affected his childhood.

I interviewed David for the first time in July 2019. By that time, we had worked collaboratively on Behind the Big House and Gracing the Table for over seven years. I'd heard bits and pieces of his life story but not in detail. After a few minutes of reflecting on his father's relationship to Texas Revolution historians in Goliad as well as to descendants of those who fought in the revolution, he shifted his narrative to recollect meeting a ninety-one-year-old Black woman on one of his recent trips to Texas. He didn't mention her name in our interview that day, but I remembered her from an email he had sent me in September 2018. He forwarded the email with a note, "J, Not sure you ever went to Goliad—coastal plains—lots of history," with a series of photos, and another note, "Lots of Texas and Spanish history here. Met Mrs. Petty age 91 who remembered lots of family and friends from long ago!!! Courthouse with Hanging Tree to left!!" I responded that I was familiar with Goliad, from my time in Texas, but didn't remember visiting. He replied, "J, Truly wonderful!!!! Feel as if something big and totally unexpected will be coming around the corner!!!! PS Mrs. Petty in pixs is 91 and knew so many folks both white and black from my past. She was always working in a German environment—she is very focused without any hint of southern influence!!! Just another example. . ."[6]

To David, something unexpected was always around the corner, something that would somehow bridge the past and the present for the better. The hanging tree was a concrete thing. He didn't expect to see it but wasn't shocked by its existence. There was no "I can't believe there's a hanging tree in Goliad" in his email. He also didn't expect to meet a Black Texan influenced by German cultures, but he wasn't surprised by her existence either. She was just another example of the cultural confluences that he found so interesting. To him, she complicated southern notions of blackness and represented the ambiguity he seemed to consistently see in people. Her complicated survival (Black life), foregrounding the backdrop of a hanging tree (Black death), is how that email read to me. It's how much of what he communicated read to me. It was all important. It was all complicated. It was all connected. It's not only how David saw Mrs. Petty's presence but how he saw his own as well. He was too enmeshed in the nuances of history to take sides. When reflecting on that experience in Goliad, he wondered about Mrs. Petty's vulnerability as a Black woman and about when Black folks came to Goliad. It was another stream of thought in his curiosity about history and how it intersected with race.

David's earliest memory of Holly Springs was visiting the city sometime in the 1950s. Some of his ancestors had moved from Holly Springs to Goliad and still had family connections in Holly Springs. To his grandmother, Holly Springs was heaven. Her husband was from Holly Springs and her mother was born in Waterford, a small town between Holly Springs and Oxford. He described his grandmother as a patrician with little tolerance for mediocrity. She didn't grow up in Holly Springs, but he thinks that she was socialized by its hierarchy, a postbellum White planter class. His grandmother culturally transmitted her love for Holly Springs to his mother who, dissimilarly, didn't want to live in the past. To her, Holly Springs was the past.

David returned to Holly Springs yearly, sometimes without his parents. He is candid about the racism that intersected with some of his elders' classism, valuing the time he spent with them while acknowledging their faults as whole people. In that way, he reminds me of Chelius—a White male with the ability to value an antebellum southern past without letting its nostalgia dupe him in the present. It's a challenge for many of us as individuals, but it's even more challenging when one's ancestors' wrongdoings (as a group) negatively affected others historically and today. For a White descendant of racists, it means accepting those ancestors' actions as individually and systemically harmful to countless Black folks then and now. Some might admit the former but not make the leap to the latter, because that would mean taking personal accountability for contemporary privilege. You can't just say that it's in the past or that it was my ancestors, but it's not me. Others never even come to acknowledge the racial harms of the past, choosing instead to essentialize their White ancestors as not racists, or good to the slaves they did have, or good to their Black sharecroppers, or poor, or more recent European immigrants, and therefore they couldn't be racists, and so on.

As a child, David accepted how his ancestors in Holly Springs normalized racial hierarchies, but his experiences with Black Americans in South Texas showed him something different. He was personally socialized, not with a sense of racial equity but with mutual respect. This was less evident in the time he spent as a child in Holly Springs. Something about David or about that life experience has caused him to face the difference between how his Texas and Mississippi families associated with Black people and what those relationships might indicate about the impacts of slave–slave owner relationships in the present. He can appreciate those ancestors who shaped his childhood and the slave-owning ancestors who influenced them, yet he can critique the effects their actions had and still have on African Americans. It's a quality that I haven't found in most people whom I consider White. I wish that I could bottle it and spread it all over the world. I don't think that David recognizes this quality in himself at all, which is what makes it seem even more genuine.

When David returned to Holly Springs in 2002, he was enamored with the place and its romantic appeal. He hadn't been there for nearly twenty years. He had been living in England just before deciding to move and was looking for a place to get a new start. The deaths of several elder family members led to disconnections from those in Holly Springs. He was partially pulled by connections to the family still there. The cousin to whom he was the closest, a trusted confidante, died when David was in the process of moving there, making his transition more difficult.

David bought Crump Place and conducted extensive restoration and renovation of the antebellum house, which was erected by one of the founding fathers of Holly Springs and later connected with the family of Edward Hull "Boss" Crump, Jr. Crump spent his late boyhood and teenage years there before moving to Memphis.[7] He controlled Memphis politics for much of the early twentieth century and became the most powerful man in Tennessee politics, with considerable influence on the state's gubernatorial races. In 2006, David purchased Burton Place, once owned by Mary Malvina Burton, one of the wealthiest antebellum plantation owners in Marshall County. Burton Place was her townhome in the city.

In 1836, Mary Burton had come to Holly Springs from Rockbridge County, Virginia, along with others from states such as Georgia and North Carolina where former Chickasaw land sales were heavily advertised.[8] She came with her husband, Dr. Phillip Patrick "Paddy" Burton, to capitalize on the sales of land there. After a troubled relationship (Paddy was abusive and promiscuous), the couple divorced in 1842.[9] Burton was a unique woman during the antebellum era. Not only was she a divorced single mother of three children, but she was able to retain her wealth and build a fortune in cotton after her divorce. To manipulate a legal system preferential to men, Burton's brother, John N. Shields, acted as trustee of her estate at the time of her divorce. As a result, she was able to become a wealthy Marshall Countian, modeling her refined house after those in her native Rockbridge County.

Mary Burton had the house and its accompanying slave dwelling built in 1848. She referred to it as the Burton home. Per the 1850 U.S. slave census schedule, Burton enslaved eight persons. By 1860, that number had increased to eighty-seven. Eighty likely lived and worked on Burton's rural plantation out in Marshall County. She made her wealth through cotton and that slave labor. Seven enslaved people were recorded as living and working at the Burton home in Holly Springs. They likely lived in the kitchen/quarters on David's property, a plainly finished brick building one room deep and three rooms wide. In addition to the kitchen, the other two rooms might have served as residences and workrooms for enslaved persons. The 1860 slave census schedule notes two slave houses, which might refer to those other two separate rooms.

The kitchen/quarters on David's property were not only featured on the Behind the Big House tour, but his main house has been a stop on the garden club's pilgrimage, which selects a few homes for presentation each year. David purchased the three-acre property for restoration and repair after hearing rumors that a developer was going to buy it to build condominiums. Not only was the antebellum townhome on his property a prime candidate for interpretation on the pilgrimage, but his more inclusive narration of its dependent kitchen/quarters comparably made his property a candidate for Behind the Big House. His persistent belief that other White elders, like him, with a passion for history could also be inspired to prioritize inclusive narratives makes him an effective race relations mediator. He is one of few people in Holly Springs whose home is, at times, an integrated space.

In October 2013, David wrote me with an inquiry about how to "have better contact with Ole Miss." He wanted University of Mississippi faculty and students to be involved in Gracing the Table. He began his email by highlighting the initiative as one of Holly Springs's most recent successes. "Its basic tenet is: until you heal the effects of slavery, racism will continue. We have been meeting for a year and a half. We discuss openly and confidentially racism and its healing. Our membership has grown from about 8 people to over 35. We have a topic and then we break out into small groups for further discussion."[10] It was succinct, as are most of his messages.

David genuinely loves people and wants them to feel appreciated. He's the epitome of what an upper-class White male showcasing his private home as a site of slavery should be: knowledgeable, gracious, sympathetic, and a good listener. He also genuinely wants people to feel included. The more, the better. I was reluctant to join the group, but David insisted. No, he didn't insist; he assumed. How could I not want to? I didn't want to. I reluctantly responded to his invitation to attend my first Gracing the Table event in November 2013. His email invitation predicted that Saturday, November 16, would be a *wonderful morning*, with a *very interesting program*, in a *wonderful place*.

David invited me to a tour, lunch, and program at Strawberry Plains, the Audubon Society's nature preserve with historic site components related to an antebellum cotton plantation. The property was willed to the National Audubon Society by Ruth Anna Finley and Margaret Finley Shackelford in 1983 and "fully turned over to" them "in 1998 by Margaret."[11] The Finleys bought the land from their cousins, the Davises, who owned it in the nineteenth century.[12] The property is most often associated with Ebenezer "Eben" Nelms Davis, a planter who, by 1860, owned 114 people. According to David, Madge Lindsay, then Strawberry Plains's director, had very generously invited Gracing the Table and friends to the program, which included a wagon tour of historic sites such as the old Davis Plantation house, old sharecropper homes, and the slave and sharecropper cemetery.

One significant facet of Gracing the Table's protocol is that all its activities must include dialogue. At the end of the tour, all guests were asked to reconvene at the visitors center. After soup and desserts, Alisea asked that we form small groups and consider a passage, printed on a sheet of paper, describing the experiences of a member of the Davis family. The passage described the initial White settlement of the property and the "goods" with which they traveled from the Atlantic Coast, including enslaved persons. She then asked a group representative to address a main question associated with the passage. This prompt was meant to promote dialogue, and it did just that. Guest comments ranged from direct reflections on the passage to thoughts of the day's experiences. Emotions ranged from discomfort to tears. Some were candid, others were silent, but it seemed that most participants were affected in some way. I wasn't uncomfortable. I didn't cry. I was surprised—surprised that what seemed to be such a small thing could elicit such bold responses.

As a Black woman, I constantly feel at risk. I'm always weighed down with the added burden of racism. White anti-racists intentionally put themselves at risk of being ostracized by family, by friends, and in community circles. I needed to believe that a White person was willing to fight on the front lines and assume those risks. It's not that I didn't have White friends who did that. As a matter of fact, it's a necessity before I can call a White person a friend. What I needed was a White person who seemed to have every desirable privilege—class, gender, retirement—to motivate me to take on the emotional labor of racial reconciliation work. I had to know that it was shared. For me, David was that person. After witnessing his compassion and the work that Alisea was able to do, I decided to join Gracing the Table.

Alisea Williams McLeod

Alisea came to work at Rust College in fall 2011, but it was not her first time going to Holly Springs. She had been doing genealogy research there since 2003. Like David, Alisea's connection to North Mississippi is deeply rooted in family. She came to Mississippi for the first time as a child, in 1974, when her family wanted to get back to their roots in the South. She describes both of her parents as "children of the migration" whose families had migrated to Detroit after World War II. Her parents hadn't been back since.

Her mother planned the trip to help reconnect to Memphis, the place where her mother was born and of which her mother had no memory. Alisea recalls that her immediate family was one of the few from her neighborhood in Detroit who didn't regularly travel back to the South in the summer. In those cases, her peers' grandparents were still in the South, and they went back to visit them. Her maternal grandmother was still living in Memphis then, but they had not met. Her paternal grandparents also lived in Detroit.

Her paternal aunt and her husband, Alisea's uncle, traveled all the time. In 1973, they were the first in her family to "go back South," and that encouraged her immediate family to do the same. Alisea thinks that people, in general, were talking about returning to pasts at that time, more than they had been before. This was before *Roots*, and she thinks that other books and films like *The Autobiography of Miss Jane Pittman* and *Sounder* helped begin a long process of healing shame around the slave past. *The Autobiography of Miss Jane Pittman* had a huge influence on her. Uncoincidentally, it later had an impact on me. It was how we both "first learned about slavery and Jim Crow and night riders."[13]

Her parents began their journey in Memphis, where both of them were born, and then headed south to several Mississippi Delta counties. Alisea, who has a photographic memory, vividly recalls the heat, and she remembers driving to her maternal great-grandmother's house at Union and Dunlap in Memphis. She remembers what the street looked like, with its small public housing units, and her great-grandmother and two other ladies sitting at the curb in lawn chairs. Her mother got out of the car and introduced herself, they embraced, and then her mother introduced the rest of them. The visit was a surprise one; her great-grandmother wasn't forewarned, but they were warmly welcomed. Alisea recalls the discussions her family had that night as bringing 1945 back together with 1974.

They spent the day with her father's family in DeSoto County, where her father had grown up. Her father, then in his early forties, was only thirteen when his parents left Mississippi. They spent the day reminiscing with his family. Her father also went to look for the family cemetery, but the area was overgrown, and he couldn't find it. Alisea found it many years later. At the time they visited Mississippi in 1974, her father did not know that he had any roots in Marshall County. Alisea also discovered those roots later on.

Alisea and her family continued farther south to Yazoo County and then to Mound Bayou in Bolivar County, where her mother had relatives. Her mother's great uncle had died shortly before they arrived. They stayed there about three days for the funeral, then turned around and went home. Her father, whom her mother had to convince to take this trip, was done with the "deep in the Delta" mosquitoes. The family concluded their trip, but the entire experience stuck with Alisea. That was her first time in the South. She says that she thinks "it was just in her blood to come back."[14]

Alisea attended Stillman College, a historically Black liberal arts college in Alabama, and then married a man from Memphis. They came through Mississippi a lot. She became more familiar with the state through Stillman peers from cities like Columbus. Ten years later, it was still typical for my Grambling peers from states like California to travel home with me and others from Louisiana, and probably it still is. What Black northern, western, and midwestern college students learn from their southern peers is a less discussed part of the return migration experience but was certainly essential to Alisea's experience. A journalism major, Alisea even came to Rust College in Holly Springs to hear famous journalist and Okolona, Mississippi, native William James Raspberry speak.[15] She says that by the end of that experience, she was fascinated with the South and with Mississippi.

After receiving her B.A. from Stillman, Alisea attended Miami University in Ohio and earned an M.A. in English, then went to the University of Michigan for doctoral work in English and education in 1990. She describes Michigan's program as a "pretty liberal" one and recalls her adviser, on their last day of rhetoric class, asking them to talk about what they wanted to work on. She said that she wanted to know more about her family, not imagining at the time how that could have been an appropriate dissertation topic. She says that her adviser could not have been more encouraging. In 1993, she began traveling back to Mississippi, including Jackson, to do archival research. She ended up writing about her family's post–World War II migration from DeSoto County and Memphis to Detroit.[16] She said that "if we want to talk about where African Americans are mentally, cognitively, we have to talk about place. We have to talk about time. We have to talk about movement. . . . It really was about constructing your sense of self and time in light of past and present and future. . . . I don't think you can talk about those things without talking about various types of move-ment. I just don't know how you can talk about that without talking about [migration]."[17]

Alisea describes that dissertation project as incomplete, saying that it's taken twenty years for her to answer most of the questions she's had about her father's family. She spent a lot of time speaking to her father's oldest sister, who remembered more about their premigration Mississippi experience than other siblings did. Those conversations with her made Alisea want to know more. She came back to DeSoto County in 2003 for additional archival research on her father's family. That trip was one of the turning points in her life. The many family documentary records aligned with what her aunt had said about family landownership. "I didn't know that they had owned their land. I didn't know anything."[18]

When she decided to take the position at Rust in 2011, part of her reason was to reconnect with family. She wanted to know as much about that past as she could because she had questions. Through her research, she had been communicating with members of the Marshall County Genealogical Society for about four years and with Chelius Carter for about two years. Chelius came across some of Alisea's writing on a blog on the Coming to the Table site and emailed her. At that time, she had been traveling to the Marshall County courthouse for about eight years. "I had kind of been dreaming about being able to be here. You know the story about the writer who lives in the place they're writing about for a while to really soak up the culture. I can't be writing about Mississippi from afar. The work at Rust just enabled that to happen."[19] It then made perfect sense to her to write that genealogy work into the college's humanities curriculum.

Alisea described incorporating a history component into her rhetoric and composition course as a natural fit. I disagreed with her, which led to what I find most fascinating about Alisea: what seems to be an innate ability to see interdisciplinary work as natural. I feel the same way about the work that I do, but my education has caused me to see it as more of a problem than she does. I'm trained as a historical archaeologist yet wrote my dissertation on museum making as a strategy for representing African American pasts. I saw that as my responsibility as a public archaeologist. I saw these things as inherently related but knew that such an interdisciplinary approach might jeopardize my job prospects in historical archaeology departments, which looked for an excavation as central to dissertation research. That bothered me. I chose to do my dissertation my way, with support from my dissertation committee, but still felt pressure to explain my decision.

Alisea unapologetically moves beyond disciplinary boundaries. I asked her about that. She took a deep breath, admitting that she didn't know where to begin to answer. It makes sense to not really think about something that you find natural. She began by saying that her English and education program at Michigan marketed itself as multidisciplinary, but that she was likely one of only a few students to take that seriously. "I never stayed in my discipline to begin with." She wrote an ethnographic paper on what she describes as a Latina study group that met each day at noon to talk about race, migration, and identity. This is what led her to think about identity and time as a dissertation approach. Her dissertation crossed the boundaries of literary theory with cultural geography, scholarship she describes as "very good about talking about time and space and constructing [those]." That shift felt organic to her, and she wasn't afraid to make it. She said that's how she probably came to think that her students at Rust didn't need to think about disciplinary boundaries.[20]

She assigned each of her forty students the task of studying one of the slave owners listed in the Civil War contraband camp log, the Register of Freedmen.[21] They were to do Internet research, including information from Ancestry.com and FamilySearch.org, but they were also to go to the Genealogy Room in the Marshall County Library. She describes that group of students as willing and trusting. A couple of those students vigorously debated whether or not they should judge slave owners. One of those students, Naomi Rahn (now Naomi Rahn-Rodriguez), helped cofound Gracing the Table along with another Rust student, Joshua Stampley-Gardner. Alisea thinks that "most of them got a whole lot out of it . . . and came to some really profound thoughts." She recalls one of her favorite students writing that "there are certain things that you should just know, and who owned your family is one of those things."[22]

I met some of Alisea's students when I attended my second Gracing the Table event, held at the Smiling Phoenix, then a coffee and sandwich shop owned by Chelius and Jenifer. As Alisea did with the Strawberry Plains event, she led a discussion with over thirty-five participants, cofacilitated by several of her students. We split into groups to discuss our thoughts about a series of photographs of plantation homes in Holly Springs. After doing that, we reconvened as a larger group for further discussion. Through that experience, I became more interested and attended more events, soon becoming absorbed into the group. I was motivated by several things, but Alisea's ability to get people to talk about race, without directly asking them to, interested me the most. It's a skill set that most don't have and one that often requires training, a training that Alisea doesn't have. At this point, I was impressed enough by what I saw of Gracing the Table's work to join. There was no official membership process, nor should there be in a racial reconciliation group. I attended a couple of events, including that one, and then I considered myself a member.

Gracing the Table Events

My first experience helping plan an event began when I served as a panelist for a film screening and discussion in December 2013. We watched *Traces of the Trade: A Story from the Deep North* about Katrina Browne, a White woman from the North who "tells the story of her forefathers [the DeWolf family], the largest slave-trading family in U.S. History."[23] Alisea gave each invited panelist discussion questions to consider. First, what kinds of symbolic and spiritual ceremonies can living descendants on both sides of the slavery issue create to recognize inhumanity or universal human failings? Second, what can we do locally? Finally, what kinds of activities can heal shame and anger? We allowed one hour for questions from the floor, but that was not long enough to meet the audience's need for additional time and space, particularly some Black participants who seemed to take this opportunity to release some of the pain of racism. We offered the opportunity for them to express themselves, and they did, seemingly with decades of pent-up frustration and pain. We learned that we needed to be more flexible about designating time for audience feedback. We sponsored one additional film: a viewing and discussion of *Prince Among Slaves*, a PBS film about a West African Muslim prince enslaved in Mississippi. We left ample time for audience feedback. At other events, we relied on small-group discussions, which seemed to allow participants, across race and age demographics, more free expression.

In October 2013, when Sue Watson, a journalist for the *Holly Springs South Reporter*, interviewed David about Gracing the Table, he stated that because the "meetings are held in a safe and confidential environment, all issues of community relations, problems, and solutions can be openly and freely discussed. . . . Where else is there such an ideal atmosphere to examine community problems, individual questions, and discovery of solutions?"[24] I think that this event was a relatively safe space for the Black folks who attended and possibly an insecure one for some of the older White folks who remained silent.

When I interviewed former Winter Institute employee Rhondalyn Peairs for this book, she mentioned the difficulty with getting some of the older White participants to push beyond a certain point in a discussion designed to be reconciliatory. She clarified that "they wanted to believe they had already arrived at reconciliation early," which one White reconciliation discussion facilitator she met from the Carolinas described to her as "White people feel like they did enough just to show up to have a discussion, but it didn't extend to participation really in the dialogue in the same way. It didn't extend to the level of introspection or the action that would come from true relationships with people. . . . We came together. It's all fixed."[25]

Alan Barton and Sarah Leonard and Dave Tell detail a similar reluctance among some White Deltians to participate in reconciliation attempts, through the biracial Emmett Till Memorial Commission, without economic incentives from tourism.[26] Doing it for the good of the common community seems to be rare. I didn't want to be part of a reconciliation effort that only required that White people show up while Black people do the work or enabled them to negotiate participation, as in the case of a White commission member who refused to publicly apologize for Tallahatchie County's role in Till's murder, citing his family's historical relatively good treatment of Black people. Dave Tell, who chronicles these events in *Remembering Emmett Till*, describes this commissioner as having a sense of the interpersonal rather than the structural inequities that "deprived Till of his life."[27] As a representative of the Winter Institute, its director, Susan Glisson, was able to negotiate with the commissioner to create a statement of regret instead of an apology.

David Person's understanding of both structural and interpersonal inequities, as an older White man, appealed to me. He is an idealist, as evidenced in his newspaper quote, but to his credit Gracing the Table was as close to that ideal as Holly Springs had come.

Early events reflected efforts to heal through dialogue with candid and sustained community conversations. Early on David, a meditator himself, sought training and assistance from Mid South Mediation Services. One of the major results was a keener understanding of constructive communication between divided parties. Conflict mediation is common in racial reconciliation initiatives, yet its incorporation in dialogues on cultural representations of African American pasts is not.

In 2012, a Behind the Big House program volunteer, a Black woman, fainted after entering the Burton Place slave dwelling. She was overcome with emotion, and program leaders were not sure how to best offer support. David sought the assistance of a psychotherapist to help the group adequately respond to any subsequent similar instances. That occurrence also prompted members' desire to learn to be appropriately sensitive as they strove to connect with other descendants of enslaved communities who might be affected in comparable ways. One answer was an African-centered libation ceremony held at Strawberry Plains in honor of ancestors buried at the slave and sharecropper cemetery there.

The pouring of libation, an essential ceremony in some African cultures, pays homage to ancestors by offering drinks, sometimes water, to ancestral spirits. One of my friends adequately captures this as "letting ancestors drink first." Libation ceremonies continue to be practiced at events in which ancestral spirits are being called to participate or are being honored for their contributions to their descendants. The first program was held in October 2013 at Strawberry Plains. Since that time, the program has been led by Rkhty and Wayne Jones, two Holly Springs residents who moved to the city in 2005.

I don't remember when I met Wayne or Rkhty, and neither do they, but I imagine that they might have been there for my first Strawberry Plains event. Of the folks in my supportive network, they have probably been most integral to developing representations of the African American past in Holly Springs.

Rkhty Jones

Rkhty and Wayne were living in Claremont, California, when they decided to move to what they considered a better place to raise their daughter. They knew that they didn't want to go back to New Jersey or Chicago. They selected Mississippi, the place where Rkhty's mother was born.

Rkhty says that she chose Holly Springs because anti-lynching activist, suffragist, and cofounder of the National Association for the Advancement of Colored People Ida B. Wells was born there and because the Ida B. Wells-Barnett Museum was there. As a teenager and young woman, Wells raised her orphaned siblings in Holly Springs. She began her activist work after moving to Memphis, where she sued a railway for having her ejected from the first-class ladies' car and later launched an anti-lynching campaign through the *Memphis Free Speech*, a newspaper she co-owned. Through her journalism, Wells exposed racism and economics as the primary motives for White mob lynchings against Black men and women, an argument antithetical to many White U.S. journalists, who framed Black people as criminals who deserved their fates. Wells's work threatened White Memphis locals so much that she was forced out of Memphis and moved to Chicago. She married attorney Frank Barnett, with whom she had four children. She continued her activist work by integrating civil rights into the women's suffrage issue, something that White suffragists were reluctant to do.

In the 1970s, Holly Springs native Reverend Leona Harris formed the Ida B. Wells Cultural Center after learning about Wells-Barnett while in college in Chicago. She wanted Wells-Barnett to be as much a part of the historical memory in Holly Springs as she was in Chicago. The cultural center became the Ida B. Wells-Barnett Museum, located at the former Spires Boling house, where Wells's mother and father met and on the property of which she was likely born.[28] Rkhty thought that she could work at the museum and her daughter could go to the local high school. Neither she nor Wayne had ever been to Mississippi.

Rkhty's family is from Grenada County and Carroll County in Mississippi, about a two-hour drive from Holly Springs. She did not realize how far away she'd be from them until she moved. It's a mistake that many who live outside the state make when trying to gauge the distance between cities. The state is imagined as a lot smaller than it really is. Rkhty's mother was one of twelve children, and many of her extended cousins still live in those counties. Rkhty visits them every now and again.

Shortly after she arrived in 2005, Rkhty made introducing herself to Reverend Harris a priority. She started volunteering and worked at the museum for about seven years. As a volunteer, she performed several tasks but had what she describes as "a few special skills" from her work as an

Rkhty and Wayne Jones at Gracing the Table's 2019 libation ceremony at Hillcrest Cemetery. Photo by Tarondal Phillips.

assistant curator at both the Brooklyn Museum and the Metropolitan Museum of Art when she lived in New York.[29]

By 2010, Rkhty and Wayne, her husband, had cofounded the Marshall County African American Living History Association with local historian Sylvester (whom she refers to as Sy) Oliver.[30] The group envisioned doing living history and historical research to tell African American stories. They traveled to churches and schools doing living history interpretations of famous Marshall Countians like Belle Caruthers, a former enslaved woman who was candid about her owners' abuse in her Works Progress Administration former slave narrative; Hiram Rhodes Revels, the first African American U.S. senator; George Washington Albright, who was born enslaved in Holly Springs and later "entered the Mississippi Senate as a member of the Reconstruction government"; and Memphis business-man, philanthropist, and community activist Robert R. Church Sr., also born in Holly Springs.[31] They also did living history interpretations at

Annie Lucas's soul food restaurant on one occasion, and Rkhty reflects on that experience as "an exciting time."[32] Six to eight people reenacted, with about twelve people involved as a whole. Even Andre DeBerry, Holly Springs's mayor from 2001 to 2013, was involved.

Unfortunately, they were unable to keep the momentum going. The reenactments required research, costuming, and people willing to invest the time and effort. Some participants were more committed than others, notably Holly Springs native Dale DeBerry, who "stayed with them 'til the end." DeBerry, a master clay craftsman, was key to helping form their brickmaking project, interpreting the experiences of enslaved brickmakers integral to Holly Springs's antebellum infrastructure. Rkhty researched the brickmaking process and talked with older brickmakers in the city, subsequently compiling a booklet for sale at historic site festivals like the Ames Plantation Heritage Festival near Grand Junction, Tennessee, just about thirty miles northeast of Holly Springs. She thought that short, accessible reading would be a good idea. "We didn't want to deal with scholars. We just wanted to do this for the people."[33]

Rkhty walked around the city looking at bricks. Through that process, she met homeowners like David Person, who advised her that the clay for the bricks came from the building site itself. She had no idea and wanted to share that information with others. She said that even the brickmakers she interviewed, who worked in local kilns, were fascinated by the work of their historical counterparts. Brickmaking was an essential part of an enslaved person's experiences in antebellum Holly Springs, yet it was a subject rarely discussed in the standard architectural narratives. "I just wanted to make people in Holly Springs proud of what they've done. Because it's not just the bricks, it's the ironworking, woodworking, it's so many things, and we haven't started to talk about those other things."[34]

On one of her walks, Rkhty had a conversation with David about the slave dwelling on his property. She recalls that he considered turning the dwelling into guest houses, and she suggested that she open it up for tours. Members of the Marshall County African American Living History Association had considered developing a tour of African American heritage sites in Holly Springs, with some plans in the works, but Rkhty says that "it never got off the ground." As a matter of fact, they identified the location of Ida B. Wells's parents' family home in Holly Springs, and Rkhty shared that location with a colleague, students, and me as we worked on an Ida B. Wells in Marshall County tour in 2019.[35] She and Sylvester Oliver also traveled around Marshall County looking for cemeteries and contraband camps, temporary residences for enslaved people who escaped across Union lines. That seed was already planted, so her suggestion to David was a natural fit. By their next meeting, David had agreed, and they started planning to develop that idea. That was the beginning of Behind the Big House for her. She also went to Chelius's house, where he told her that he had considered an interpretive program but was also thinking about using the space as his architecture studio. It seems that they were all thinking about this at the same time and were encouraged by each other's thoughts. Rkhty began giving tours of the slave dwelling at Burton Place during the first Behind the Big House program year and has volunteered for the program ever since.

Although an Egyptologist, Rkhty was so touched by African American history in Holly Springs that she dedicated much of her time to making it more accessible to others. Part of that effort filled a void that began in childhood. "My parents never ever *ever* mentioned Mississippi or talked about enslavement or slavery. Umm, they just didn't want to have anything to do with it. So, I knew practically nothing before I came here. And when I came here and I saw this, I was in shock. Like, look at all I've missed." I asked Rkhty if she thought that her parents were trying to disconnect themselves from the state while trying to protect her. She wholeheartedly agreed. Her mother said little about Mississippi. Her mother "had a living mother and a living father and most of her sisters, but they never wanted to bring their children here to Mississippi."[36] As a result, Rkhty never saw her grandparents. She had no communication with them. Her father, who was from Georgia, never went back there either. Her mother took most of what she knew about Mississippi to her grave.

Rkhty and Wayne began participating in Gracing the Table in 2013, its second year. They "liked the idea of talking to people and trying to have some healing, bringing White and Black folks together." They figured that if they were going to do anything in Holly Springs, "it would be good for all people to be involved in it because all of the big houses were owned by White people, not us."[37] Rkhty didn't quite remember when she became involved but did recall doing a libation ceremony at Strawberry Plains in 2013. I hadn't recalled that, but our memories combined to generate that fuller picture.

Rkhty started the Gracing the Table tradition of pouring libation to honor ancestors. She'd traveled to the African continent many times and participated in libation ceremonies there, as well as through the Kemetic Institute in Chicago. She humbly stated that she had participated through the institute, minimizing her role as one of its founding members. According to the institute's website, it is "a research organization concerned with the restoration and reconstruction of African civilization through scholarly research, African centered education, artistic creativity and spiritual development."[38] Rkhty was part of the antecedent Communiversity there. According to historian Charles Russell Branham, the Communiversity was "a kind of grassroots group of people . . . who would basically teach little mini-classes, often included with indoctrination classes, to other young people who were just interested in learning about black history and black culture . . . they began to understand history as perhaps a central part of any African American culture or curriculum." They were "on the ground floor . . . of reclaiming a past that nobody had actually spent a lot of time looking for."[39] Rkhty was among a group of scholars at the Kemetic Institute who had begun studying Medu Neter, "the language of ancient Egypt as called by the people who spoke it," on their own.[40]

As a child, Rkhty had a desire to learn and study languages. Her uncle James, a World War II vet, spoke a little German and taught the children in the family some. Rkhty thought it was a lot of fun but didn't pursue the study of languages until she was a student at the University of Illinois. She majored in linguistics, with classes mainly focusing on the origins of European languages. On her own, she sought out the African students on campus who spoke Yoruba, Kikuyu, and Kiswahili and paid them to teach her. She also studied German, French, and Hebrew. She became fascinated with Egyptology, an interest she developed from hearing Yosef Ben-Jochannan's (also known as Dr. Ben) lectures to the Black Student Union.[41] According to her, "he was talking about Kemet. He called it Ancient Egypt, but that's what he was talking about."[42] She attended the University of Chicago in the Egyptology PhD program from 1979 to 1982. That is where she learned the language, history, and culture of Ancient Egypt and became an Egyptologist.

Rkhty left Chicago after Leonard Jeffries, his wife, Rosalind, and a few others brought her to the City College of New York to teach.[43] The Kemetic Institute was also connected with Dr. Ben as well as with African American historian John Henrik Clarke, who were both in New York at the time. She set up the first Association for the Study of Classical African Civilizations study groups in Harlem.[44] She also spent three months studying with Senegalese historian Cheikh Anta Diop. She translated two of Diop's books from French to English.

Rkhty understands ancestor veneration, what she describes as "calling the ancestors and giving praise and honor and respect to them" as an essential part of all that work. She introduced it to people in Holly Springs, whose largely Christian population, she thought, didn't know anything about it. "Or they do it but don't know that they're doing it," I responded. She agreed.[45] I was one of those who unknowingly witnessed libation practices through cousins who poured out a little beer before they drank it, or through pop culture representations in films like *Cooley High*, or through R & B groups like Dirty Rotten Scoundrels, whose hit "Gangsta Lean" tipped 40s to the memories of their friends gone too soon. I also remember some Black Graduate Student Association events at Florida State beginning with libation ceremonies, but I can't say that I felt particularly emotionally connected to them. I think that I understood it as a good or respectful thing to do but not a necessary one. As a result, I didn't make the practice a habit.

As I reflected on my conversation with Rkhty, I realized that part of my disconnect from African rituals of pouring libation was part of an emotional disconnect from my Afrocentric Grambling roots. My anthropological training, as decolonial as I thought it was, led me to come to see the essentialized mythical Africa linked to intellectual pan-Africanist thought as just as dangerous as traditional Eurocentric schools of thought. I think that I had completely disregarded it, in practice, because I forgot what that early work meant to me.

I had reaped the benefits of work that folks like Rkhty put in. Some of them were self-taught; others, like Rkhty, supplemented their training in Western universities with networks of scholars who did the vindicationist Black history work that those institutions failed to do. At Grambling, I'd read *The Great Oracle of Tehuti and the Egyptian System of Spiritual Cultivation*, the first volume of Ra Un Nefer Amen's *Metu Neter* series, as well as Ivan Van Sertima's *They Came Before Columbus: The African American Presence in Ancient America* and John Jackson's *Introduction to African Civilizations*, but I couldn't put a finger on what they meant to me.

Through my conversation with Rkhty, I remembered. I wasn't sure how to capture that sentiment but came across a quote by Ta-Nehisi Coates that did, reflecting on the contributions of self-taught historians like Dr. Ben as giving him his "first sense of skepticism."[46] Rkhty's work had laid the groundwork for my first sense of skepticism.

Wayne Jones

Wayne and Rkhty had been living in Claremont for about ten months when they decided to move to Holly Springs. Wayne describes Claremont as an aesthetically beautiful place but too expensive, with too much traffic and not enough Black people. Rkhty surprised him with the suggestion to move when he came home from work one day, and he replied, "I'm not moving to Mississippi, 'cause nobody's gonna lynch me."[47] That was 2004. He reluctantly went to Holly Springs to check it out, and they decided to move there in 2005.

Wayne didn't know much about Mississippi. His maternal and paternal grandparents had settled in Woodstown, in southern New Jersey, as part of a community migration from King and Queen County, Virginia. He has no family in Mississippi but found rural Marshall County similar to the environment in which he grew up in South Jersey. His mother's family had a farm and his father's family also did farmwork. His first jobs were working on farms. Rural life was familiar to him. During the interview, Wayne shifted between his family's more specific postemancipation move from the Gresham plantation in Virginia to the broader enslaved community's postemancipation efforts "to create a hundred and twenty something–odd colleges in less than a hundred years. No other people on the face of the Earth have done that. That story doesn't get told."[48] He not only liked the idea of being in a majority Black city, but he was intrigued by the historically Black Rust College, founded the year after the Civil War ended, and what he later discovered to be its role as a headquarters for civil rights workers who came from the North.[49]

Racist or racially segregated spaces weren't foreign to Wayne. He said:

> At the time that I grew up in South Jersey, we saw White folks, but my parents didn't visit white people, and none of them visited us. We went to school with White folks, and I, you know, played with the children, but you

didn't go to their house. Not when I was young. That only happens when I get into high school. A family moved out next door and built a house out next to where we were. And so, they had two sons. Naturally my mother and father had two sons and the boys got together and we did what boys do. . . . So I grew up like that and, uh, when it comes to racism or being Black my mother would tell us things like you know you got to be twice as good. You got two strikes against you already.[50]

Wayne is nearly twenty years my senior, but we seem to have had similar childhood experiences. My parents worked with White people but didn't visit them, nor did they visit us. I vaguely remember one of my mom's White coworkers coming to pick up a sack of okra, but I don't recall her coming into the house or being invited in. I grew up in a post–White flight neighborhood on what was and still is considered the Black side of town. The last White family left when my older sister was a child in the early seventies. I played with White children in school up until the fifth grade, before we racially segregated ourselves in middle school. I can't say that my experience was the norm or that Wayne's was. I knew Black kids, my age, who had White friends. Most came from parents with higher education backgrounds or those who drove their kids to majority-White schools. Like Wayne's mother, mine told me that, as a Black person, I had to be twice as good and that I already had strikes against me. Unlike Wayne, I wasn't oblivious to it. Personal experience proved what my mother said (see chapter 1). I left home because the little contact I did have with White people seemed to be too much, and my experiences with them always seemed to occur through a racist lens. I wanted to get away from it. I was hyperaware of race.

Wayne's contact with White people was limited, and his experience with racism was only through his parents' warnings. He says, "I was Black, but I wasn't Black in the mind." That changed when he joined the Marine Corps in 1975, after he got out of high school. He was overlooked for a promotion after two years of service. "All of a sudden, it hit me one night. The reason they're not promoting you is because you're Black." He expected a meritocracy. He expected things to be fair if "you do everything you're supposed to do." He became the Black ideal to which other soldiers compared themselves when making arguments about systemic racism. He reflected: "They would look at me and tell the officers in charge, 'Look, okay, you got me over here [talking about themselves] and I know I didn't do what I was supposed to do but that guy over there, Jones, he do everything y'all say and y'all still won't promote him.' And they were right, but I didn't see it that way. The White folks didn't even know I existed. That's another example of White supremacy."[51]

Wayne's examples were meant to show me that he wasn't always the Black activist man I met nearly eight years before. It was a process rooted in experience. After leaving the military in his early twenties, he attended Salem Community College in Salem County, New Jersey, where he trained as an electrical instrumentation technician. He admitted, "Now, I'm still not this Black guy though," except for getting exposed to some Black history programs after school and being one of the few people in the room at Black history speeches. At moments, he tended to see what he considers parts of racism, "running into White folks" and trying to understand why some are "so damn mean" or "how come some Black folks are so bitter," but he couldn't put it together yet.[52] He didn't have the sociohistorical contexts necessary to make sense of those parts.

Wayne is a technical person, evident in how he reminisces about taking his father's lawn mower apart as a child, his studies at Salem Community College, and his electrical engineering training at the New Jersey Institute of Technology. It's also evident in how he talks about racism—in parts that need to be put together. Wayne's a reasonable and practical thinker. He moves on from things that don't seem to be working; he doesn't like beating around the bush; he doesn't seem to be a people pleaser (Rkhty's an exception); and he's also willing to take risks. He said that he believed that he could do anything, because that's what his mother told him. He had no reason not to believe it. Yet he was admittedly a poor sociology student, managing to avoid a failing grade with an impressive late paper on how public schools failed to educate Black children "in their own best interests." He added, "But I'm still not this guy," meaning still not the guy I met and know, the guy who held everyone in the room accountable when they didn't seem to understand how racism shaped their and others' lives.[53] I wanted to know how he had the idea for the paper in the first place, the question that would eventually get to how Wayne became *that* guy.

In the early 1980s, Wayne was staying in the dorm at the YMCA while he attended the New Jersey Institute of Technology in North Jersey. There were other young Black guys there who went to Harlem for a lecture series,

First World Alliance, every Saturday from two to eight. "They would have people come in and they were taught African American history, African literature, science, uh, sociology, anything. Yosef Ben-Jochannan would come there. Ivan Van Sertima would come there. James Turner would be there. Rkhty came and spoke. Jacob Carruthers. . . . And I was going and latched onto it. The first time I went, I was hooked. And they were talking about things I didn't know as far as history was concerned and it made sense. It was providing me with answers about my experiences that I didn't have in life."[54] That experience put Wayne's parts together.

Every Saturday for three or four years, he had college professors giving him a free education for hours. "It was standing room only. People were sitting in the aisles. You couldn't pay for that kind of education at the time. That's where I saw Rkhty for the first time. I was TAKEN!"[55] Wayne started to read any Black history books that he could get and still does. When I arrived at his house for an interview, he was reading *Wilmington's Lie: The Murderous Coup of 1898 and the Rise of White Supremacy*, David Zucchino's account of the Wilmington race riot, White terrorism as a response to Black enfranchisement. He's always sharing a new read. I think that it's a socialized practice, from his Saturdays in Harlem with folks who generously shared knowledge with him.

He was still in engineering school then, which he says created a "furious dichotomy" when he entered the workforce and engaged issues of company equity and diversity that others couldn't or wouldn't respond to. He felt like he had to raise those questions "for the other Black folks in the room." Wayne still has that sense of ancestral descendant accountability. "You fulfill your honor and obligation to those that have come before you and you make a way and fulfill your honor and obligations for those that'll come after you."[56] His early introduction to Holly Springs reflects that same sense of obligation.

After arriving in Holly Springs, Wayne became part of the Marshall County Democratic Executive Committee and attended Marshall County Board of Supervisors meetings. He also participated in a men's breakfast group, in which local men met at four different churches on Sunday mornings to discuss community issues and, with Rkhty, volunteered at the Ida B. Wells-Barnett Museum. He was also part of *Voices of Time*, a radio program, with Dale DeBerry, George Zinn III, the city's District Four supervisor, and Reverend Edward C. Moses, Sr., of Asbury United Methodist

Church. It was a forum to discuss community issues and was on the air for about two years.[57]

Wayne describes his first impression of the Holly Springs Pilgrimage as a mythical South with southern belles and a genteel society, "nothing about the actual reality."[58] This was expected, but it was not a deterrent. Wayne and Rkhty have toured pilgrimage sites as well as participated in other pilgrimage events. The mythic representations of the pilgrimage do not supersede their general interest in local history, but they clearly understand its shortcomings.

Like Rkhty, Wayne's participation in Behind the Big House began after meeting David Person. Wayne mostly does brickmaking demonstrations, based on invaluable knowledge that Rkhty gained through her booklet project research. He remarked:

Now I knew that they had done the work, cleared the land and everything, but I didn't know the degree of how they had gone about actually making the bricks and the amount of knowledge that it took. In about '86 or '87, I started to realize that you didn't bring no "slaves" from Africa. What you brought from Africa were artisans, craftsmen, doctors, lawyers, medicine people. They came with the knowledge.[59]

He added:

The fingerprints, the names, the marks on the bricks. These people wanted to be remembered. It's all there. Like Dave's [what he calls David Person] house. I started thinking about that. How long does it really take to make a house like this? It takes years. You making them bricks by hand. There's no bulldozers. There's no engines. You ain't got nothing but labor. You got these men and women who can look at a fire and tell you that's the right temperature . . . and nobody taught them that. They under pressure at the same time too. That, if the thing blow up I could lose my life out here. And the house is standing here in front of you and it's built and you don't want to give those people no credit. How can you not? They were dumb, ignorant, didn't know nothing? That's so far from the truth.[60]

As an example, Wayne shared the story of Cato Govan, a former enslaved carriage driver in Holly Springs. In a claim submitted to the Southern Claims Commission, Govan describes his process of hauling cotton to Memphis:

I commenced hauling cotton the year after the Yankees took Memphis [after 1862] and continued to haul cotton until the close of the war. I got through the rebel lines by traveling at night. Sometimes the federals occupied all the way to Memphis. I never brought anything out without a permit. I never hauled for anybody but myself. I mean I always drove my own team, but I hauled cotton for any who would pay my price. At first I got $60 per bale, and afterwards $50 per bale freight. I could haul two bales. I could go to Memphis in a day and at night. Oh it's fifty miles. It took the same to come back. I got the privilege of going in and coming out of the lines. I never was delayed any by them.[61]

Wayne continued:

I mean you got a Black man carrying all this cotton. He just ain't carrying cotton, he carrying money through lines of soldiers. There's no way he did this by being weak. He had people working with him. They was carrying guns. They was ready to fight at the drop of a hat. But he got it done in such a way that he didn't have to fight. When he's coming back, he's got people's money in his pocket, on his person, and he's bringing them back their money. And there's not that many people that can do that at the time. But he's doing it. Now, what gives this Black man, this ex-slave, the wherewithal to be able to do this? 'Cause these kinds of people aren't supposed to exist. He's not real. They can't do this. Yet they do. It's them kind of things that you can't put together without this kind of work.[62]

Wayne complicates Govan's experiences and characterizes them as an example of Black experiences being simplified in the broader sphere of historic site representations. In that way, his thought process resembles that of David and his understanding of Mrs. Petty as a Black woman whose experiences have been essentialized in the present. Wayne explicitly makes this case about historical actors. It is critical to him that you talk about people's minds and how they thought about themselves in the past, not what people say about them in the present. To Wayne, "The truth is better than the lie."[63]

"The Truth Is Better Than the Lie"

I agree with Wayne in more ways than one. I recently argued for representations of slavery that ask visitors to consider hypothetical circumstances or imagine the possibilities of lived experiences at sites of slavery.[64] Here is where my historian friends will likely cringe, if they haven't already. I understand the significance of historical documentation and site-specific narratives but have tempered my need to have such evidence in order to represent sites of slavery years ago.

Maybe that compromise began when I was a graduate student working with the National Park Service, and a park employee at the Melrose Estate in Natchez asked our archaeology crew to "help him find the slaves." I got the impression that he needed the material culture proof to justify talking about slavery and wondered what he would do if we or anyone else could not find it. I continued to worry that not having enough material culture indicative of slavery to display at a historic site could give these site managers, already reluctant to interpret slavery, an excuse not to do so. I also learned that excavating material culture related to slavery didn't necessarily mean that the general public would ever see it.

Much of the critique that comes from historians who want to hear site-specific narratives—narratives detailing the experiences of enslaved people who actually lived on site—doesn't consider the research obstacles or the lack of support that limit some sites' abilities to be fully interpreted. It doesn't excuse those historic sites that fail to interpret or that poorly interpret, but these complications caused me to sympathize with the nuances of interpretation across historic sites, especially those with disparities in access to human and economic resources. I came to value the effort more than the information. I came to value those who pooled all their resources possible to prioritize displaying the experiences of enslaved people, even if that didn't meet the standards of professional historians. Many times, that effort comes from only one or two people. Other times, it comes from an eclectic mixture of employees and volunteers.

My supportive network and I are a mixed bag of talents and experiences. We value research but don't prioritize it, especially in an all-volunteer effort. I used to lament that but haven't in a while. I've come to think that what many historic sites of slavery miss is the opportunity to include audience members in the meaning making, asking them to think about what might have happened given a limited set of circumstances. We'll never have all the answers, even less so for those enslaved. This means that so many things can be true outside of what we think we know, not simply better than the lie in misrepresentations but better than the "truth" we seek in historical documents. It's not that the latter isn't valid. It's just that it needs to be complicated—to be seen as only part of a very complicated whole. My experience has also shown that many historic site managers tend to postpone slavery interpretations until they find historical truths. If they don't find anything, then the site doesn't get interpreted, leaving gaps in the landscape of slavery interpretations. I've met folks who fear the repercussions of putting historic sites on display when they don't have enough historical documentation. I often ask them what's enough. I think that informed hypotheticals are better than nothing. Here's an example.

In June 2017, I attended Transforming Public History from Charleston to the Atlantic World, a conference hosted by the College of Charleston Avery Research Center for African American History and Culture, the Carolina Lowcountry and the Atlantic World Program, the Addlestone Library, and the Race and Social Justice Initiative. The conference's special focus was to "highlight speakers and topics relevant to transforming practices of interpreting the history of slavery and its race and class legacies in Charleston and historically interconnected local, regional, and international sites."[65] I traveled to Charleston with a team of University of Mississippi Slavery Research Group students and colleagues interested in networking and sharing our local public history projects. The conference was a refreshing mix of public history professionals, scholars, educators, librarians, and artists participating in roundtables, panels, individual paper presentations, and workshops. I signed up for Kristin Gallas's workshop "Giving Voice to Long-Silenced Millions: Interpreting Slavery on Historic Sites." Her coedited collection, *Interpreting Slavery at Museums and Historic Sites*, was published a couple of years earlier. Gallas's workshop ended with a visit to the Aiken-Rhett House, a townhouse complex built in 1820, once occupied by South Carolina governor William Aiken. The house spent 142 years in the Aiken family before being sold and opened as a house museum in 1975. The complex includes the original slave quarters.

Gallas divided workshop participants into small groups for an exercise that I think she called Hack the House. Each group was assigned a space or a room in the complex. My group was assigned the ballroom, what I remember as a mostly empty space with a few historic furnishings. There were no interpretive signs. Gallas gave us a sheet of paper with minimal descriptions and asked that we think about the role of enslaved people in those spaces. It was genius! Without such a cue, I think that ballroom visitors might shift to a fancy dance with twirling hoopskirts and a myriad of smiling faces. She made us imagine an alternate experience, one of tired hands and feet quickly and quietly moving in and out of the space, others standing along the walls for hours just waiting, thinking, hoping. We did not need the historical documentation to know what happened, but we had a powerful experience nonetheless. It wasn't mythical. It wasn't a lie. It was an imagined experience. I was so moved by that experience that I wanted to immediately go to Alisea, David, Wayne, and Rkhty to share. Maybe it was already too late to do this in Holly Springs. This was nearly three years after Gracing the Table's collaboration with the garden club.

Working with the Garden Club

In 2014, Gracing the Table and the Holly Springs Garden Club began discussing how to better integrate Behind the Big House with the pilgrimage and provide more inclusive representations of community history for tourists. From 2012 to 2014, the tours coexisted with intersecting tourists and little to no collaboration. This environment was and still is confusing to tourists. Some intentionally toured the slave-dwelling sites. Others accidentally toured them, assuming they were part of the pilgrimage.

Gracing the Table mediated talks among a few members of the garden club and Chelius Carter. David's established relationship with garden club members through his participation in several of their home tours made this collaboration possible. For one pilgrimage season, Gracing the Table helped successfully transform the pilgrimage into the more inclusive Holly Springs Home and Heritage Festival (and Pilgrimage). This included intentional marketing of Behind the Big House events by the garden club and narratives of slavery presented at several pilgrimage house sites. Rkhty created a docent training orientation guide, focusing specifically on the experiences of African Americans in Marshall County. She also interpreted at Montrose, the garden club's home base. Other Holly Springs residents, including Chester Lesueur and Marcus Daniels, helped with interpretations at the Davis House at Strawberry Plains and at Herndon House, another historic site, respectively. Herndon is a two-story brick house in Federal and Greek Revival styles built in 1845. Since 2013, it has been owned by Suzanne James, a Gracing the Table supporter, and Randy Hayes, a local artist who uses the home as a studio and exhibit space.[66] University of Mississippi history and southern studies graduate students also assisted with interpretations.

In November 2014, Gracing the Table began meeting with seven garden club members as part of this collaborative effort.[67] Through several meetings at the Kirkwood National Golf Club, we hashed out what this new collaboration would be called, Michael Twitty's potential role in the pilgrimage's Sunday brunch, and how to make the marketing materials reflect the goals of this united undertaking. I can't say that this was a smooth process. I don't think that we expected it to be. But I will say that the garden club women who embarked on this collaborative journey seemed fully committed to the process. They were committed despite major differences in how and why the garden club and Preserve Marshall County functioned: the pilgrimage was a fundraising venture, and Behind the Big House was a free grant-funded program. Behind the Big House relied on grants, which precluded it from charging or accepting fees, and Preserve Marshall County had already stipulated in its grant applications how the money would be spent.

These differences brought up issues about cost sharing and institutional values; the garden club hoped that Preserve Marshall County could more equitably share programming costs, while Chelius and Jenifer saw interpreters Michael Twitty and Joseph McGill as gifts to the pilgrimage that Preserve Marshall County funded. They argued that as the visitor numbers increased for Behind the Big House, so would the pilgrimage attendance. The conversation that they hoped to have about race shifted to economics. These were unforeseen issues that Gracing the Table tried its best to navigate, particularly because Chelius was residing at the family home in Virginia much of the time. It was not a perfect negotiation, but we were all motivated to stay the course.

Interviewed by the *Jackson Sun* in 2015, Jennifer Barkley, then president of the garden club, described its partnership with Gracing the Table as "making history" and offering "a more inclusive view of Holly Springs' history and antebellum perspective." She cited Gracing the Table members as "instrumental in gathering stories from the perspective of former slaves and finding docents to tell those stories at each of the houses," a first for the pilgrimage. She added, "We believe that these voices need to be heard. . . . We want our young people to be educated about all of their history and heritage."[68]

In 2015, interpreting the main houses from the perspectives of the enslaved was a first and last for the garden club. The next year, the pilgrimage returned to its traditional format after some club representatives determined that the collaboration was no longer feasible. I was disappointed that we seemed to have come so far and then took so many steps back. For some members, their nostalgic connections to the pilgrimage triumphed over the potential to broaden its scope with a more inclusive narrative. Others were ready to make that commitment. I'm not sure what went on behind closed doors, just that the former sentiment won over. In 2016, the tours again coexisted without collaboration.

After visiting Charleston, I still had hope that Gracing the Table would reconnect with the garden club at some point. I saw Kristin Gallas's exercise as one possible way to do that. I thought that a Hack the House effort might minimize backlash from members still uncomfortable with fully incorporating narratives of slavery. That was, at times, a point of contention between Gracing the Table and some of the on-site garden club docents. We planned but did not practice interpretations. At times, it seemed like there were two separate interpretations going on in the same space. Maybe getting garden club folks to begin to imagine the possibilities of experiences of enslaved people, rather than feeling pressure to prove that slavery happened at pilgrimage sites, was the answer. As I write now, I don't think that's what Gallas intended. Imagining isn't possible without believing.

Claiming Histories

The next year, 2016, Gracing the Table's focus was more inward. The temporary relationship with the garden club had been rewarding and then defeating. We decided to broaden our libation ceremony with a two-day symposium, "Claiming Histories: Slavery and Remembrance in North Mississippi," held on the campus of Rust College. The program, funded by the Mississippi Humanities Council with a grant from the Kellogg Foundation, began on Friday, October 21, with performing artist Alex Mercedes and lectures on slavery and public memory and the Register of Freedmen. Anthropology graduate students Suzanne Davidson and Robert Waren created displays of archaeological and historic sites for the event. History graduate student Justin Rogers gave a talk titled "'Plum Sanctified': Enslaved Women and Religious Life in North Mississippi, 1820s–1860s," based on his dissertation research. Saturday's program included a libation ceremony to honor enslaved ancestors led by Memphis drummer Ekpe. The program concluded with what was probably the most enriching segment: group discussions about slavery and our shared histories led by Gracing the Table members.

As we had with past discussion sessions, we organized participants into small groups of four to six people, gave them a list of discussion questions (see appendix B), and assigned a facilitator to each group to guide the sessions. The facilitator was always a Gracing the Table member who encouraged the groups to assign a transcriber and reporter to share what each group learned from their discussion. David always began each discussion by reviewing standard protocol and then emphasizing the need for respect for anonymity after the discussions. We expected people to learn something and share what they learned but not to attribute statements or ideas to people in the group. That was our attempt at making the discussions relatively safe spaces.

David considered the event successful and submitted a complimentary piece to the local paper. He tends to see any project that we complete that way. I wasn't quite sure how I felt about the event. The program attendance didn't reflect the effort that we put in and we still don't know exactly why. Alisea had worked hard to submit a Kellogg Foundation Racial Equity grant application on the group's behalf. The Mississippi Humanities Council's executive director, Stuart Rockoff, and board member Wilma Mosley Clopton attended and fully participated in the two-day program. Their attendance seemed to be part of a broader interest by the council in racial reconciliation work in Holly Springs, including Behind the Big House. Holly Springs was also planning its first Chickasaw festival, honoring its original inhabitants, to be held the next year. David was also on that planning committee.

Our Kellogg Racial Equity grant was a welcome addition to our planning process, especially since we normally worked with no budget or with some support from Strawberry Plains for the libation ceremony or funds that David personally contributed for food or entertainment. Now that we had a food budget, we thought critically about what we would serve, opting for gumbo, an African diasporic food. We spent hours and hours trying to find a historic photo that would capture what we hoped the event would be. After meeting in person for several hours and four days of email discussions, we decided on what seemed to be an antebellum photo of a White man, his children, and an enslaved woman, possibly their nurse. The image is displayed on many websites with no context. I searched and searched for the origin of the photo, so we could credit the source, but with no success. I even contacted the Maryland Historical Society, which also displayed the photo on its website, with no luck.

The problem was resolved for us when Alisea showed up at one of our meetings with a sketched interpretation of the Black woman in the image. I thought that it was perfect. It wasn't historic, but I think that her interpretation in the present more adequately captured what we hoped the event would accomplish.

We spent a lot of time on publicity and marketing, including posters with Alisea's drawing on them, but we didn't attract the local participation that we hoped for, especially from Rust College where the event was held. Some faculty members and administrators attended but not many students. We lured a few students in with our free lunch. Most of them stayed for the discussions. We do know that our event competed with a series of other college events, which might have limited student and faculty attendance. The content was rich, but few saw it.

Although we learned much about event planning, I think that we learned more about our limitations as individuals and as a group. We were still exhausted from 2015 and likely didn't have the energy to support each other through the 2016 event. I don't think we realized that until it was too late. No one argued or explicitly admitted to being worn out. We just took a break without announcing one.

When I interviewed Alisea four years after Claiming Histories, she reflected on Gracing the Table's founding: "We had no idea how much work it was going to be. Oooh! Oh my God! Have we recovered?" I added that I should title this chapter "Gracing the Table: Oh My God!"[69] We both laughed. I admitted to her that I was overwhelmed by how to show how much work it was. What I didn't share with her is that I soon realized that shifting the narrative from how much work it took to what it took to sustain the work was a more useful frame.

CLAIMING HISTORIES

Which histories will be remembered and why?

Slavery and Remembrance in North Mississippi

Friday, October 21, 2016, 5:30 p.m.—8:00 p.m.
HEARD AUDITORIUM—RUST COLLEGE
Sat., October 22, 2016: 12:00 p.m.—2:45 p.m. on grounds of Rust—ceremony

Guest speakers: Ekpe Abioto of Memphis and Performing Artist Alex Mercedes of Holly Springs
Information at www.gracingthetablems.wix.com; gracingthetablems@gmail.com

Gracing the Table's Claiming Histories promotional poster with Alisea's sketch.

Challenges and Successes

When I interviewed Alisea, she said that she was pleased with Gracing the Table's first three years, particularly because of the level of Rust College student involvement. Their participation was dependent on whether she taught a course with content that aligned with the group's purpose and the level of student interest. Alisea's work never translated to the rest of the college as we hoped it would, and I am not sure why it didn't. She continued to be Gracing the Table's main connection to Rust. She lamented the loss of student participation but also admitted that "you got to have support for this kind of work. You can't do this and have a full-time job. I'm not just talking about myself. I'm talking about all concerned. This is real work. It's not something you just do on the side. It'll wear you out."[70] I described it as part of our gig economy, with no income.

I'm not sure what advice I would go back to give us if I could. I don't know that we would've listened. People surviving on passion often don't realize it until they can't give anymore. It's that drive that I wanted to understand. I wanted to understand these determinations for historical truths.

Gracing the Table is still together. We still plot and plan. We're just more practical about it. I think that, over the years, we got smarter about how to distribute labor and about our limitations. That also meant doing less work. More work would have been possible only with steady growth, I think.

Alisea lamented the fact that we never really attracted the local descendants of slave owners. Our support mostly came from relative newcomers or friends of Gracing the Table members. I don't think that we didn't attract them from a lack of effort on our part, because David constantly invited and reinvited many of them. Sometimes they came. Sometimes they applauded our efforts, but they rarely continued to invest in the work. We both agreed that we still had some local impact.

I think that our most successful result has been our relationship with Black descendants of those enslaved by Mary Burton. That relationship began when Deborah "Deb" McClelland Neely Davis, a genealogist from Edwardsville, Illinois, stopped by David's house in 2014. She had a feeling, an unexplained connection to the house, each time she passed by while visiting family in Holly Springs. She soon realized that that feeling was rooted in history, a history that connected her enslaved ancestors to Mary Burton, who had enslaved some of them.[71] David invited Deb into his house that first visit, and proceeding conversations led to an invitation for the family members to visit Burton Place during their 2014 reunion. That year, forty-seven family members visited the home place, interpreted by members of Gracing the Table, including myself. They were given tours of the main house and the kitchen/quarters. Those visits were repeated from 2015 to 2019, the time of this writing.

Thanks to Deb Davis, we know the names of sixty-seven of those enslaved in 1860. Those names are on display in one of the quarters along with the slave census schedule. Deb has also consistently traveled from Illinois to Mississippi to help with Behind the Big House interpretations at Burton Place. She has been joined by her brother Alco "Al" Patton and his wife, Linear. All have been invaluable to the work that Gracing the Table has tried to do: the work of reconciling the past with the present.

I've learned a lot from my experiences with and observations of Gracing the Table. I'm still thinking through critical questions about how and why people come to do this work, how and why some are adamant not only about seeking historical truths but about sharing them, even to their own detriments. My interviews made some things clearer. I learned that David understands his life history as being so broad that, like Chelius, he doesn't feel pressure to take sides with historical actors. His ancestors simply helped make him who he is. They don't define him. Alisea and Rkhty show conscious attempts to reconnect to Mississippi family—historical and contemporary—yet I think that these are also subconscious attempts

Deb Davis (right) showing Burton Place displays to visitors in 2016.

to heal the pains of migration. They have taken on the brave work of healing generational trauma. Maybe each of us is doing that in some way.

Wayne reminded me that there are always gems in the local experience. When reflecting on Holly Springs, he rhetorically asked, "So what is it about these people here that's special?"[72] He already knew the answer: Black life, ingenuity, and survival are special. Wayne also knows that, although he is Black in Holly Springs, he's always an outsider. He mentioned that several times. That's the case for all of us. None of us was born or raised in Holly Springs. Maybe that emotional distance allows this kind of work. I don't yet know that I'd have the emotional fortitude to sustain this type of work in my home parish in Louisiana. Maybe being too close makes this work too hard.

And then I think of Deborah "Debbie" Cosey, who purchased Concord Quarters, a former slave dwelling built in 1820. The Natchez woman and her husband, Greg, purchased the property specifically hoping that it would inspire dialogue about slavery. Cosey, who worked in the tourism industry much of her life, and her husband renovated the property for several years. The Coseys live on the property, which they operate as a bed-and-breakfast. I stayed there when I was invited by the Natchez director of Cultural Heritage Tourism, Darrell White, to participate in the Natchez Heritage Tourism: New Narratives conference, the second part of Visit Natchez's attempt to help local individuals and institutions think through broader interpretations of slavery across the city, including the Natchez pilgrimages. That was in September 2019, and it was a long time coming. Cosey had already started showing her property during Natchez's fall pilgrimage two years prior, envisioning it as what some might consider a contradictory mix of bed-and-breakfast, wedding venue, and tour space. Somehow it works. Cosey's personality is infectious; she's unapologetic about her purpose, seems to wear her heart on her sleeve, and periodically breaks out in song to express how she feels. She's also the only Black woman I know interpreting slave quarters that she purchased.

I haven't worked with Cosey but, in the short time that I spent with her, her spirit reminded me of that unnamed thing that moves people to do this kind of work. Maybe the past is calling them, calling us. I initially described this force as a haunting, and my good friend Celeste reminded me that "the only people who need hauntings are the ones who refuse to see."

Academic Values and Public Scholarship

In 2011, I began working at the University of Mississippi with a joint appointment in the Department of Sociology and Anthropology and the Center for the Study of Southern Culture. Much of my work at the university can be framed as community-campus engagement, which is service-learning and community-based research "premised on mutually beneficial partnerships, integrating teaching and/or research with discovery, theory, action, and reflection."[1] In chapter 3, I discussed the development of the Behind the Big House program and the service-learning components of my courses, which merged "in a single mission the traditionally separate duties of research, teaching, and service."[2] In chapter 4, I considered the development of Gracing the Table and my relationships with its members. For me, these relationships formed a central approach to my scholarship that intersected with and linked teaching, research, and service. In many fields, community-campus engagement is perceived "as only service to the community or community activism and not research."[3] This chapter details the difficulties of sustaining my community work while attempting to be successful in a tenure-track position that not only divided research from teaching and service but devalued the latter two. This chapter is about the campus side of community-campus engagement and about how my experiences in academia often made public scholarship a contradiction in terms.

Research: Publications by Another Name

I don't recall all the details of my first campus-wide faculty meeting in 2011, but one thing stands out. Then chancellor Dan Jones stressed the additional responsibility of being a faculty member at the flagship institution in the poorest state in the country and emphasized that our work was not just about academics but about service. Jones's inauguration theme for 2010 was "transformation through service," and it seems that he reinforced some of the same points that he had made the year before: "we are a successful flagship liberal arts university in the poorest state in our nation. . . . We must seek opportunities to fulfill our responsibility to transform not just individual lives, but to transform the world around us through our service."[4] This "transformation through service" was proposed as an integral component of the university's 2020 strategic plan, introduced in spring 2012, which states that "through civic engagement and service, the University [would] purposefully apply its talent and knowledge so as to transform individuals, communities, and regions."[5] I heard a call for service and assumed that my service work would be valued.

Even with my hesitancy to return to North Mississippi, Jones's statement made me feel at home. For me, academic research and service are inextricably linked. I was too naive to recognize at that moment, however, that my university was at least five years behind several others in institutionalizing community engagement, a necessary part of the process to be able to promote faculty engagement with communities in the state. In 2006, the Carnegie Foundation for the Advancement of Teaching began selecting colleges and universities for a nationally and publicly recognized classification as "institutions of community engagement." This Classification for Community Engagement not only defined but helped by offering a template for community engagement practices as the "collaboration between institutions of higher education and their larger communities (local, regional/state, national, global) for the mutually beneficial exchange of knowledge and resources in a context of partnership and reciprocity."[6] According to Amy Driscoll, a consulting scholar with the foundation:

> The composite profile of these colleges and universities represents the best practices that have been identified nationally. The framework enabled participating institutions to assess the presence or absence of such prac-

tices, identify and reflect on both the strengths of and the gaps in their approaches, and strengthen their programs. Thus, Carnegie began to achieve its intention to honor achievements while promoting ongoing improvement.[7]

It would be another five years before I began to see community engagement institutionalized, as proposed in the 2012 strategic plan. I struggled for most of those intermediate years.

When I was a graduate student at the University of Texas, several anthropologists practiced activist anthropology approaches and encouraged their students to do the same. An activist scholar reaches out to communities to help them achieve already-established goals. The scholar's academic background is an asset to the community, but the scholar's research aspirations are not the top priority in the collaborative effort.[8]

This approach influenced my dissertation work on St. Paul United Methodist Church in Dallas, in which I collaborated with a church committee and a community advisory committee to create a public exhibition on the church's history. My project was not a typical archaeology one. Maria Franklin and two of her other students, Jamie Brandon and James Davidson, had excavated a shotgun house site on the church's property. I joined the project after that excavation was over. I wanted a public archaeology project. Maria knew how political those projects could be and thought that St. Paul would be a relatively uncontentious space in which to work. The church community requested an exhibition of their recovered artifacts. *They* wanted the work done. That was not necessarily typical for public archaeology projects, which at times could cause antagonism between communities and archaeologists when the goals of one group diverged from those of the other. I'd heard about those conflicts, and my previously mentioned experience with Fred McGhee and others in Houston had proved that.

I knew early on that I wanted to apply to academic positions in archaeology, so I had worked with private archaeology firms as a graduate student to get more practical experience. One of my dissertation committee members expressed concern that I might be compromising future opportunities for employment, because I was not doing my own excavation, but supported the community engagement focus of my work nonetheless. At the least, I felt that I had spent enough time doing archaeology work and following others' projects to be able to critique archaeologists' abilities to share authority with publics or their potential to have long-lasting impacts on local communities associated with archaeological sites. I had concerns about what archaeological excavations, in general, offered African American descendant communities, whose members often had no say in project plans or ownership of artifacts. Even public archaeology projects were often not the result of the ideal of shared authority they proposed to be. I wanted to do post-archaeology work to understand public archaeology's full potential, and St. Paul was a private entity in control of its narrative and its material culture. I chose to take an academic risk, as a graduate student, and stray from more standard practice.

As a graduate student, I had the privilege of time. I moved to Dallas for Martha Norkunas's Project in Interpreting the Texas Past fellowship in 2005 and began getting to know members of the St. Paul community and historic preservationists in Dallas outside the church community. The exhibition opening in February 2009 established time restraints and, eventually, so did my inability to fund myself through graduate school. At Maria's strong suggestion, I moved back to Austin to put necessary efforts into dissertation writing. I rushed the writing process but had not rushed my collaboration with St. Paul. Academia's tenure clock would not give me that same flexibility.

I heard University of Texas faculty talk about activist scholarship but didn't engage in the conversations that would have been necessary to understand what that work looked like for them as faculty on the ground. I took classes, heard them speak, and understood activist scholarship as a necessary practice, but I didn't understand its methodological and practical constraints until I read Charlie Hale's collection, *Engaging Contradictions: Theory, Politics, and Methods of Activist Scholarship*, several years after its publication. The book featured contributions from five scholars then on the Texas faculty. I left the university wondering how it could be possible that anthropologists would not do work with and for the communities they serve; I didn't understand what pursuing activist scholarship might mean for me as an academic personally and professionally.

Activist scholarship assumes that I, as a researcher, must heed the knowledge of those with whom I collaborate, regardless of how well educated and steeped in "authoritative knowledge" I might think I am. This shared authority takes time. What I didn't realize is the fact that my work might have value to community groups, like St. Paul and my supportive network in Holly Springs, but little to no value "to the academy," my new workplace, regardless of what Dan Jones said.[9]

My Academic Career

By the end of my first academic year, I was meeting department standards for teaching and service. I'd prepped for four classes, all taught that academic year. Although I had presented papers at a couple of conferences, one in anthropology and one in southern studies, I had not communicated a clear plan for publication to my primary department. Senior department colleagues stressed that I seek publishing mentorship from tenured anthropology colleagues, who included a range of southeastern Indian archaeologists and ethnohistorians, Mesoamerican archaeologists, and cultural anthropologists working in the Middle East and South America. None of them explicitly offered that type of mentorship, and I didn't know that I needed it. I was accustomed to figuring things out on my own. I also had no idea how long the article-publishing process could take or how complicated it would be to find a book publisher. I was too independent to ask. The "double-edged" independence that worked for me as a graduate student did the opposite for me as a tenure-track academic.[10]

Working across Black feminist and womanist constructs like the Superwoman Schema, the Sojourner Truth Syndrome, and the Sisterella Complex, psychologists Jasmine Abrams, Morgan Maxwell, Michell Pope, and Faye Belgrave theorized my experiences as those of a Strong Black Woman who is "resistant to vulnerability or dependency" and who "displays strength, suppresses emotions, succeeds despite inadequate resources, and assumes responsibilities as a community agent."[11] This schema was culturally transmitted, and I had seen so many examples of these women in my upbringing in Louisiana. My approach to my academic career wasn't strange. I had normalized it. Even with attempts to contest racist and gendered notions of who I was, later in my life, I still felt obligated to assume those responsibilities. I almost couldn't help myself. By the next academic year, I was meeting department expectations in teaching and now thriving in service, which was not surprising for a "community agent." I had begun my collaboration with Behind the Big House, which senior colleagues noted as impressive in my evaluations. They saw my collaborative work as the type of scholarship that the department hoped to develop in the future. I didn't know how to reconcile my belief that the department wanted to build something in the future that I didn't think it was planning for in the present.

I excelled in my service commitments for two reasons. First, I didn't know how to say no, especially when senior colleagues suggested or requested that I do department or university service. I was on three search committees and the university's Faculty Senate in my first two years. Second, I felt that I "must work toward changing the institution" I was in.[12]

In *The Black Academic's Guide to Winning Tenure—Without Losing Your Soul*, Kerry Ann Rockquemore and Tracey Laszloffy "acknowledge that just saying no is more complicated for black faculty than it appears."[13] A senior colleague nominated me for the Faculty Senate and, through an email, asked if that was okay with me. That colleague asked if it was okay as the nomination was being made, not beforehand. I asked another senior colleague if I had to do this, and that colleague said that I could decline but that some of the department faculty had served in the senate during their first couple of years. This gave me the impression that this service wasn't much of a burden and also that it was a department expectation, without that being explicitly stated. What I remember feeling is that I didn't want to add this to my list of things to do and that even though the colleague who nominated me asked if it was okay with me, that person would be making future decisions about my tenure.

Even if one of them had told me to say no, I had encountered what Rockquemore and Laszloffy describe as a common practice by White faculty "with the best of intentions" that "seemingly simple advice too often fails to acknowledge the sheer volume of requests that the average black faculty member receives over and above majority faculty. It neglects the complex equation of work you may feel obligated to do on top of research and teaching, and the differential costs associated with saying no to various administrators' requests for participation in a never-ending stream of diversity work."[14]

By my second year, I had begun collaborating with Behind the Big House, but although I was a professor, as a Black female anthropologist critiquing race and racism I was struggling with classroom hostility in an introductory southern studies course; these difficulties were abetted by the sociopolitical environment of racism on campus, which I will discuss shortly. My response was to work to change the culture of the university and of southern studies. In 2011, I joined the Critical Race Studies Group, which I saw as a support system. It began as an interdisciplinary reading group of faculty members mainly in the College of Liberal Arts. The group started before I came to the university but began to shift to a more politically active body shortly after I arrived. Overtly racist acts on campus generated that shift.

I also co-organized a symposium to help think through the culture of teaching and practicing southern studies. I needed help dealing with the hostility. The human resources support wasn't there, and I thought that the symposium would help create a less antagonistic environment for other faculty and for me. I did all this still thinking that I was going to meet my publishing requirements, which Rockquemore and Laszloffy state is "impossible to do . . . in your first, second, or third year on the tenure track."[15]

I wish that I had read their book sooner. By that second academic year, senior colleagues still saw my contributions in teaching and service as integral to the department's community engagement future but stressed that I had not yet made research contributions, which is to say that I had no published research. I felt like the work that I had done in the past year didn't matter and that I was integral to the department's future but not its present.

Although I did seek advice from senior colleagues on several issues, I did not consult anyone on a regular basis, a commitment I have come to understand to be crucial to a productive mentorship relationship. I had one sociology colleague, a Black woman, take on what Rockquemore and Laszloffy describe as the role of a sponsor—a department advocate—for some junior faculty members, especially those of color and women and those doing race work.[16] She tried her best to help me navigate the department and the university as she understood them. I didn't comprehend what mentorship relationships were supposed to be and largely relied on another junior faculty member, also a Black woman, to help me make my way through the department.

Contrary to my University of Mississippi experience, I was immediately assigned a mentor as a graduate student at the University of Texas. Peggy Brunache, another Black archaeologist, was waiting for me at the anthropology office the same day that I arrived in 2002. She took her role seriously. Peggy was part of a mentor matching program for incoming graduate students there. The matches weren't always ideal ones, but the program did send a message that mentorship was significant. Peggy and I sustained a mentor-mentee relationship throughout my time there. My experience at Texas might have caused me to assume that mentorship was institutionalized. My Mississippi department later required mentoring for junior faculty members, after my colleague and I expressed frustration with the lack of structured mentoring. I wish that I had known to ask earlier.

Race, Racism, and the Tenure Track

What I did know is that race and racism shaped my tenure-track experience, as it did everything else. I felt the passive-aggressive behavior of those White students who didn't want me to analyze race and racism in the classroom. That was clear in student evaluations, especially in southern studies classes: "She seemed to talk about white racism 90% of the time. This class is about Southern Studies and the only thing we talked about all semester was about race in the South." There were suggestions that I talk less about racism and more about culture. Or what became redundant in evaluations: "This isn't a black culture studies class this is a 101 Southern Studies class that should be about the Civil War and interesting things about the South. I didn't take African American Studies for a reason."

Teaching southern studies to majority-White students, many of whom had whittled the field down to normalized whiteness and Black cultural forms of expression, was hard. It was stressful, even with the few enthusiastic students who seemed to get it, to get us.

I also didn't feel like I belonged in Oxford. A Black female professor in another department told me that I wouldn't fit in with some Black folks because I was a Black woman with natural hair, I was liberal in my clothing choices, and I didn't belong to a church community. I felt like I fit in only with her and a few others, all struggling with comparable issues. Oxford never felt like a safe space, especially when I received a warning from one White colleague who suggested that I avoid eating at a certain restaurant. I still don't know if it's safe to eat there. I never tried because restaurant-negotiating work is hard. I'm never sure if the White person behind the counter's greeting to me is lukewarm because I'm Black, or if she's just a lukewarm greeter. Then a White person comes in and I spend a few seconds watching their interactions to see if there's any difference. Then if it's different, meaning better, I wonder if they already had an informal relationship. If they're treated the same, then I'm relieved. If it's obviously different, then I decide whether I'm going to leave or eat there just that one time and never return. It happens way too often, and it requires way too much work. Whether or not an Oxford restaurant displayed the Gateway Tire Ole Miss football schedule, featuring Colonel Reb, or the old state flag on the wall was an added point of contention. Choices, in such a small city, are already limited.

By the time I began writing this book, three out of the four Black women I depended on for emotional support had left the institution. Two of them received a disproportionately high number of service requests because we were so few in number. Black students depended on them, and the institution depended on all of us to give Martin Luther King Day speeches and to meet Equal Opportunity Review Commission search committee requirements. The emotional labor was toxic. It is toxic. Despite those challenges, we worked. Maybe we worked because our existence, as Black women, had been "constructed in such a way that we felt like we should naturally endure 'stress and pain'" as we carried "on the onerous weights and trickle down effects of society's oppressive systems."[17] I have "naturally endured" longer than they had and am still uncomfortable with that. I envy the strength that it took for them to leave.

Early on in my tenure-track process, I was unfamiliar with two of Kerry Ann Rockquemore's lessons. One: "Black faculty cannot wait for others to welcome, mentor, or assist them because it may never happen." Two: "Because black faculty are under-represented they must be extra vigilant about formal and informal service demands that can cripple their ability to become productive researchers and count little towards their promotion."[18] What I did know how to do was avoid conflict. Rockquemore cites not avoiding conflict as a common mistake that faculty members of color make. What I didn't know is that the stress and anger from my conflict avoidance had to go somewhere. I internalized it.

I did know that I didn't want to compromise my values as an activist scholar, but I struggled to reconcile my practice of slow research with what was supposed to be a quick turnaround of journal articles. Through Behind the Big House, I found a racially diverse group of people in Mississippi who prioritized the lives of enslaved persons and who clearly understood the impacts of antebellum slavery on the present. I had shifted from a public archaeology approach to a broader critical heritage approach that included all material culture representations of the past, not just those underground. All had potential for interpreting slavery and for complicating the narratives of Mississippi antebellum history that were stuck in Susan Falck's "moonlight and magnolias" time warp. I was in awe that folks in Holly Springs were independently doing something different that I knew could change both heritage tourism in Mississippi and the way that tourism scholars, broadly, understand tourism as a form of community development. I wanted to stick with it. I wanted to work there. I wanted to help. I wanted them to help me understand.

I also knew that one basic tenet of activist scholarship is showing up. I felt that some senior colleagues understood research in a compartmentalized way. You teach in the fall and spring, do research at your convenience, and then make a concentrated research effort in the summer. My "field" was only a thirty-minute drive away, and I had continuous contact with the folks there by email and over the phone. I couldn't cut them off to focus on writing, as senior colleagues seemed to suggest. I wouldn't cut them off. Inconsistency could mean compromising my relationships altogether, and cultivating those relationships took insurmountable amounts of time.

My relationships with folks in Holly Springs were clearly not one-sided. My students gained invaluable experiences with each Behind the Big House program, and I secured a safer space in which to do race work. To me, the university was not safe at all. My various attempts to participate in collaborative university diversity initiatives, usually as responses to violence incited by White males, were ongoing but with few to no gains. My department was flexible about my research projects, yet any attempts to make systemic changes that might constructively change the lives of people of color on campus were met with institutional wait-and-see approaches or a combination of behind-closed-door discussions and public forums that did not lead to any substantive change.

Among the faculty, I had several actors and allies and, to a lesser extent, accomplices. Actors expressed disgust with racist incidents on campus in private conversations but made few to no appearances at public protests. Allies not only attended those events but, at times, got other White folks who wouldn't normally attend to participate. At times, these allies were long-established actors who were inspired to engage other White people about their actions, even if this risked discomfort. There were not enough allies and certainly not enough accomplices, an essential position for those attempting to "enact social justice from positions of privilege."[19] Accomplices are more apt to put themselves and their positions in hierarchies on the line. They "purposefully disrupt White spaces, meaning, create discomfort in places where other White people and Whiteness would otherwise exist in comfort," whether it be in a meeting room or on social media.[20] What I saw were people full of good intentions, claiming "to support the principles of diversity, equity, and inclusion," but few "courageous enough to put their own jobs on their line."[21] Still, I can count White accomplices at my workplace on one hand and often worry about their emotional constraints. Most of them waver between their commitments to their core values and their abilities to remain in a space with a different value system.

The University and Me

Eventually, my relationship with the University of Mississippi felt like I was choosing to be in an abusive relationship with someone who wouldn't change no matter how hard I tried. For several years, I worked with other faculty in the Critical Race Studies Group, including several in my department, who attempted to make the university a safer space to work. We spent many hours meeting with each other, then planning to meet with administrators, then meeting with administrators, then thinking we had made some headway, and then not hearing from administrators until another racial incident occurred. Although university administrators had done nothing to prevent or mitigate the circumstances and attitudes that led to these incidents, they continued to make the hollow claim that they greatly regretted the incidents themselves.

In his 2012 fall address to the faculty, Chancellor Dan Jones mentioned the university's history of racial injustice and its contemporary responsibility to remedy that past with diversity and inclusion efforts. His comment followed a year of events commemorating the fiftieth anniversary of James Meredith's integration of the University of Mississippi.[22] Jones challenged faculty to consider what each might do individually, as well as part of the university collective, to deal with its difficult history.

In 2011, my sociology colleague Willa Johnson wrote a proposal for an

Association for Jewish Studies–Legacy Heritage Jewish Studies Project grant to explore the complex relationships between African Americans and Jews in the Deep South. She wrote the grant on behalf of the university's Critical Race Studies Group, which received it for a 2012–13 lecture series designed to bring together scholars, students, and community members to explore anti-Semitism, racism, and the collaborative as well as the fraught relationships between the two groups. As a testament to the race studies group's good faith in Dan Jones's speech, its members invited him to give a greeting at Rabbinic scholar W. David Nelson's "Say Again! Race, Religion and Realities of Reading the Bible," a talk and discussion about the Bible and its historical use as a tool to promote racist ideologies. Jones, also in good faith, accepted.

Almost exactly two years later, the university hosted Symbols of Exclusion: The Semiotics of Race in Public Spaces, an interdisciplinary symposium on race and historical memory also organized by Willa Johnson, who did the bulk of the planning work with some support from other members of the race studies group, including me. One of the goals of that symposium was to bring in race scholars, like sociologist Joe Feagin, and memory studies scholars, like professor of English and Judaic studies James E. Young, to help the university think about how its history and its efforts to remember its history fit into other national efforts to commemorate difficult pasts. Jones was so impressed with the lecture series and the subsequent symposium that he invited the group's members to engage him in deeper discussions about race, privilege, and inequality.

In 2012, several of the members met with Jones, who was clearly on a reflective journey to understand how race and racism intersected with his personal life and his role (at times a conflicting one) as a university leader seeking to address historical and contemporary racism on campus. I remember that conversation around the chancellor's coffee table as a refreshingly candid one. We gave him individual and group advice about how the university could move forward to address some of these issues, and we shared our personal experiences as counternarratives to some of his understandings of how racism manifests itself on campus. The meeting ended with the chancellor committed to sustaining these discussions with a subsequent meeting at his home.

That meeting did not happen. As a matter of fact, members of the Critical Race Studies Group later discovered that Jones chose to periodically meet with select members of the group, not as representatives of the group but as individual advisers on campus race relations. It became clear that university administrators, although seeming to have good intentions, made promises to do better in private and then went behind our backs to consult with faculty members with whom they felt most comfortable. It was a waste of a lot of my time.

Discomfort is a necessary feeling for people considered White who are seeking to do anti-racist work. Although Jones didn't explicitly say that he was trying to promote an anti-racist agenda, anti-racist is how I understood the work that we were trying to do. It also became clear to me that being anti-racist was not an essential part of the university's "transformation through service." It was, and it is, too threatening to the status quo.

Working with my Behind the Big House and Gracing the Table supportive network gave me the feeling that change was possible if I worked hard enough. This was a healthier space for me, but it clashed with department values, which indicated that junior scholars should wait until they were no longer junior scholars to call for systemic change. This assumed that the skills and approaches needed to call for change could be learned overnight, after the state's tenure-granting board approved my tenure application. This reality reflects a broader academic wait-and-see value. It made no sense to me, even as I witnessed how it seemed to make sense to others.

I had also not taken the more expected academic route of turning my dissertation into a book, instead publishing a combination of journal articles on my dissertation research and, eventually, on the Behind the Big House project. I felt that by alienating myself from my activist politics and grassroots communities, just until I was able to write the necessary number of articles, I could become even more lonely in my department, in Oxford, in Mississippi. What if I compromised my values and still didn't get tenure?

By the next academic year, senior colleagues still saw my work as important but not as research. What seemed most significant to my department is that whatever I was doing be affirmed by other academics through one medium: publications. Whether or not those outside the university would continue to benefit from my work was contingent on tenure and promotion. I wouldn't be allowed to continue to make an impact otherwise. I acquiesced.

I had a few manuscripts in the publication pipeline. Senior colleagues recommended that I consult with a senior sociology colleague, who helped me think through my work as a form of community development. It was helpful to publish with community development scholars in mind, as I perceived their scholarship to be more aligned with my activist anthropological training. More importantly, I wanted to show that, as expected, I was seeking help from senior colleagues, and thus I asked a few other senior anthropology and sociology colleagues to review article drafts. I supplemented that with reviews from those in my trusted University of Texas anthropology cohort, who best understood me and my work.

That summer, I typed myself into carpal tunnel syndrome, knowing that most of those publications didn't directly matter to the folks in Holly Springs or to anyone else on the ground seeking to better the lives of those affected by representations of the past in the present. The publications were a means to an end, and I'm still very uncomfortable with that.

What I didn't know at the time was that there was a relatively nascent field of tourism anthropology with a working group of scholars who convened at the American Anthropological Association annual conference.[23] My public archaeology training had not intersected with this scholarship. There were also academic activists in tourism studies whose work could help give me the language to articulate what I was doing.[24] They understood that activist tourism scholars might receive "considerable positive attention from a wide range of nonacademic sources, [but have] been systematically devalued by the academy," especially if their activist work does not have academic value to the university; more specifically, "while university rhetoric supports the concept of community engagement, the activity [might not be] valued in promotion and tenure decisions."[25] Such work is complicated and requires individual assessment of potential benefits and drawbacks as well as the impact of prevalent issues on practice. Academics who attempt to do such work should consider those issues before getting involved in comparable community projects. I don't think that a deeper assessment and understanding of these considerations would have eased me through my department's tenure process, but I might have felt less alone.

Sensitivity and Respect on Campus

In 2012, Chancellor Dan Jones created a Sensitivity and Respect Committee on the heels of several public displays of overt racism on campus. Some received national attention. For example, White students hurled racial epithets at Black students after President Obama's reelection on Tuesday, November 7.[26] I remember getting an early morning text from a Black colleague. She texted several of us in what we considered our sister circle, other Black female faculty we could trust with our feelings. She was afraid to go to campus that day. So was I. I remember feeling fortunate that I didn't have to go because I didn't teach that day. I didn't want to be on the receiving end of students' rage. I'd normalized their passive-aggressive behavior when I said the word "White" or mentioned Confederate ideology or any seemingly negative critique of the South.

That Wednesday morning, Dan Jones sent a campus-wide email assuring us that the campus was safe and quiet for all students. But what about faculty like me? It was an issue of safety for faculty considered of color and for those who dealt with race and racism in the classroom. The university had no structural way of protecting me, of protecting us. As of this writing, in 2020, it still doesn't.

The events on November 7 and 8 were being described as a riot, with a crowd of four hundred students.[27] I wasn't there. I didn't want to see it. I wanted to protect our most vulnerable students but was clouded by historical memories of university riots to stop James Meredith's integration in 1962, half a century ago. That October, the university had commemorated the fiftieth anniversary of its integration. In between texts of fear and phone calls of concern, I decided to keep my distance, as I had done many other times.

We expressed our concerns about safety to our department chair, who took them seriously, passing them along to those higher up in the hierarchy. One result was a visit from a now former college dean, who stopped by my office to see how I was doing. My outpouring of concerns, ranging from my safety to the safety of colleagues in interracial relationships, went on and on. I even mentioned the restaurant negotiating and a colleague's warning that there was one restaurant in particular that I should not visit. Shocked, the dean said that he ate there all the time and that we should go together. Somehow, that would make me feel safer. He never followed up on the invitation.

I was reassured when a colleague and friend, Michele Coffey, co-organized a We Are One unity walk in the hopes that it might be comforting to students and others who needed to feel massive love and support. I trusted Michele, as a White accomplice, and enthusiastically shared her plans with others with the caveat that this was not an administrative action but had administrative support. Michele and Susan Glisson, then director of the Winter Institute, located on campus at the time, did the work. At the least, Michele was worried about us, her Black female friends. She was hurting but knew that our experiences as Black women were much more unbearable. We were growing weary. The vigil, with around six hundred people in attendance, calmed me down for a moment.

Outside of the sister circle, I had an email exchange with faculty allies who discussed these events with action plans. This gave me some hope. We wrote the chancellor with offers of group support, while stressing the need for a university-supported organization to address the systemically racist environment. At the time, I didn't know that this would set a precedent for redundancy. We offered support and asked for change, to no avail.

That same month, my former sociology colleague, Zandria Robinson, published an article in the *Griot* in response to the November events through the context of her lived experiences as a Black woman on the faculty at the University of Mississippi. She wrote:

> I was neither shocked nor surprised by the events, as the University of
> Mississippi encourages this kind of behavior through its consistent inaction
> against a host of bad behaviors, from racial slurs scrawled in graffiti in dorm
> elevators to gross mishandling of cases of sexual harassment and rape. This
> institutional inaction is bolstered by the University's identity as a bastion
> of the traditional, Old South: a white South where Dixie plays, confederate
> flags wave, and black people are subservient.[28]

Zandria was hired by the university two years before I was. By her third year, she had decided to free herself from its reluctance to change. She had left for the University of Memphis earlier that year. I was still convinced that change was possible. Zandria wrote that if faculty of color "all push, the institution may move a centimeter." She also recognized that institutions like the University of Mississippi can and do move slowly, "especially in response to external threats."[29] University administrators seemed to respond to the external threat of media shame, narratives of students as bad actors, that were outside their institutional control.

University administrators eventually organized the Sensitivity and Respect Committee charged with developing solutions to address the cultural climate on campus. In 2013, Dan Jones hired two consultants, Ed Ayers, then president of the University of Richmond, and Christy Coleman, then president of the American Civil War Center at Historic Tredegar, to review "the university's environment on race and related issues."[30] Part of the review included Ayers's and Coleman's discussions with groups like the Sensitivity and Respect Committee and southern studies faculty members. Ted Ownby, then director of the Center for the Study of Southern Culture, invited me to come to one of the discussions and I agreed.

I then completely forgot about the meeting. I was physically exhausted from planning the southern studies interdisciplinary symposium and the 2014 Behind the Big House program and emotionally drained after some White students hung a noose on the university's statue of civil rights pioneer James Meredith that month.[31] I was disappointed that I had committed to something and didn't come through, especially because I had promised Ted. I knew that Ted was sympathetic enough to understand. What I recall feeling less guilty about was not participating in another university process that I didn't think would go anywhere. I felt like I was in the same place that I was in two years prior; I was simply better at creating boundaries with administrative processes. In my absence, other southern studies faculty recommended that the university rename streets reminiscent of the Confederacy and noted that they found "the name 'Ole Miss' problematic, preferring to use 'The University of Mississippi' instead," and that "some resented the fact that 'olemiss.edu' was used for the email system versus 'UMiss.edu.'" They elaborated that "they viewed the email address as a signal to the outside world that the university is a place that embraces notions of the old south and its historically exclusionary practices."[32] Since then, the university has changed the name of Confederate Drive to Chapel Lane, even after the Sons of Confederate Veterans filed suit to prevent it from renaming Civil War monuments and statues on campus.[33] The olemiss.edu address is still the official one.

Slavery and the University

In late 2013, a few of my colleagues, across disciplines, developed a Slavery and the University group to connect acts like the ones in November 2012 to the manifestation of White supremacist ideologies rooted in slavery. As an initial step, Craig Steven Wilder, author of *Ebony and Ivy: Race, Slavery, and the Troubled History of America's Universities*, was invited to discuss his book with a faculty reading group organized specifically for that purpose. Those conversations inspired faculty to propose several initiatives in addition to a working group to help prioritize and undertake some of those initiatives. I became one representative of this group of faculty, staff, and students whose participation numbers have ranged from thirty to fifty or so.

Early on, the group decided to form subgroups in three main areas—research, teaching, and community outreach—to identify best first steps. Our campus struggled with ubiquitous symbolic representations of those who fought for the Confederacy. Some alumni and students had a "possessive investment" in Confederate iconography.[34] We were concerned about how those images affected the health of our campus community as a whole and how these reinforced legacies of the Civil War, whether accurate or not, continued to present themselves through daily student life and, further, expanded to influence statewide inequality. The group's main concern was how to most effectively unmute the experiences of those who were enslaved and more broadly represent them on campus.

Some group members traveled to the University of Virginia for a national conference, Universities Confronting the Legacy of Slavery, and invited Nancy Bercaw, then curator for the Smithsonian Institution's new National Museum of African American History and Culture, to give a presentation to the group. In addition, group members completed a workshop led by representatives from the Digital Archaeological Archive of Comparative Slavery. The group had eleven projects in progress by the 2015–16 academic year. My participation in a National Council on Public History Campus History as Public History working group was one of them.

In 2016, I had suggested that the Slavery Research Group participate in this working group to learn more about academics at other institutions who were doing comparable work. Coleaders Jeff Jackson and Chuck Ross agreed. Our group had some funding from university administrators, which helped get me to Baltimore for the conference. Administrators like Dan Jones were, by that point, moved by the recommendations of those like Ayers and Coleman, who had clearly articulated the fact that some of the university's systemic problems were rooted in antebellum Confederate ideals.

I was also still a member of the Critical Race Studies Group. Several of us framed university responses to more public racist incidents in an article published in 2016.[35] I still struggle with the term "incidents," which seems to be void of the campus context that encourages such behavior, but I haven't come up with a more suitable one. Maybe "expected" or "probable occurrences"?

The collaborative process was helpful to me. It counted as an additional publication and gave us a voice in a process that seemed to invite the opinions of campus groups that seemed less political. The Slavery Research Group became one of those. It seemed like a more comfortable space for faculty who didn't align with a social science theoretical framework, as most of us in the Critical Race Studies Group did. That group's attempts to respond to ongoing acts of racism on campus were demanding and exhausting. We were meant to be a support system for each other. We were proactive thinkers fighting reactive battles. "Racial battle fatigue" eventually set in.[36] We became overwhelmed with helping university administrators think through how to prevent and respond to those probable occurrences.

The Slavery Research Group had participation from more faculty in history, English, and other units like the university library than the Critical Race Studies Group had. There was then a broader Slavery Research Group support system to do research on the university's slavery legacy and to eventually make that research available. To me, this meant understanding how to interpret the legacy of slavery in the present and how to work with Black Oxonians, those most directly affected by that legacy. I didn't want community authority to be forgotten. I didn't feel like my university colleagues had clearly understood that about my work in Holly Springs.

Other academics did. I met many of them at Joe McGill's first Slave Dwelling Project conference in 2014, which attracted a who's who of slavery historic preservationists, of whom academics were just a few. I attended several talks, the most memorable of which was Nicole Moore's "Interpreting Slave Life." Moore, a museum educator, was so thoughtful, candid, and articulate about her experiences as a docent at sites of slavery that I wanted a piece of anything she was part of. She mentioned that she would be part of an edited collection, *Interpreting Slavery at Museums and Historic Sites*, to be released later that year. I don't recall ever being so excited about a book's release. I not only assigned the book as a how-to guide in my Southern Heritage Tourism course but shared it with Slavery Research Group leaders.

The Slavery Research Group had clear goals that connected the past to the present, key research and practice points for me. What was missing was the local community engagement that I felt was necessary to understand the impacts of the campus's and city's systemic racism on Black Oxonians. To many of us on the faculty, Oxford was new. In reality, Black communities there had a long history of developing family, religious, and civic coalitions to get them through, but many of us on campus didn't have a comprehensive understanding of that. After all, they are the most direct descendant community. Up to that point, not many of us had bothered to get their input.

That changed when the Slavery Research Group decided to include the Rowan Oak site in its exploration of slavery and the university. William Faulkner's former home, Rowan Oak, is owned by the university and is interpreted through his time there. Unknown to many is the fact that it was once the site of the Sheegog Estate, built and sustained through slave labor.

In 2013, Chelius Carter and Joe McGill proposed Rowan Oak as a possible site for one of Joe's sleepovers, as part of his Slave Dwelling Project, but had no luck. I supported them but had little hope that the university would see this as an opportunity. The structure of the Slavery Research Group, as a university entity, changed that dynamic, making possible the research necessary to tell the site's antebellum history. The group also facilitated Joe's sleepover in 2017, four years after his initial request.

Several of my anthropology colleagues agreed to support research efforts through archaeology. Jillian Galle, project director for the Digital Archaeological Archive of Comparative Slavery, was brought in to help the group think through an archaeology excavation on site. Anthropology colleagues Tony Boudreaux and Maureen Meyers executed that through a field school course, which taught students basic archaeological excavation techniques, in addition to archival research. Galle recommended that we bring in noted architectural historians Ed Chappell and Carl Lounsbury to examine the structures on site, especially a small brick structure behind Faulkner's main house. They not only did that but enthusiastically traveled to Holly Springs and other sites of urban slavery in the state so that we could have a comparative data set of slave dwellings. What we didn't have were the descendant community connections necessary to make this work worthwhile to me. The knowledge of African American Burton Place descendants, like Deb Davis, had made our work in Holly Springs easier and more complete. We had been lucky.

I'd personally experienced the pains of wanting to connect to ancestral sites of slavery in Louisiana and being blocked by contemporary site owners, some descendants of those who enslaved my ancestors. Not knowing, not connecting, left me feeling empty. I also knew that, contrary to popular belief, I am not all Black people and that emotions about connections to slavery run the gamut. What was most important to me is that Black Oxonians who want to connect always feel welcome and that the Slavery Research Group's work is always accessible. This was not *my* work to do but the group's.

The Slavery Research Group would need to take a "critical service-learning" pedagogical approach of "academic service-learning experiences with a social justice orientation." That would include contemplating "institutional contributions to social problems" in Oxford and taking "measures that may lead to social change. This praxis brings to light the political nature of a pedagogy aimed to address and contribute to dismantling structural inequality." In the research group's case, the university institution participated in the institution of slavery, one social problem, and then subsequently left the local African American descendant community out of public efforts to hold the university accountable for its participation in the institution of slavery. As Tania Mitchell makes clear, "critical service-learning must focus on creating true community-university partnerships where community issues and concerns are as important (in planning, implementation, and evaluation) as student learning and development."[37]

I add that community issues and concerns should also be as important as research. The Slavery Research Group still has some way to go, but it's made significant strides with the establishment of the Lafayette Oxford Community Archive and Legacy group, L.O.C.A.L. I think that what became L.O.C.A.L. began meeting in the summer of 2018. Jeff Jackson and Chuck Ross, who facilitated most of the research group's initiatives, worked in collaboration with Black Oxford community leaders to think through collaborative projects and events centering African American history in Oxford and Lafayette County. That collaboration is ongoing. As of July 2019, I've attended meetings and participated in L.O.C.A.L. events. I've also made attempts to integrate some of those events into those in Holly Springs. Slavery Research Group colleagues like Jay Watson, who runs the summer Faulkner and Yoknapatawpha Conference, have helped with that. Watson included a slavery tour of Holly Springs as an optional tour for 2018 conference participants that David Person and I co-organized. Rhondalyn Peairs helped facilitate our busload of guests on the tour day. L.O.C.A.L. members were invited to participate, and several took us up on the offer. Some said that the tour of slave-dwelling sites was life changing for them. My newfound relationships with them have been life changing for me.

What I've benefited from most is the passion of Black Oxonians and others in Lafayette County whose love for history and their heritage surpasses mine. I'd observed Rhondalyn's passion for years and then witnessed other native Oxonians like Annie McEwen, who attends almost every liberal arts university event with a video camera in tow, and her sister Gloria McEwen Burgess, who chronicled their father's lifelong commitment to education and subsequent relationship with William Faulkner in her children's book *Pass It On!* Their father, Earnest McEwen, Jr., spent the early 1950s working as a custodian at the University of Mississippi and later attended Alcorn University with Faulkner's tuition assistance. I also met Sheila Howard-Baker, who returned to Oxford after years outside the state and who has participated in several events, some more than once. Each time she hears something new in the story. Her presence reminds me that people like me doing the work *with* her is important. It's important for mutual sustainability.

The university still has a lot of work to do, but my colleagues in the Slavery Research Group have helped it make a good start toward bridging a town-gown divide. There are still disproportionately too many local Black folks working in university restaurants and making sure that the campus is clean. These are respectable jobs but never pay enough. I've been privileged not to have to do this but know that my dad needed an additional full-time job at a loading dock to help make ends meet with his job as a custodian at what was then the University of Southwestern Louisiana. Disproportionately, Black folks did that work then and, in too many places, they still do, for wages that are still very low. These are the systemic issues around race, racism, wealth, and class rooted in slavery. Doing the research is not enough. People need to be made more whole in the present.

The Payoff

Just three years after Behind the Big House began, it received a Mississippi Humanities Council Preserver of Mississippi Culture Award, recognizing "outstanding efforts to interpret and promote the cultural assets and traditions of" the state, as well as a Mississippi Historical Society Award of Merit.[38] The program was then selected by the National Humanities Alliance Foundation as a model for collaborative publicly engaged work. Chelius and Jenifer always made sure that I felt part of these award ceremonies. I accepted the Mississippi Historical Society's award along with Chelius at the annual meeting in Corinth.

Our College of Liberal Arts publicized this award with the headline "Professor Jodi Skipper Receives Award of Merit." I literally received the award, but it was not mine. It belonged to Preserve Marshall County. The article clarified that I received the Award of Merit *to* Preserve Marshall County and Holly Springs, but the heading is what stood out to me and, I assume, to others. As a result, I tried to make sure that my role as a scholar-in-collaboration with the program was clarified in all subsequent publications. At the least, I was relieved that the program was finally getting state and national attention.

By the time I went up for tenure, my community work had also gained state and national attention. In February 2017, I received the Mississippi Humanities Council's Humanities Scholar Award, which "honors a scholar in a traditional humanities field who has participated in MHC programs, serving as an interpreter of his or her discipline to public audiences."[39] Later that year, I was awarded a Whiting Foundation Public Engagement Fellowship.

The Whiting Foundation's application process began as an internal one, through which university departments nominate candidates and then administrators choose a candidate to apply. I was that candidate. The paradox is that the work that ultimately brought national attention to the university and to me is not the work that got me tenure. The publications that I struggled to write did. I'm still not sure how to make sense of that.

When I attended the 2016 National Council on Public History conference in Baltimore, I took advantage of a workshop, "Putting Theory into Practice: Making Your Case for Promotion and Tenure," facilitated by public scholars Melissa Bingmann, Larry Cebula, Michelle Hamilton, Modupe Labode, Allison Marsh, and Gregory Smoak. For the first time, I heard other academics who seemed to understand tenure and promotion processes as I did. Their workshop was based on a 2010 report, "Tenure, Promotion, and the Publicly Engaged Academic Historian," a report with which I was not familiar.[40] I was attracted not only to the idea of critically thinking through my place as an academic, one I wrestled with all the time, but to the workshop's goal to "discuss strategies to help educate colleagues and administrators to understand and evaluate the scholarly production of public historians."[41] I wanted these folks to save me, unaware that their disciplinary restrictions could only take me so far. I didn't have the advocacy necessary to speak to these issues in my field and certainly not in my department. I felt reassured, to some extent, but still alone. That began to change when the Whiting Foundation fellowship affirmed my work as unique yet exceptional scholarship. I met others, even anthropologists, in comparable positions.

The Whiting fellows' process consisted of two convenings, one before and one after the proposed fellowship project. The convenings created not only a space for camaraderie but access to some of the top public humanists in the country who were evaluating my work. I even had a new term for myself: a public humanities scholar. Those in my cohort and in others presented a range of problems, but many shared the difficulty of negotiating tenure and promotion while balancing public humanities projects. It was the one issue that seemed the most difficult to rectify. We couldn't do it in two Whiting convenings.

In 2018, I was invited to present at a National Humanities Alliance annual meeting discussion titled "Changing Narratives about Humanities in Higher Ed." The meeting coincided with Humanities Advocacy Day in Washington, D.C. I was on a panel with four other scholars who gave very brief introductions to their projects, followed by a half-hour question-and-answer period. One of those scholars was David Trowbridge, a historian at Marshall University who developed Clio, a public historic and cultural sites website and mobile app. Trowbridge was also part of my Whiting cohort. It was the first time that I noticed conference overlap with scholars outside my discipline but not the last. I met Rhondda Thomas, a literature professor well known for her research on Black Clemson, at the National Council on Public History meeting in 2016; I then saw her again as part of the 2018–19 Whiting cohort.[42] It was clear that Whiting was building a public humanities cohort across disciplines.

My prep for the National Humanities Alliance talk began with a phone call with staff member Daniel Fisher. He reminded me of Imagining America's 2008 Tenure Team Initiative on Public Scholarship, which was also mentioned at a Whiting convening. The subsequent report, *Scholarship in Public: Knowledge Creation and Tenure Policy in the Engaged University*, offers advice on how to best communicate the significance of public work to scholarly audiences (especially tenure and promotion committees) alongside those of public ones.[43]

Aware that some archaeologists in comparable positions might find such a report useful, I decided to present these issues as part of a 2018 American Anthropological Association session titled "Changing Archaeology: Building a More Diverse and Inclusive Discipline." I focused on the things I wish I had known during my time as a junior scholar.

1. Articulating my training and negotiating the value of my work during the hiring process might have led to more reasonable expectations from all parties involved.

2. My intellectual goals and publicly engaged scholarship would inevitably clash with institutional tenure policies.

3. My university's professed public mission did not guarantee a strong commitment to the civic potential of its faculty.

4. Sustained community engagement is more often considered an academic risk, not a benefit.

And what I hope senior faculty and administrators facilitating the careers of junior public humanities scholars consider.

1. Creative scholars committed to the public good and with the "social idealism that leads them to want to engage in this kind of work" are frequently faculty of color and women.[44]

2. If we genuinely want to encourage and retain them, then we must reward their work at tenure time.

3. Discouraging junior faculty members from collaborative work that is interdisciplinary and publicly engaged, while privileging publications as output, does not make them better senior faculty members. It only makes them feel detached and lonely.

This was one of the most personal and meaningful things that I've done as a public humanities scholar.

Institutionalizing Diversity and Community Engagement

One direct result of recommendations made by Dan Jones's Sensitivity and Respect Committee was the hiring of a vice chancellor for diversity and community engagement in 2017. Her staff came to include an assistant vice chancellor for community engagement. Since the creation of a Division of Diversity and Community Engagement, the university has shown some institutional commitment to community engagement. One university goal was to obtain the nationally recognized Carnegie Foundation's Classification for Community Engagement for the 2020 cycle. I noticed Diversity Division efforts to create programs and collect data to support that application process. One program was a campus award celebration through which Behind the Big House received a University Excellence in Community Engagement Award. There were monetary prizes for projects in the areas of research, learning, service, and engaged scholarship and a $5,000 award for the most outstanding project. I applied for the award based on Carolyn Freiwald's and my work with Behind the Big House. We received a $5,000 award to further the community engagement work, a university reward that I could not have fathomed just a few years earlier.

Through the Carnegie application process, institutions must show that community engagement is a priority, formally recognize community engagement through campus-wide awards and celebrations, and "have mechanisms for systematic assessment of community perceptions of the institution's engagement with community."[45] The pessimistic side of me felt like this was just a university attempt to check off points on an application while community members, other colleagues, and I did the work. It was hard for me to integrate myself into the goals of a university that I didn't feel had done the work others and I had done. On the other hand, am I not the university?

The students in my Southern Heritage Tourism and African diaspora courses supported Behind the Big House through service-learning, and this effort was supported by both departments. So did students in archaeology classes that Carolyn and I taught. The Center for the Study of Southern Culture provided student transportation to Holly Springs when needed. A History Department colleague, Shennette Garrett-Scott, and students in her Experiences of Black Mississippians class completed research for a Behind the Big House teachers' guide. Behind the Big House was a university-supported program that still largely depended on the voluntary service labor of committed faculty. That labor made the work possible, and there was little to no university recognition for that. We made it happen, but that labor, in addition to other university responsibilities, is not sustainable.

Even with my skepticism, I applied for and accepted the award because I wanted to be able to honor my supportive network, Chelius and Jenifer, Gracing the Table, and Carolyn Freiwald, who are often left out of Behind the Big House success narratives. The award gave money to the project and tangible trophies to everyone.

We all make choices as academics. Choices about what we will commit our time to. I made lots of them, with few regrets about spending much of my time as a scholar-in-collaboration. What I do regret is not knowing that, since 2006, there was a formal classification for "institutions to have their community engagement acknowledged" and that other academics and institutions had been thinking critically about how to incorporate this work into faculty reward systems.[46] I hope that the latter doesn't get left out of University of Mississippi diversity initiatives, especially when so much about diversity work depends on understanding the impacts of the past on the present. I also continue to reject the assumption that I should have to wait until I prove that I'm a scholar to be an activist scholar. What I have come to accept is that my "work is an offering" but that I'm not "supposed to be sacrificed in the process."[47]

I realize that my academic experiences are not the experiences of all or most, but they are likely the experiences of many. Some of them have chosen to leave academia for some of the reasons that I have discussed. I've chosen to stay. It's not a final decision, and I'm not always sure why.

I like the process of learning through teaching and respect the credibility that it gives to my community work. I've watched too many friends, more intellectual than I am, not get the respect that they deserve because they are not in academia. They struggle to make connections and struggle to garner economic and human resources support, even with the best intentions and ideas. The only thing that I'm sure of is that I don't want to give anyone else the power to tell my story, if I do leave, and that I will likely be perceived as more of an authority on the matter if I tell that story while I'm in it. I hope that my candor empowers others to make the best decisions possible about what academia can and can't do for them and the communities they hope to serve.

Epilogue

What to Throw Away and What to Keep

In June 2020, I came across a Facebook meme of an antebellum house on fire. One of my cousins posted it. It was captioned "burn down the house." He didn't offer an explanation, but the few follow-up comments indicated that the meme was a direct call to burn historic sites of slavery, aligned with protests in response to the death of George Floyd, killed by Minneapolis police just a month earlier. Until that moment, I felt like I had aligned myself with the protesters, whether framed as violent or not, because I understood their frustration and anger.

I was appalled by my cousin's seeming inability to distinguish between what's okay to damage and what's not. The angry Black woman in me saw the spaces damaged during the protests as unfortunate consequences in a nation that refused to value Black lives, but I felt a commitment to protecting sites of slavery. I didn't want those burned and, until that point, I had not discriminated between places that should be protected and those that should not. I felt like a hypocrite. At the same time, I wondered how my cousin could not understand what was so obviously clear and important to me.

For over twenty years, I have worked to preserve antebellum sites, investing in their abilities to help us tell stories that historic documents often would or could not. I personally knew people who owned antebellum properties and had acted as advocates for telling the stories of enslaved people, often forgotten in historic site narratives.

When I saw my cousin's Facebook post, I wanted to tell him about my work, hoping that it would matter. I wanted my spiel to encourage him to dissuade others from burning down plantation houses and the other buildings on the properties that sustained them. Still, I knew that I might not be as convincing about saving the Holly Springs Garden Club's properties as I was about saving Chelius and Jenifer's house. I also realized that he and others would likely not see any of these homes as different from the many

Confederate monuments and other symbols caught up in our broader narratives about what to throw away and what to keep. At some level, they all represent White supremacist ideologies rooted in Black oppression—some built in the eighteenth and nineteenth centuries as landscapes of labor by an enslaved workforce used to sustain plantation economies, others built in the late nineteenth and early twentieth centuries to perpetuate a Lost Cause ideal of dedicated slaves, benevolent masters, and glorified Confederate war heroes. The former was the system, the latter a reminder to Black Americans that the system still exists. I understood that protesters would not necessarily be concerned about deciding what properties to damage. They're not easy spaces to differentiate. It takes more work to think through the different values of these spaces but, I argue, it's worth the effort.

I may be one of few Black Americans who hoped for some public discussion about which of those monuments should be canceled. I'd given up on that fight, often responding to those who asked how I as a historic preservationist could support destroying Confederate symbols by saying that "they're not actual symbols of the Confederacy but White affirmations of Jim Crow era power," or that "Black folks wouldn't be so bothered by them if what they represented wasn't still all too real." I'd personally let those monuments go, realizing that with no national conversation cancel culture might win the Confederate symbol debate. For me, letting go of historic sites of slavery is much more difficult. It's not an all or nothing game.

Outside of more recent viral articles about White visitors' disappointment when hearing too much about slavery on plantation tours at sites like the Whitney Plantation in Louisiana and the McLeod Plantation in South Carolina, most online readers seem to be most concerned about people still choosing to wed at plantation sites.[1] There's little discussion about historic preservation efforts, leaving them vulnerable to cancel culture during recent protests in the Movement for Black Lives or simply destruction by neglect.

The reality is that most historic sites of slavery don't interpret the experiences of enslaved people and are not held accountable for not doing so. The reality is also that those that do represent slavery depend on events like weddings to supplement the funds required for those historic narratives. The public support necessary to keep those sites operating just isn't there.

Yes, the spaces in which I work are sites of systemic oppression and at times monuments to the Confederacy. Yet they are also spaces where Black life was in full existence, and that should matter, too. My point *is* to understand them as Black life. There is a way to value that history.

Brent Leggs, the executive director of the African American Cultural Heritage Action Fund, wrote that "our collective reverence and respect for Black people should be measured by the cultural assets that we preserve now and into the future." He also felt that it "was critically important to acknowledge that the nation may be rich in diverse history, but it has often been poor in representation of that history and in funding its protection, conservation, and recognition."[2] My experience has been that people are generally quick to call for the removal of Confederate monuments and other symbols like them and slow to respond to the critical needs of historic preservation efforts that support Black heritage sites.

Even our national historic preservation institutions are constrained by funds and by tendencies to support sites of significance, often meaning those connected to recognizable persons, places, or events. That doesn't do much for the people with whom I work who interpret sites of slavery connected to ordinary places with ordinary people, many of whose names we don't yet know. I've thought a lot about what it might take to bridge that gap. Here are two things to consider: we can think through what sites of slavery can teach us about the present to deepen our understanding of systemic racism, and we can complicate generalized responses to dealing with public symbols.

One of the most blatant characteristics of the Holly Springs slave-dwelling sites is their proximity to the main houses, a literal representation of constant surveillance by slave-owning families. These sites have the unique ability to show how embedded the policing of Black bodies is in our national history, made even more relevant with the nationwide protests of 2020 that took place in response not only to police violence against Black bodies but to the policing of Black bodies by ordinary White people in general. When Amy Cooper called the police on a Black bird-watcher, Christian Cooper, in New York City's Central Park after he politely asked her to follow the law and leash her dog, this incident was highly publicized, along with a slew of other recorded confrontations between Black people and the White people who were policing them for doing ordinary things.

One of the biggest historic preservation challenges is communicating preservation's value to different stakeholders and convincing those who may not consider themselves stakeholders that they, indeed, are. Why should people care about a historic site? Making such connections can deepen our understanding of systemic racism and, by default, encourage local communities to be more invested in this material culture and the possibilities of the stories they can tell. Simply arguing that antebellum structures symbolize racism just doesn't work, and neither will arguments about preserving historic sites of slavery just because it's the right thing to do. Regardless of what side of the debate you are on, we are left without productive conversations about which symbols of our slavery past we choose to throw away and which we choose to keep. Without such conversations, we risk the destruction of Black heritage sites as a form of neo-Confederate resistance.

In July 2019, an image surfaced of several University of Mississippi students holding firearms and posing next to a marker commemorating the location where Emmett Till's body was believed to have washed up three days after being thrown into the Tallahatchie River in 1955. The marker was riddled with bullets. As a result of the destruction of that marker and several others, those putting in the hard work to make sure that what happened to Till is not forgotten resorted to a bulletproof marker. In addition, the Emmett Till Interpretive Center has installed multiple cameras and sensors at this memorial site as a form of surveillance. Since that time, several groups of neo-Confederates have been recorded meeting at the site. This type of vandalism continues nationwide. In 2020, an African American museum in Phoenix was vandalized with swastikas; nearly fifteen headstones at Evergreen Cemetery in East Austin, Texas, were defaced; and a historic African American library in Polk County, North Carolina, was damaged. Unfortunately, the list goes on.

In addition to White neo-Confederate backlash, we also risk the publics' inabilities to discriminate between sites designed to complicate history and those doing the work of silencing it. Without protocols for holding the American public responsible for thinking through what represents us publicly, we risk a vicious cycle of destruction with no means of recovering sites that mattered to us, as well as an ongoing cycle of replacing and reproducing historic sites at costs not likely to be sustainable for most historic preservation entities. I suggest that we think through what to throw away and what to keep by asking these questions.

1. Why does the site exist? How did it come to be? Who is responsible for it?

2. What kind of work does it do? Does it do harm to members of the public, and can that harm be mitigated?

3. What kind of work do we want it to do, and can it do that work, with support? If not, then can something else do that work in its stead?

4. What might cause us to have to rethink this site in the future?

These questions are meant not to provide quick answers but to facilitate discussions, rare in this contemporary moment but crucial if we hope to have a historic preservation future.

Appendix A
Historic Site Evaluation

I used this Historic Site Evaluation in my class The Past in the Present: The Politics of Southern Heritage Tourism prior to working with Behind the Big House. I used a Historic Site Evaluation project that Martha Norkunas assigned in her Cultural Representations of the Past course as a model. One of her class goals was to interpret the Civilian Conservation Corps' role in developing Bastrop State Park in Bastrop, Texas. Before working with Behind the Big House, I did not have one specific site focus for the class as Norkunas did, so I asked students to visit a local site of their choice and evaluate it based on the following guidelines.

Site Visit

The goals of historic sites are to generally enhance learning in American history by connecting significant events, people, ideas, stories, and traditions with specific places. Within this context, this historic site evaluation project and paper require you to summarize and evaluate the contents of one historic site that played a significant role in Southern history. The site may be one that you have visited, but you should revisit this site to do this analysis. Be prepared to describe the assets of the site(s) (e.g., buildings, natural features, landscape, collections of objects, images, documents) and how they convey the site's history. If photos are allowed at the site location, then please take them. I also suggest that you take at least one docent-led tour of the site, if offered. Speaking with site managers and docents could be a bonus.

Your written report should identify the site you interpreted and explain what makes it significant. What happened there and why is it important? What central themes or issues in Southern history did the site address? You should place the information presented at the historic site within the context of more recent scholarly information on events or persons relevant to the site and determine how myths and stereotypes about the South are expressed in your research. Your research will be presented in a critique that addresses why you chose that site; a summary of the persons, places, or events related to the site; a description of the scholarly references you explored and how they compare/contrast to the information presented at the site; and a description of the overall effectiveness of the site as a learning tool, including what you would change about the historic site.

Things to Consider about the Historic Site as a Learning Tool

1. How well did the site address central events, themes, and issues in Southern history?

2. Is the site accessible to the general public?

3. Did you feel that your guide or docent communicated the subject matter in ways that were appropriate to your needs or the needs of this project? Please indicate any ways in which they could improve.

4. Did you feel that the exhibits, demonstrations, and/or other presentations were accessible, as well as informative? Please suggest any ways that the site interpreters could enrich the experience.

5. Did you feel that site activities were ones that made good use of the unique facilities and resources that the site has to offer? What could have been done differently?

6. Would you say that your visit to the site offered a significant experience that could not be duplicated in the classroom? Did it help to expand and/or supplement the knowledge in your scholarly resources?

7. Is the signage sufficient?

8. Were there interactive components?

9. Were brochures or other published materials available for the general public?

10. Did the staff seem knowledgeable and well trained?

11. Note significant awards or designations (e.g., National Historic Landmark, National Heritage Area, state-designated historic landmark or heritage area).

12. Think about whether the site broadens public understanding of Southern history and culture. Describe, to the extent possible, the expected audiences for each site component, including any targeted or hard-to-reach groups.

Other Things to Consider

If a historical structure/site or monument, when was the structure originally built? Has this structure been preserved or reconstructed? If so, then how? Who visits the site and why do they visit? What kind of audience is this site attempting to attract? How can you tell? Is the structure associated with any historical figures or any historical events? What other purposes has the structure served? Does it host any special events? If a monument, when was it dedicated, by whom, and for whom?

If a cemetery, how old is the cemetery? Are any notable figures buried there? If so, then who? Is this cemetery segregated by religious, cultural, or racial groups? How do you know this? What specific information can be determined from the cemetery markers? Does the cemetery host any special events? If so, are these events related to particular holidays or celebrations? Is the cemetery still active?

If a museum, who or what is the major focus of the museum? Observe the displays. For at least one display, describe what is being displayed and what is being portrayed. Be sure to note the specific material items and the text accompanying them. Are any artifacts included in the exhibition? Are the text and placement of artifacts and other items clearly communicating the intended messages? Determine the intended audience for the exhibit and another audience for whom this exhibit might say much less. Were there any other visitors there when you arrived? If so, then what were the visitor demographics?

Some Suggested Places to Visit

1. Rowan Oak

2. Burn's Belfry Church & Freedmen Town

3. J. E. Neilson Co.

4. Square Books

5. The Lyric

6. Barnard Observatory

7. First Presbyterian Church

8. Lafayette County Courthouse

9. Lamar House

10. St. Peter's Cemetery

11. St. Peter's Episcopal Church

12. Ventress Hall

13. The University of Mississippi Museum

14. Oxford Cemetery

15. Buford Cemetery

16. Church Grove Cemetery

17. College Hill Cemetery

18. Confederate Cemetery on the Campus of the University of Mississippi (including the memorial to Confederate soldiers)

19. North Oxford Cemetery

20. Saint John's Cemetery

21. South Oxford Cemetery

22. Toby Tubby Cemetery

23. Memorial Cemetery of Paris, MS

24. Magnolia Tree Memorial

25. Oxford University United Methodist Church

16. The Courthouse Square (including the Confederate memorial)

Appendix B
Small-Group Discussion Questions

This is a list of group discussion questions about slavery and shared histories from Gracing the Table's "Claiming Histories: Slavery and Remembrance in North Mississippi" symposium. The discussions began with David Person reviewing standard protocol and then emphasizing the need to respect anonymity after the discussions. We then organized participants into small groups of four to six people, gave them a list of discussion questions, and assigned a Gracing the Table member as a facilitator to each group to guide the sessions. The facilitator encouraged the groups to choose a transcriber and reporter to share what each small group learned with the larger group.

• What are your initial thoughts about the people in the photograph's relationship to each other? What are some other possibilities? Do their positions in the photograph indicate anything about their status? How might each of the persons in the image want to be remembered, and why? Do we share a responsibility in this remembrance? Why or why not?

• According to LeVar Burton, star of the original *Roots* series, "Slavery is the original sin that America has never atoned for and has never recovered from. And unless and until we are really able to roll up our sleeves and talk about those things that are difficult to talk about, we will forever be bound by the ghosts of our past." How do you feel about Burton's statement? Is it more comfortable to talk about slavery today than it was 10–15 years ago? Can you offer specific examples? If it is more comfortable, then for whom? The Census Bureau predicts that, by 2060, the nation's foreign-born population will reach nearly 19 percent of the total population, up from 13 percent in 2014. What role might these changing demographics play in telling the story of slavery? What reasons do more recent immigrants to this country, and their descendants, have to get involved in telling this story?

• The Smithsonian National Museum of African American History and Culture opened last month. The city of Jackson is planning to open the Mississippi Civil Rights Museum in December of 2017. That museum is being paired with the Museum of Mississippi History. Some state leaders expect that the museums will facilitate economic and community development throughout the state. Do the state museums' successes hinge on presenting honest, forthright, and transparent views of history? What might be some of the social benefits to candidly presenting slavery? What can the museums do to help heal contemporary racial divides?

• What groups in your local community seem to be remembered? What groups seem to be forgotten? Where are the stories of those who came before us told (historic sites, etc.)? What are some of the other ways that we remember those who came before us? How can we, in this region of the country, honor everyone's contributions to our shared history? What can you personally do to honor the history of everyone in your community?

Notes

Introduction

1. See Joyce Ehrlinger, E. Ashby Plant, Richard P. Eibach, Corey J. Columb, Joanna L. Goplen, Jonathan W. Kunstman, and David A. Butz, "How Exposure to the Confederate Flag Affects Willingness to Vote for Barack Obama."

2. The flag was removed in November 2011. See Sean Staggs, "Confederate Flag Removed from Caddo Courthouse Overnight."

3. Catherine D. Kimball, "State v. Dorsey."

4. Ibid. The oral argument before the Louisiana Supreme Court on May 9, 2000, can be heard on the Internet Archive at "State of Louisiana versus Felton Dejuan Dorsey Confederate Flag Capital Case" at https://archive.org/details/StateOfLoui sianaVersusFeltonDejuanDorseyConfederateFlagCapitalCase. In 2012, the Louisiana Association of Criminal Defense Lawyers submitted a motion for leave to file an amicus curiae brief, arguing racial discrimination in jury selection, in support of Dorsey's petition for a writ of certiorari to seek judicial review of the lower court decision. Dorsey was represented by famed Equal Justice Initiative attorney Bryan A. Stevenson. The U.S. Supreme Court denied the writ of certiorari. See Supreme Court of the United States, "Docket No. 11-8470."

5. American Civil Liberties Union, "ACLU Amicus Brief in Support of New Trial for Felton D. Dorsey."

6. George Lipsitz, "Breaking the Chains and Steering the Ship," 91.

7. Carolyn Ellis, Tony E. Adams, and Arthur P. Bochner, "Autoethnography: An Overview," 273.

8. Ibid., 279.

9. Brent Leggs, "Expanding the American Story, Clip 3."

10. Kathryn Radishofski, "Last (Un)fair Deal Goin' Down: Blues Tourism and Racial Politics in Clarksdale, Mississippi," 215–216.

11. Heewon Chang, *Autoethnography as Method*, 76–77.

12. Ellis, Adams, and Bochner, "Autoethnography," 276. See also Elissa Foster, *Communicating at the End of Life*; Amir Marvasti, "Being Middle Eastern American: Identity Negotiation in the Context of the War on Terror"; and Lisa M.

Tillmann-Healy, *Between Gay and Straight: Understanding Friendship across Sexual Orientation.*

13. Carolyn Ellis, Christine E. Kiesinger, and Lisa M. Tillmann-Healy, "Interactive Interviewing: Talking about Emotional Experience," 121.

14. Ibid., 121–122.

15. Ellis, Adams, and Bochner, "Autoethnography," 281–282. See also Lisa M. Tillmann, "Body and Bulimia Revisited: Reflections on 'A Secret Life'"; Tillmann-Healy, *Between Gay and Straight*; and Mechthild Kiegelmann, "Ethik."

16. Tami Spry, "Performing Autoethnography: An Embodied Methodological Praxis," 723. See also Carolyn Ellis and Arthur P. Bochner, eds., *Composing Ethnography: Alternative Forms of Qualitative Writing.*

17. Spry, "Performing Autoethnography," 713.

18. Ellis, Adams, and Bochner, "Autoethnography," 276. See also Carol R. Ronai, "Multiple Reflections of Child Sex Abuse" and "My Mother Is Mentally Retarded."

Chapter 1   Thank You, Cousin Geneva!

1. Alexandra Giancarlo, "'Don't Call Me a Cajun!' Race and Representation in Louisiana's Acadiana Region."

2. Festival International de Louisiane, "What Is Festival International de Louisiane?"

3. The University of Southwestern Louisiana is now the University of Louisiana at Lafayette.

4. The Nation of Gods and Earths (or the Five Percenters), a Black nationalist religious organization based in New York City, made an impact on the hip-hop genre between the mid-1980s and the early 1990s. See Michael Muhammad Knight, *The Five Percenters: Islam, Hip Hop and the Gods of New York*, and Jarrett L. Carter, "'A Different World' Minimizes a Different Age for HBCUs."

5. So much of what I learned at Grambling, outside the classroom, was rooted in Africanist understandings of ancient Egyptian symbols like the Eye of Horus, "sometimes called the all-seeing eye as a reference to the third eye." See Charlotte Zobeir Ali, "The Eye of Horus and Our Brain: Ancient Egyptians Gave Us the Key to Reach Enlightenment." Grambling students who studied the philosophies of ancient African civilizations understood the third eye as accessing the part of the brain that seeks spiritual enlightenment; for students like me, this meant educating myself beyond socialized Western, Eurocentric worldviews.

6. See Ta-Nehisi Coates, *Between the World and Me.*

7. See, for example, Gary B. Mills, *The Forgotten People: Cane River's Creoles of*

Color. Robert Maguire's doctoral research culminated in "Hustling to Survive: Social and Economic Change in a South Louisiana Black Creole Community."

8. Carolyn Ellis, Tony E. Adams, and Arthur P. Bochner, "Autoethnography: An Overview," 274.

9. Tami Spry, "Performing Autoethnography: An Embodied Methodological Praxis," 723.

10. Mary Turner Project, "Remembering Mary Turner." See also Julie Armstrong Buckner, *Mary Turner and the Memory of Lynching*.

11. See Owen J. Dwyer and Derek H. Alderman, *Civil Rights Memorials and the Geography of Memory*. See also Stephen A. King, *I'm Feeling the Blues Right Now: Blues Tourism and the Mississippi Delta*. King and Roger Davis Gatchet make a similar argument about the Mississippi Freedom Trail markers: the state's "selective efforts to present the people, events, and prominent locations that are part of its civil rights history—what is referred to as the Mississippi Movement—via official trail markers . . . present the struggle for civil rights as something that is confined to the past. In doing so official memory workers in Mississippi limit the MFT's ability to speak to contemporary racial struggles in the present"; see "Marking the Past: Civil Rights Tourism and the Mississippi Freedom Trail," 104.

Chapter 2   Heritage Tourism in Mississippi

1. "Unite Mississippi," https://unitemississippi.com, website no longer accessible. See Ashton Pittman, "Gov. Bryant Declares April 'Unity Month,' Not 'Confederate Heritage Month.'" See also Michelle Liu, "Dubbed a '21st Century Billy Graham Crusade on Steroids,' Revival Aims to Unite Mississippians."

2. Pittman, "Gov. Bryant Declares April 'Unity Month'. . . ."

3. Emanuella Grinberg, "These States Are Observing Confederate Memorial Day This Month."

4. J. Sather-Wagstaff, "Heritage and Memory," 191–192.

5. Michel Rolph Trouillot, *Silencing the Past: Power and the Production of History*, 195.

6. Christine N. Buzinde and Carla Almeida Santos, "Representations of Slavery," 471.

7. Giacomo Bologna, "Mississippi Flag Is Not a Banner That Unifies Us, So Change It, AG Hopeful Says."

8. Adam Ganucheau, Bobby Harrison, and Geoff Pender, "After Waffling for Years, Gov. Tate Reeves Signs Bill to Change State Flag."

9. Tate Reeves, "FY22 Executive Budget Recommendation."

10. W. Ralph Eubanks, "'Manufactured Ideas of History': Patriotic Education Fund in the Playbook of Totalitarian Leaders."

11. Stephen A. King, *I'm Feeling the Blues Right Now: Blues Tourism and the Mississippi Delta*, 172.

12. See Georgette Leah Burns, "Anthropology and Tourism: Past Contributions and Future Theoretical Challenges." Burns and others cite several reasons for this relatively late interest: tourism is not seen as a serious area of study, host communities are not distinguishing between traveling anthropologists and tourists, anthropologists desire to distinguish themselves from tourists, and scholars see tourism as primarily an economic activity that is not about human relations.

13. The Anthropology of Tourism Interest Group, a section of the American Anthropological Association established in 2012, has done much to change that. It offers a literal and virtual space for collaboration around anthropological tourism research, intersecting scholars who've had the benefits of tourism studies training with those, like me, who haven't.

14. Dallen J. Timothy and Stephen W. Boyd, "Heritage Tourism in the 21st Century: Valued Traditions and New Perspectives," 5.

15. Visit Mississippi Travel Blog, "Find Your True South in Mississippi." Visit Mississippi is the tourism division of the Mississippi Development Authority, the state's leading economic and community development agency.

16. See James C. Cobb, *The Most Southern Place on Earth: The Mississippi Delta and the Roots of Regional Identity.*

17. Mississippi Development Authority, "Mississippi—Find Your True South."

18. See Stephen Small, "Still Back of the Big House: Slave Cabins and Slavery in Southern Heritage Tourism." See also Jennifer L. Eichstedt and Stephen Small, *Representations of Slavery: Race and Ideology in Southern Plantation Museums.*

19. For more on slavery tours at the Myrtles Plantation, see Tiya Miles, *Tales from the Haunted South: Dark Tourism and Memories of Slavery from the Civil War Era.*

20. See Stephen J. Whitfield, "Emmett Till," for general information. Bryant changed her story about what happened in the grocery store several times, most recently (in 2008) admitting to Tim Tyson that "the circumstances under which she told the story were coercive." See Richard Pérez-Peña, "Woman Linked to 1955 Emmett Till Murder Tells Historian Her Claims Were False." No one responsible for the lynching, including Bryant, was held accountable for the crime.

21. See https://www.winterinstitute.org. The Winter Institute became one of the initiative's most successful measurable results.

22. B. Brian Foster, *I Don't Like the Blues: Race, Place, and the Backbeat of Black Life*, 24.

23. Ibid., 23.

24. Haley Barbour, quoted in Carlie Kollath Wells, "Barbour: Mississippi Is 'Birthplace of America's Music.'"

25. See King, *I'm Feeling the Blues Right Now,* 169.

26. Ibid., 168–169.

27. The quoted phrase is Rhondalyn Peairs's.

28. The Mississippi, Believe It! program launched in 2005 and relaunched the campaign with four new public service ads in 2016. See https://www.mississippibelieveit.com.

29. Kathryn Radishofski, "Last (Un)fair Deal Goin' Down: A Case Study on the Racial Ideologies and Projects Advanced by the Blues Tourism Industry in Clarksdale, Mississippi," 81, and King, *I'm Feeling the Blues Right Now,* 168.

30. Debra Devi, "Can the Blues Rescue the Mississippi Delta?"

31. Ibid. The Mississippi Blues Trail includes over two hundred markers dedicated to people, places, events, locations, and themes significant to the development and proliferation of blues music. "Out-of-state markers that denote the cities and states where significant numbers of Mississippi blues performers have migrated, or that denote areas that have a documented history (25 years or more) of presenting numerous Mississippi blues artists in clubs or festivals, or of recording Mississippi blues artists, if such activities have raised the levels of appreciation and public recognition for Mississippi blues are also eligible for inclusion." See Mississippi Blues Trail, "Mississippi Blues Trail Selection Criteria."

32. Devi, "Can the Blues Rescue the Mississippi Delta?"

33. Ibid.

34. Foster, *I Don't Like the Blues,* 66, and King, *I'm Feeling the Blues Right Now,* 171. See also Charles W. Eagles's coverage of University of Mississippi student versus outsider responses to James Meredith's fight for integration in "'The Fight for Men's Minds': The Aftermath of the Ole Miss Riot of 1962."

35. Lynell L. Thomas, *Desire and Disaster in New Orleans: Tourism, Race, and Historical Memory,* 7–8, 14.

36. See Dave Tell, *Remembering Emmett Till,* as a case study on historical memory and the tourism economy in the North Mississippi Delta.

37. See St. Louis Convention and Visitors Commission, "Explore St. Louis."

38. See City of Clarksdale, "Clarksdale Musicians and Artists," and Joel Nathan Rosen, "Mound Bayou."

39. Alana Dillette, "Roots Tourism: A Second Wave of Double Consciousness for African Americans," 412.

40. See Patricia Pinho, "African-American Roots Tourism in Brazil."

41. See Jodi Skipper and Suzanne R. Davidson, "The Big House as Home: Roots Tourism and Slavery in the U.S."

42. See Eugene Yiga, "How the Black Travel Movement Is Gaining Momentum."

43. See Mississippi Development Authority, "Fiscal Year 2018 Annual Report."

44. Travel South USA, "Showcase History: Celebrating 38 Years of Travel South Showcase."

45. Laurajane Smith, *Uses of Heritage*, 4.

46. Tell, *Remembering Emmett Till*, 25.

47. Stephen A. King and Roger Davis Gatchet, "Marking the Past: Civil Rights Tourism and the Mississippi Freedom Trail," 107.

48. Ayisha Jeffries Cisse, quoted in Kim Severson, "New Museums to Shine a Spotlight on Civil Rights Era."

49. Brakkton Booker, "Trump Attends Opening of Mississippi Civil Rights Museum Despite Controversy."

50. Ayisha Jeffries Cisse, quoted in Severson, "New Museums to Shine a Spotlight on Civil Rights Era."

51. See Eric Bradner and Andrew Kaczynski, "Mississippi Sen. Cindy Hyde-Smith Pushed Resolution Praising Confederate Soldier's Effort to 'Defend His Homeland,'" and Ashton Pittman, "Tate Reeves Spoke at Event Where 'Yankees' Were Compared to 'Nazis.'"

52. Derek H. Alderman, "Introduction to the Special Issue: African Americans and Tourism," 377.

53. Chelius Carter, interview with the author, Holly Springs, Mississippi, December 29, 2019. Although I interviewed Chelius and Jenifer together, in the interest of streamlining the notes, I am citing only the person I am quoting.

54. Jenifer Eggleston, quoted in Joseph McGill, Jr., "Back of the Big House: Slave Dwelling Project a Stop on Holly Springs, MS Pilgrimage Tour."

55. Susan T. Falck, *Remembering Dixie: The Battle to Control Historical Memory in Natchez, Mississippi, 1865–1941*, 308n16. Falck makes notes of another possible naming source, "a Wisconsin club delegate who made the suggestion to create 'an annual pilgrimage to Natchez . . .' during a garden club convention attended by Katherine Miller." Miller is most credited with creating the Natchez Pilgrimage.

56. Ibid., 168–169.

57. Mrs. Vadah Cochran, "First Pilgrimage Is a Big Success."

58. See Hubert H. McAlexander, *A Southern Tapestry: Marshall County, Mississippi, 1835–2000*, 130, 132.

59. Cochran, "First Pilgrimage Is a Big Success."

60. "Local People Enjoy Garden Pilgrimage." Walter Place was built in 1859 by Colonel Harvey Washington Walter, who served as the first president of the Mississippi Central Railroad. The house, a fusion of Greek and Gothic Revival styles, was constructed by local architect Spires Boling, who also owned a young Ida B. Wells, later known as a famed civil rights activist and anti-lynching advocate. See Phillip Knecht's *Hill Country History* blog for a more detailed historical and architectural description. The Holly Springs Main Street Association nominated the home for the Mississippi Heritage Trust's 10 Most Endangered Historic Places in Mississippi list, on which it was included in 2017. For more on "Heaven Bound," see Gregory D. Coleman, "Heaven Bound."

61. Steven Hoelscher, "Making Place, Making Race," 666, 673, 669.

62. Charles Reagan Wilson, "The Religion of the Lost Cause: Ritual and Organization of the Southern Civil Religion, 1865–1920," 238. See also Paul A. Shackel, *Memory in Black and White: Race, Commemoration, and the Post-Bellum Landscape*, 21–50, 175–179.

63. Falck, *Remembering Dixie*, 3–4.

64. King, *I'm Feeling the Blues Right Now*, 28.

65. Jack E. Davis, "A Struggle for Public History: Black and White Claims to Natchez's Past," 52–53.

66. Stephen Lloyd, "Sacrilisation of Secular Pilgrimages as Archetypal Transformational Journeys: Advancing Theory through Emic and Etic Interpretations," 28.

67. Cochran, "First Pilgrimage Is a Big Success." Falck details this publicity campaign in *Remembering Dixie*, 153–210.

68. See "Paved Route to Picturesque Spring Pilgrimages" in the *Durant News*.

69. See "On the Calendar" in the *Washington Evening Star*.

70. See McAlexander, *A Southern Tapestry*, 131, and Martha Swain and Roger D. Tate, Jr., "Great Depression."

71. Refer to the list of manuscript sources in McAlexander, *A Southern Tapestry*, 171.

72. Neil R. McMillen, "Feature Story: WPA Slave Narratives."

73. See Mrs. J. A. Donaldson, "Interesting Interviews: Henry Walton"; Netty Fant Thompson, "Lizzie Fant Brown," "Alice Shaw," 1920, and "Liza McGhee," 1402; and "Callie Johnson."

74. Netty Fant Thompson, "Belle Caruthers," 364–368.

75. Ann Fant Rozell, "Fant History," typescript courtesy of Nancy Fant Smith, cited in McAlexander, *A Southern Tapestry*, 14.

76. This information is summarized from the general "History of Marshall County and Holly Springs" panels at the Craft House.

77. Mississippi Encyclopedia Staff, "Pontotoc County." For more information on the history of the Chickasaws, see Robbie Ethridge, *From Chicaza to Chickasaw: The European Invasion and the Transformation of the Mississippian World, 1540–1715* and "The Making of a Militaristic Slaving Society"; David S. Newhall, "Chickasaw-European Relations," "Chickasaw-U.S. Relations," and "Chickasaw War"; Justin Rogers, "Constructing and Crossing Color Lines: Race and Religion in the Southern Confluence, 1810–1865"; Jeffrey D. Washburn, "Chickasaw Gender Roles and Slavery during the Plan for Civilization"; Theda Perdue, *"Mixed Blood" Indians: Racial Construction in the Early South*; Greg O'Brien, "Chickasaws: The Unconquerable People"; Charles Bolton, "Social and Economic History, 1817–1890"; and Mack Cameron, "Sixteenth Section Lands."

78. McAlexander, *A Southern Tapestry*, 15.

79. John Hebron Moore, *The Emergence of the Cotton Kingdom in the Old Southwest: Mississippi, 1770–1860*, 177.

80. McAlexander, *A Southern Tapestry*, 32.

81. Jenifer Eggleston, email message to author, May 31, 2012.

82. See Preserve Arkansas, "Behind the Big House."

83. Ira Berlin, "American Slavery in History and Memory and the Search for Social Justice," 1263.

Chapter 3   The Behind the Big House Program

1. St. Joseph's was consecrated as a Catholic church in 1857, although it was built for an Episcopal congregation in 1841. Now the Yellow Fever Martyrs Church and Museum, the building honors the priest and nuns who died helping victims of the yellow fever epidemic in 1878. See Phillip Knecht, "Yellow Fever Martyrs Church and Museum (1841)." According to the museum's website, the last church service was held in the building in 1981. The building fell into disrepair after the congregation moved to a new building and was rehabilitated in the 1990s. See Yellow Fever Martyrs Church and Museum, "The Church Episcopalian Beginnings."

2. Chelius Carter, interview with the author, Holly Springs, Mississippi, December 29, 2019. Although I interviewed Chelius and Jenifer together, in the interest of streamlining the notes, I am citing only the person I am quoting.

3. Chelius Carter, Behind the Big House tour narrative, in author's possession. For information on the Panic of 1837, see Bradley G. Bond, "Panic of 1837."

4. Hubert H. McAlexander, *A Southern Tapestry: Marshall County, Mississippi, 1835–2000*, 33.

5. Ibid., 65–67.

6. Chelius Carter, tour of the Hugh Craft House recorded for the author's Best Practices for Interpreting Slavery Workshop tour, April 19, 2018.

7. Edward A. Chappell and Carl Lounsbury, "Hugh Craft House Kitchen-Quarters," unpublished manuscript, August 3, 2017, annotated March 25, 2019, in author's possession. Courtesy of the University of Mississippi Slavery Research Group.

8. Chelius Carter, "Craft House Talking Points," unpublished manuscript, April 2012, in author's possession.

9. See Bernard L. Herman, "Slave and Servant Housing in Charleston, 1770–1820," 90.

10. Carter, "Craft House Talking Points."

11. Ibid.

12. Jenifer Eggleston, interview with the author, Holly Springs, Mississippi, December 29, 2019. Although I interviewed Chelius and Jenifer together, in the interest of streamlining the notes, I am citing only the person I am quoting.

13. I witnessed the same thing when I visited the garden club's home, Montrose, in 2015, ultimately sympathizing with the preteens eager to please their audience with narratives of interior furnishings. They are not the only docents; some adults do serve as guides, offering more detailed mentions of family names and anecdotal family histories. The guides, regardless of age, are in antebellum-era dress.

14. Eggleston, interview with the author, December 29, 2019.

15. Ibid.

16. Ibid.

17. It is believed that Wells-Barnett was born on the property to Elizabeth Warrenton, an enslaved cook, and James "Jim" Wells, a carpenter and apprentice to Spires Boling. Boling built the house in 1860. For more information on Wells's early life in Marshall County, see Beth R. Kruse, Rhondalyn K. Peairs, Jodi Skipper, and Shennette Garrett-Scott, "Remembering Ida, Ida Remembering: Ida B. Wells-Barnett and Black Political Culture in Reconstruction-Era Mississippi." The house was owned by the Gatewood family for nearly one hundred years. Members of the family "deeded the house to Brian K. Frazier, who deeded the house to the City of Holly Springs in 2000. Soon after, the Boling-Gatewood House became the home of the Ida B. Wells-Barnett Museum"; see Phillip Knecht, "Boling-Gatewood House."

18. Eggleston, interview with the author, December 29, 2019.

19. Carter, interview with the author, December 29, 2019.

20. Ibid.

21. Rhondalyn Peairs, interview with the author, Oxford, Mississippi, June 19, 2019.

22. Carter, interview with the author, December 29, 2019.

23. Hugh Craft's child from his first marriage, Martha Craft (1826–1885), married James Fort (1822–1878), and in 1868, after the death of Hugh Craft, Martha and James Fort moved into the house. James Fort and his daughter Mary Fort both died in the yellow fever epidemic of 1878. The widowed Martha Craft Fort continued to live in the house with her surviving daughter, Fannie Fort Daniel (1856–1934), until Martha's death in 1885. Fannie had married Dr. Chesley Daniel (1849–1914); Chesley Thorne Smith is their granddaughter. See Phillip Knecht, "Hugh Craft House (1851)."

24. Chesley Thorne Smith, *Childhood in Holly Springs: A Memoir*, 74.

25. See Willie H. Mallory, *The Strawberry Story: When I Can Read My Title Clear.*

26. Joe McGill chronicled that first experience in Holly Springs in "Back of the Big House: Slave Dwelling Project a Stop on Holly Springs, MS Pilgrimage Tour."

27. Eggleston, interview with the author, December 29, 2019.

28. In 2005, Chelius Carter spearheaded the move of the Stephenson-McAlexander plantation office, the only one still standing in Marshall County, to the Strawberry Plains Audubon Center for restoration and use in the center's educational programs and history interpretation. The building, originally the office for a plantation adjoining Strawberry Plains, was moved a short distance to save it from destruction. See Phillip Knecht's *Hill Country History* blog for brief historical time lines of Burton Place, the Magnolias, McCarroll Place, Polk Place, and Featherston Place.

29. For a discussion about visitor responses to the Behind the Big House program, see my essay "Hidden in Plain Sight: Contested Histories and Urban Slavery in Mississippi."

30. Carter, interview with the author, December 29, 2019.

31. Eggleston, interview with the author, December 29, 2019.

32. For information on broader issues involved in engaging African American students in public history work, see Jodi Skipper, Kathryn Green, and Rico D. Chapman, "Public History, Diversity, and Higher Education: Three Case Studies on the African American Past."

33. Carter, interview with the author, December 29, 2019.

34. See Skipper, Green, and Chapman, "Public History, Diversity, and Higher Education."

35. Dan W. Butin, "The Limits of Service-Learning in Higher Education," 482.

36. Tania D. Mitchell, "Traditional vs. Critical Service-Learning: Engaging the

Literature to Differentiate Two Models," 50. See also Karen D. Zivi, "Reflections on Integrating Service Learning into the Curriculum."

37. Michael W. Twitty, "An Open Letter to Paula Deen."

38. Southern Foodways Alliance, "Smith Fellows."

39. Elaine Bennett, "A Simple, Practical Framework for Organizing Relationship-based Reciprocity in Service-learning Experiences: Insights from Anthropology," 9.

40. Erica K. Yamamura and Kent Koth, *Place-Based Community Engagement in Higher Education: A Strategy to Transform Universities and Communities*, 10.

41. Carter, interview with the author, December 29, 2019.

42. For more information, see https://www.sankofatravelher.com.

43. Tammy Gibson, "We Grew Up Together."

44. Joseph McGill, Jr., "We Grew Up Together."

45. Gibson, "We Grew Up Together."

46. I am currently coauthoring a book chapter on that workshop process with Jodi Barnes, who adopted the Behind the Big House program model to develop a similar program in the state of Arkansas. For that reason, I have left it outside the scope of this text.

47. Chelius Carter, quoted in Ashley Norwood, "Mississippi Edition."

48. For more on Gracing the Table's key role in dealing with racial divisions in Holly Springs, see my "Community Development through Reconciliation Tourism: The Behind the Big House Program in Holly Springs, Mississippi."

49. Chelius Carter and Jenifer Eggleston, interview with the author, December 29, 2019.

50. *In Living Color* is an American sketch comedy created by Keenan Ivory Wayans. The show launched the careers of many, including Jennifer Lopez, Jamie Foxx, and Jim Carrey. It consisted of a diverse cast, approaching contemporary issues through comedy. Other members of the Wayans family had regular roles, including Kim Wayans, who played the Benita Butrell character.

51. Conversation with Chelius Carter, Jenifer Eggleston, and Rhondalyn Peairs, Holly Springs, Mississippi, December 29, 2019.

52. Lynell L. Thomas describes this as one consequence of African American participation in the tourism industry in New Orleans. See *Desire and Disaster in New Orleans: Tourism, Race, and Historical Memory*, 13.

53. Stephen A. King, *I'm Feeling the Blues Right Now: Blues Tourism and the Mississippi Delta*, 18–19.

54. Representing Enslavement in Public: Louisiana's Past in the Present, "About."

55. Takuna Maulana EL Shabazz, "Un-Cajun Committee," in *"Black I Am!" Cajun/ Creole I Am Not!*, 30, 34. The institution's original mascot was a bulldog; then the Cajun Man, also contested on the grounds that "Cajun" was used as a racial slur by Black residents, as White residents used the slur "Nigger"; then the Cajun Chicken; and then the Cayenne, described as the essence of Cajun people. For a summary, see Lisa Wade, "Sociological Images: The Ragin' Cajuns." As of this writing, the university had formed a secret committee to search for a new mascot. See Aaron Gonsoulin, "UL Officials, Students Silent on Secret Committee."

56. Eggleston, interview with the author, December 29, 2019.

57. See "Behind the Big House, Arkansas" at https://behindthebighouse.org/ programs/behind-the-big-house-arkansas and Preserve Arkansas's link to this Behind the Big House program on its website at https://preservearkansas.org/ what-we-do/education/behind-the-big-house.

Chapter 4   Reconciling Race

1. For more on this history of the Confederate battle flag at the South Carolina State House, see Charles Joyner, "Furling that Banner: The Rise and Fall of the Confederate Flag in South Carolina, 1961–2000."

2. Gracing the Table shares the general mission of Coming to the Table but is not affiliated with it, nor is it related to any religious group. Coming to the Table's mission is to provide "leadership, resources, and a supportive environment for all who wish to acknowledge and heal wounds from racism that is rooted in the United States' history of slavery." Its website lists its four approaches to this mission: researching, acknowledging, and sharing personal, family, and community histories of race with openness and honesty; connecting to others within and across racial lines in order to develop and deepen relationships; exploring how we can heal together through dialogue, reunion, ritual, ceremony, the arts, apology, and other methods; and actively seeking to heal the wounds of racial inequality and injustice and to support racial reconciliation between individuals, within families, and in communities. See https://comingtothetable.org/about-us.

3. Alisea Williams McLeod, Zoom interview by the author, March 28, 2020.

4. I detail this argument in "Community Development through Reconciliation Tourism: The Behind the Big House Program in Holly Springs, Mississippi."

5. Preserve Marshall County and Holly Springs, Inc., 2012 project director's report and evaluation, in author's possession.

6. David B. Person, email to author, September 7, 2018.

7. See Phillip Knecht, "Crump Place."

8. See Gene Dattel, *Cotton and Race in the Making of America: The Human Costs of Economic Power,* and Hubert H. McAlexander, *A Southern Tapestry: Marshall County, Mississippi, 1835–2000.*

9. See McAlexander/Marshall County Collection, Finley-Davis Letters.

10. David B. Person, email to author, October 3, 2013.

11. LeeAnne J. Wendt, "Understanding Strawberry Plains through Landscape Archaeology," 3.

12. See Hubert H. McAlexander, *Strawberry Plains Audubon Center: Four Centuries of a Mississippi Landscape.*

13. Williams McLeod, interview by the author, March 28, 2020.

14. Ibid.

15. See Kathleen Woodruff Wickham, "William Raspberry."

16. Alisea Charmain McLeod, "Living Detroit (on the Edge of Disorder): Time and Space in the Twentieth Century."

17. Williams McLeod, interview by the author, March 28, 2020.

18. Ibid.

19. Ibid.

20. Ibid.

21. For a description of this class project, see Alisea Williams McLeod, "Student Digital Research and Writing on Slavery."

22. Williams McLeod, interview by the author, March 28, 2020.

23. For more information, see *Traces of the Trade: A Story from the Deep North* at tracesofthetrade.org.

24. Sue Watson, "New Group Focuses on Healing Wounds of History."

25. Rhondalyn Peairs, interview by the author, Oxford, Mississippi, July 19, 2019.

26. See Alan W. Barton and Sarah J. Leonard, "Incorporating Social Justice in Tourism Planning: Racial Reconciliation and Sustainable Community Development in the Deep South," and Dave Tell, *Remembering Emmett Till,* 102–118.

27. Tell, *Remembering Emmett Till,* 116.

28. For more on Leona Harris and the museum's founding, see Danny McArthur, "Leona Harris: Director of Ida B. Wells Museum."

29. Rkhty Jones, interview by the author, Holly Springs, Mississippi, November 7, 2019.

30. Oliver published a Black History Month feature in the local paper. See Sylvester Oliver, Jr., "African-Americans in 19th Century Holly Springs."

31. Wayne Jones, interview by the author, Holly Springs, Mississippi, January 25, 2020. For more information, see Netty Fant Thompson, "Belle Caruthers"; Mary Frances Marx, "Hiram Rhoades Revels"; Elizabeth Lawson, "George Washington Albright"; and Ronald A. Walter, "Robert R. Church Sr."

32. Wayne Jones, interview by the author, January 25, 2020, and Rkhty Jones, interview by the author, November 7, 2019.

33. Rkhty Jones, interview by the author, November 7, 2019. The popular fall festival ended in 2017 after a twenty-year run. The festival, which featured folk artists, nineteenth-century reenactors, musicians, and educational activities, became too large to manage. For historical information on the Ames Plantation, see http://www.amesplantation.org/historical-research.

34. Rkhty Jones, interview by the author, November 7, 2019.

35. Ibid. And see Beth R. Kruse, Rhondalyn K. Peairs, Jodi Skipper, and Shennette Garrett-Scott, "Remembering Ida, Ida Remembering: Ida B. Wells-Barnett and Black Political Culture in Reconstruction-Era Mississippi."

36. Rkhty Jones, interview by the author, November 7, 2019.

37. Ibid.

38. Ifé Carruthers, "History of the Kemetic Institute."

39. Larry Crowe, "Charles Russell Branham Remembers the Communiversity."

40. Rkhty Jones, interview by the author, November 7, 2019.

41. A popular Black nationalist and anticolonialist, Yosef Ben-Jochannan is considered the Father of African Studies to many Black political and intellectual activists, influencing a variety of folks including Cornel West and Ta-Nehisi Coates, as noted in Sam Kestenbaum, "Contested Legacy of Dr. Ben, a Father of African Studies." Ben-Jochannan touted the Afrocentric roots of Western civilizations at the height of the civil rights movement.

42. Rkhty Jones, interview by the author, November 7, 2019.

43. Ibid. Leonard Jeffries, former chair of Black studies at the City University of New York and former president of the African Heritage Studies Association, was a leader in the early field of Black studies.

44. For more information, see the Association for the Study of Classical African Civilizations, "Our Significance."

45. Rkhty Jones, interview by the author, November 7, 2019.

46. See Kestenbaum, "Contested Legacy of Dr. Ben."

47. Wayne Jones, interview by the author, January 25, 2020. July 1, 2019, population estimates show a 5 percent Black or African American population for Claremont. See United States Census Bureau, "QuickFacts: Claremont City, California."

48. Wayne Jones, interview by the author, January 25, 2020.

49. For more information, see Ishmell Hendrex Edwards, "History of Rust College, 1866–1967."

50. Wayne Jones, interview by the author, January 25, 2020.

51. Ibid.

52. Ibid.

53. Ibid.

54. Ibid. James Turner was integral to the Black studies movements of the 1960s and 1970s. He pushed for the integration of the African Studies Association's executive leadership, helped organize the African Heritage Studies Association, was founding director of the Africana Studies and Research Center at Cornell University, and conceptualized Africana studies as a widely used and accepted paradigm. Turner was president of the African Heritage Studies Association from 1972 to 1976 and from 1982 to 1984. Wayne might have been introduced to him during the later period. See Shirley Hawkins, "10 Things to Know about Dr. James Turner, Africana Studies Pioneer at Cornell University," and Jonathan B. Fenderson and Candace Katungi, "'Committed to Institution Building': James Turner and the History of Africana Studies at Cornell University, an Interview."

55. Wayne Jones, interview by the author, January 25, 2020.

56. Ibid.

57. Ibid.

58. Ibid.

59. Ibid.

60. Ibid.

61. The Southern Claims Commission "was created by an Act of Congress on March 3, 1871, to receive, examine, and consider claims submitted by Southern Unionist citizens. Claimants sought compensation for supplies that had been confiscated by or furnished to the Army of the United States during the Civil War. After an additional act in 1872, the SCC also considered claims against the Navy." See U.S. National Archives and Records Administration, "Southern Claims Commission Records." Cato Govan sought $1,610 in compensation for eight mules, a wagon, harnesses, and a saddle. He was awarded $500 of that. See Southern Claims Commission Approved Claims, "Cato Govan." Govan's claim was certified on August 11, 1874. The cited response is on page 7 of that claim.

62. Wayne Jones, interview by the author, January 25, 2020.

63. Ibid.

64. See my essay "Hidden in Plain Sight: Contested Histories and Urban Slavery in Mississippi."

65. College of Charleston Avery Research Center, "2017 Conference: Transforming Public History from Charleston to the Atlantic World."

66. See Phillip Knecht, "Herndon."

67. The garden club members were Jennifer Barkley, Dianene Fant, Jacque Kazemba, Linda Seale, Kathy Elgin, Christine Walker, and Nancy Jones.

68. Jennifer Barkley, quoted in Lyda K. Ferree, "Holly Springs 77th Pilgrimage Home and Heritage Festival."

69. Williams McLeod, interview by the author, March 28, 2020.

70. Ibid.

71. For detailed information on Deb Davis's genealogical research and its relationship to the Burtons, see Suzanne R. Davidson, "African American Roots Tourism at 'Home': History, Memory, and Heritage in Holly Springs, Mississippi," and Jodi Skipper and Suzanne R. Davidson, "The Big House as Home: Roots Tourism and Slavery in the U.S."

72. Wayne Jones, interview by the author, January 25, 2020.

Chapter 5   Academic Values and Public Scholarship

1. Nadine Changfoot, Peter Andrée, Charles Z. Levkoe, Michelle Nilson, and Magdalene Goemans, "Engaged Scholarship in Tenure and Promotion: Autoethnographic Insights from the Fault Lines of a Shifting Landscape," 239.

2. Ellen Cushman, "The Public Intellectual, Service Learning, and Activist Research," 331.

3. Changfoot, Andrée, Levkoe, Nilson, and Goemans, "Engaged Scholarship in Tenure and Promotion," 242.

4. Daniel W. Jones, "Chancellor Dan Jones Inauguration Speech."

5. University of Mississippi, "UM/2020 Strategic Plan."

6. Carnegie Foundation for the Advancement of Teaching, quoted in Amy Driscoll, "Analysis of the Carnegie Classification of Community Engagement: Patterns and Impact on Institutions," 3.

7. Amy Driscoll, "Carnegie's Community Engagement Classification: Intentions and Insights," 40.

8. See Craig Calhoun, "Foreword," xvii.

9. Ross A. Klein, "Breaking Loose from the Ivory Tower: The Challenges for Academic Researchers with an Activist Agenda in Tourism," 1.

10. Barbara Smith, "Doing Research on Black American Women," 25.

11. Jasmine A. Abrams, Morgan Maxwell, Michell Pope, and Faye Z. Belgrave, "Carrying the World with the Grace of a Lady and the Grit of a Warrior: Deepening Our Understanding of the 'Strong Black Woman' Schema," 504.

12. Kerry Ann Rockquemore and Tracey Laszloffy, *The Black Academic's Guide to Winning Tenure—Without Losing Your Soul*, 118.

13. Ibid.

14. Ibid.

15. Ibid.

16. Ibid., 181.

17. Cailyn Petrona Stewart, "The Mule of the World: The Strong Black Woman and the Woes of Being 'Independent,'" 32.

18. Scott Jaschik, "The Black Academic's Guide to Winning Tenure—Without Losing Your Soul," interview with Kerry Ann Rockquemore.

19. Colleen Clemens, "Ally or Accomplice? The Language of Activism."

20. Jonathan Osler, ed., "Opportunities for White People in the Fight for Racial Justice."

21. Kimberly Harden and Tai Harden-Moore, "Moving from Ally to Accomplice: How Far Are You Willing to Go to Disrupt Racism in the Workplace?"

22. Jerry Mitchell, "Ole Miss Reflects on the 50 Years since Integration."

23. See Antonio Miguel Nogués-Pedregal, "Anthropological Contributions to Tourism Studies."

24. See Rob Hales, Dianne Dredge, Tazim Jamal, and Freya Higgins-Desbiolles, "Academic Activism in Tourism Studies: Critical Narratives from Four Researchers."

25. Klein, "Breaking Loose from the Ivory Tower," 4.

26. See Robbie Brown, "Anti-Obama Protest at Ole Miss Turns Unruly."

27. Ibid.

28. Robinson republished the piece, "Riots and Rumors of Riots: Lessons from the University of Mississippi," on her New South Negress website.

29. Ibid.

30. Edward L. Ayers and Christy Coleman, "Three Recommendations to the University of Mississippi."

31. See Barbara Combs, Kirsten A. Dellinger, Jeff T. Jackson, Kirk A. Johnson, Willa Johnson, Jodi Skipper, and James M. Thomas, "The Symbolic Lynching of James Meredith: A Visual Analysis and Collective Counter Narrative to Racial Domination."

32. Ayers and Coleman, "Three Recommendations to the University of Mississippi."

33. See Jimmie E. Gates, "Confederate Group Loses Fight over Ole Miss' Civil War Monuments Changes."

34. Phrase from George Lipsitz, *The Possessive Investment in Whiteness*.

35. See Combs, Dellinger, Jackson, K. Johnson, W. Johnson, Skipper, and Thomas, "The Symbolic Lynching of James Meredith."

36. Ibid., 10–11.

37. Tania D. Mitchell, "Traditional vs. Critical Service-Learning: Engaging the Literature to Differentiate Two Models," 51, 54, 52.

38. See the Mississippi Humanities Council's nomination form at http://mshuman ities.org/wp-content/uploads/2017/01/2019-Public-Award-Nomination-Form.pdf.

39. Ibid.

40. See https://www.oah.org/insights/archive/historical-associations-issue-recom mendations-about-rewarding-public-history-work-for-promotion-and-tenure for access to the full report.

41. Joint Annual Meeting of the National Council on Public History and the Society for History in the Federal Government, "2016 Program," https://ncph.org/wp-content/uploads/2016/02/2016-Annual-Meeting-Program-Final-Web.pdf.

42. For more on her research, see Rhondda Robinson Thomas, *Call My Name, Clemson: Documenting the Black Experience in an American University Community*.

43. See Julie Ellison and Timothy K. Eatman, *Scholarship in Public: Knowledge Creation and Tenure Policy in the Engaged University*.

44. Orlando Taylor, quoted in ibid., 18.

45. Swearer Center at Brown University, "The Carnegie Foundation for the Advancement of Teaching, 2020 Classification Carnegie Elective Community Engagement Classification, First-Time Classification Documentation Framework."

46. Driscoll, "Carnegie's Community Engagement Classification," 39. See also KerryAnn O'Meara, "Encouraging Multiple Forms of Scholarship in Faculty Reward Systems: Have Academic Cultures Really Changed?"

47. Chani Nicholas, "Horoscopes for the Full Moon in Aquarius."

Epilogue

1. For more on responses to these plantation tours, see Jodi Skipper and James M. Thomas, "Plantation Tours." For more on the plantation wedding controversy, see Michael T. Luongo, "Despite Everything, People Still Have Weddings at 'Plantation' Sites"; John R. Legg, "A Romantic Union? Thoughts on Plantation Weddings from a Photographer/Historian"; and Malaika Jabali, "Plantation Weddings Are Wrong: Why Is It So Hard for White Americans to Admit That?"

2. Brent Leggs, "Out of Crisis, an Opportunity."

Bibliography

Abrams, Jasmine A., Morgan Maxwell, Michell Pope, and Faye Z. Belgrave. "Carrying the World with the Grace of a Lady and the Grit of a Warrior: Deepening Our Understanding of the 'Strong Black Woman' Schema." *Psychology of Women Quarterly* 38, no. 4 (December 2014): 503–518, doi:10.1177/03616843 14541418.

Adams, Tony E. "A Review of Narrative Ethics." *Qualitative Inquiry* 14, no. 2 (March 2008): 175–194.

Alderman, Derek H. "Introduction to the Special Issue: African Americans and Tourism." *Tourism Geographies: An International Journal of Tourism Space, Place and Environment* 15, no. 3 (2013): 375–379.

Ali, Charlotte Zobeir. "The Eye of Horus and Our Brain: Ancient Egyptians Gave Us the Key to Reach Enlightenment." Medium, October 1, 2020, https://medium.com/la-biblioth%C3%A8que/the-eye-of-horus -and-our-brain -ce1d7b82a62a.

American Civil Liberties Union. "ACLU Amicus Brief in Support of New Trial for Felton D. Dorsey." https://www.aclu.org/legal-document/aclu-amicus-brief-support-new-trial-felton-d-dorsey.

Association for the Study of Classical African Civilizations. "Our Significance." https://ascac.org/about.

Ayers, Edward L., and Christy Coleman. "Three Recommendations to the University of Mississippi." In *Chancellor's Action Plan on Consultant Reports and Update on the Work of the Sensitivity and Respect Committee*, August 1, 2014, http://chancellor.olemiss.edu/wpcontent/uploads/sites/17/2013/08/2014Action PlanonConsultantReportsandUpdateontheWorkoftheSensitivityandRespect Committee.pdf.

Barton, Alan W., and Sarah J. Leonard. "Incorporating Social Justice in Tourism Planning: Racial Reconciliation and Sustainable Community Development in the Deep South." *Community Development* 41, no. 3 (2010): 298–322, doi.org/10.1080/15575330903444051.

Bennett, Elaine. "A Simple, Practical Framework for Organizing Relationship-based Reciprocity in Service-learning Experiences: Insights from Anthropology." *International Journal of Research on Service-Learning and Community Engagement* 6, no. 1, article 2 (2018): 1–15, https://ijrslce.scholasticahq .com/article/6999-a-simple-practical-framework-for-organizing-relationship -based-reciprocity-in-service-learning-experiences-insights-from-anthropology.

Berlin, Ira. "American Slavery in History and Memory and the Search for Social Justice." *Journal of American History* 90, no. 4 (March 2004): 1251–1268.

Bologna, Giacomo. "Mississippi Flag Is Not a Banner That Unifies Us, So Change It, AG Hopeful Says." *Clarion Ledger*, April 9, 2019, https://www.clarionled ger.com/story/news/politics/2019/04/09/mississippi-flag-ag-candidate-says -state-flag-should-change/3398978002.

Bolton, Charles. "Social and Economic History, 1817–1890." In *The Mississippi Encyclopedia*, ed. Ted Ownby and Charles Reagan Wilson. Jackson: University Press of Mississippi, 2017. Article updated April 26, 2018, http://mississippien cyclopedia.org/overviews/social-and-economic-history-1817-1890.

Bond, Bradley G. "Panic of 1837." In *The Mississippi Encyclopedia*, ed. Ted Ownby and Charles Reagan Wilson. Jackson: University Press of Mississippi, 2017. Article updated April 14, 2018, https://mississippiencyclopedia.org/entries/ panic-of-1837.

Booker, Brakkton. "Trump Attends Opening of Mississippi Civil Rights Museum Despite Controversy." *National Public Radio*, December 9, 2017, https://www .npr.org/2017/12/09/569621998/trump-attends-opening-of-mississippi-civil -rights-museum-despite-controversy.

Bouie, Jamelle. "Bonus: How Can We Get Americans to Talk Honestly about Slavery?" Interview with LeVar Burton. *Slate Plus*, October 8, 2015, https://slate .com/podcasts/history-of-american-slavery/2015/10/history-of-american -slavery-episode-bonus-talking-about-slavery-jamelle-bouie-levar-burton.

Bradner, Eric, and Andrew Kaczynski. "Mississippi Sen. Cindy Hyde-Smith Pushed Resolution Praising Confederate Soldier's Effort to 'Defend His Homeland.'" *CNN Politics*, November 26, 2018, https://www.cnn.com/2018/11/24/politics/ cindy-hyde-smith-confederacy-mississippi-senate-race/index.html.

Brown, Robbie. "Anti-Obama Protest at Ole Miss Turns Unruly." *New York Times*, November 7, 2017, https://www.nytimes.com/2012/11/08/us/anti-obama -protest-at-university-of-mississippi-turns-unruly.html?auth=login-email&log in=email.

Buckner, Julie Armstrong. *Mary Turner and the Memory of Lynching.* Athens: University of Georgia Press, 2011.

Burgess, Gloria J. McEwen. *Pass It On!* Kingston, Wash.: Two Sylvias Press, 2018.

Burns, Georgette Leah. "Anthropology and Tourism: Past Contributions and

Future Theoretical Challenges." *Anthropological Forum* 14, no. 1 (March 2004): 6–7.

Butin, Dan W. "The Limits of Service-Learning in Higher Education." *Review of Higher Education* 29, no. 4 (2006): 473–498.

Buzinde, Christine N., and Carla Almeida Santos. "Representations of Slavery." *Annals of Tourism Research* 35, no. 2 (2008): 469–488.

Calhoun, Craig. "Foreword." In *Engaging Contradictions: Theory, Politics, and Methods of Activist Scholarship*, ed. Charles R. Hale, xiii–xxvi. Berkeley: University of California Press, 2008.

"Callie Johnson." In *The American Slave: A Composite Autobiography*, supplement, series 1, vol. 8, Mississippi Narratives, part 3, Contributions in Afro-American and African Studies, no. 35, ed. George P. Rawick, Jan Hillegas, and Ken Lawrence, 1151. Westport, Conn.: Greenwood Press, 1977.

Cameron, Mack. "Sixteenth Section Lands." In *The Mississippi Encyclopedia*, ed. Ted Ownby and Charles Reagan Wilson. Jackson: University Press of Mississippi, 2017. Article updated May 1, 2018, https://mississippiencyclopedia.org/entries/sixteenth-section-lands.

Carruthers, Ifé. "History of the Kemetic Institute." http://www.ki-chicago.org/about_us.htm.

Carter, Jarrett L. "'A Different World' Minimizes a Different Age for HBCUs." *HuffPost*, August 9, 2011, https://www.huffpost.com/entry/a-different-world-minimiz_b_915035.

Chang, Heewon. *Autoethnography as Method*. Walnut Creek, Calif.: Left Coast Press, 2008.

Changfoot, Nadine, Peter Andrée, Charles Z. Levkoe, Michelle Nilson, and Magdalene Goemans. "Engaged Scholarship in Tenure and Promotion: Autoethnographic Insights from the Fault Lines of a Shifting Landscape." *Michigan Journal of Community Service Learning* 26, no. 1 (Winter 2020): 239–264, http://dx.doi.org/10.3998/mjcsloa.3239521.0026.114.

Chappell, Edward A., and Carl Lounsbury. *Architectural Report on the Hugh Craft House Kitchen-Quarters*. Oxford: University of Mississippi Slavery Research Group, 2017.

City of Clarksdale. "Clarksdale Musicians and Artists." https://www.cityofclarksdale.org/music-culture-history.

Clemens, Colleen. "Ally or Accomplice? The Language of Activism." *Teaching Tolerance*, June 5, 2017, https://www.tolerance.org/magazine/ally-or-accomplice-the-language-of-activism.

Coates, Ta-Nehisi. *Between the World and Me*. New York: Spiegel and Grau, 2015.

Cobb, James C. *The Most Southern Place on Earth: The Mississippi Delta and the Roots of Regional Identity*. New York: Oxford University Press, 1992.

Cochran, Mrs. Vadah. "First Pilgrimage Is a Big Success." *Holly Springs South Reporter*, October 22, 1936, http://archive.southreporter.com/2007/wk16/first_pilgrimage.html.

Coleman, Gregory D. "Heaven Bound." In *New Georgia Encyclopedia*. Article published July 24, 2002; updated August 22, 2013, https://www.georgiaencyclopedia.org/articles/arts-culture/heaven-bound.

College of Charleston Avery Research Center. "2017 Conference: Transforming Public History from Charleston to the Atlantic World." https://claw.cofc.edu/2017-conference-schedule.

Combs, Barbara, Kirsten A. Dellinger, Jeff T. Jackson, Kirk A. Johnson, Willa Johnson, Jodi Skipper, and James M. Thomas. "The Symbolic Lynching of James Meredith: A Visual Analysis and Collective Counter Narrative to Racial Domination." *Sociology of Race and Ethnicity* 2, no. 3 (2016): 338–353.

Crowe, Larry. "Charles Russell Branham Remembers the Communiversity." Interview with Charles Russell Branham. *HistoryMakers Digital Archive* A2008.119, November 3, 2008, session 1, tape 5, story 3, https://www.thehistorymakers.org/digital-archives.

Cushman, Ellen. "The Public Intellectual, Service Learning, and Activist Research." *College English* 61, no. 3 (January 1999): 328–336, https://www.jstor.org/stable/379072.

Dattel, Gene. *Cotton and Race in the Making of America: The Human Costs of Economic Power*. Lanham, Md.: Ivan R. Dee, 2009.

Davidson, Suzanne R. "African American Roots Tourism at 'Home': History, Memory, and Heritage in Holly Springs, Mississippi." Master's thesis, University of Mississippi, 2018.

Davis, Jack E. "A Struggle for Public History: Black and White Claims to Natchez's Past." *Public Historian* 22, no. 1 (2000): 45–63.

Devi, Debra. "Can the Blues Rescue the Mississippi Delta?" *HuffPost Arts and Culture*, March 11, 2013, http://www.huffingtonpostE.com/debra-devi/delta-blues_b_2313109.html.

———. *The Language of the Blues from Alcorub to Zuzu*. Jersey City, N.J.: True Nature Books, 2012.

Dillette, Alana. "Roots Tourism: A Second Wave of Double Consciousness for African Americans." *Journal of Sustainable Tourism* 29, nos. 2–3 (2021): 411–426, doi: 10.1080/09669582.2020.1727913.

Donaldson, Mrs. J. A. "Interesting Interviews: Henry Walton." In *The American Slave: A Composite Autobiography*, supplement, series 1, vol. 10, Mississippi Narratives, part 5, Contributions in Afro-American and African Studies, no. 35, ed. George P. Rawick, Jan Hillegas, and Ken Lawrence, 2168–2169. Westport, Conn.: Greenwood Press, 1977.

Driscoll, Amy. "Analysis of the Carnegie Classification of Community Engagement: Patterns and Impact on Institutions." *New Directions for Institutional Research*, no. 162 (2014): 3–15, doi:10.1002/ir.20072.

———. "Carnegie's Community Engagement Classification: Intentions and Insights." *Change: The Magazine of Higher Learning* 40, no. 1 (2008): 38–41.

Dunworth, J. R. "Letters to the Editor: The Culture, Flag." *Holly Springs South Reporter*, July 9, 2015.

Dwyer, Owen J., and Derek H. Alderman. *Civil Rights Memorials and the Geography of Memory*. Athens: University of Georgia Press, 2008.

Eagles, Charles W. "'The Fight for Men's Minds': The Aftermath of the Ole Miss Riot of 1962." *Journal of Mississippi History* 71, no. 1 (Spring 2009): 1–54.

Edwards, Ishmell Hendrex. "History of Rust College, 1866–1967." PhD dissertation, University of Mississippi, 1993.

Ehrlinger, Joyce E., Ashby Plant, Richard P. Eibach, Corey J. Columb, Joanna L. Goplen, Jonathan W. Kunstman, and David A. Butz. "How Exposure to the Confederate Flag Affects Willingness to Vote for Barack Obama." *Political Psychology* 32, no. 1 (February 2011): 131–146.

Eichstedt, Jennifer L., and Stephen Small. *Representations of Slavery: Race and Ideology in Southern Plantation Museums*. Washington, D.C.: Smithsonian Institution Press, 2002.

Ellis, Carolyn, Tony E. Adams, and Arthur P. Bochner. "Autoethnography: An Overview." *Historical Social Research/Historische Sozialforschung* 36, no. 4 (2011): 273–290.

Ellis, Carolyn, and Arthur P. Bochner, eds. *Composing Ethnography: Alternative Forms of Qualitative Writing*. Walnut Creek, Calif.: AltaMira Press, 1996.

Ellis, Carolyn, Christine E. Kiesinger, and Lisa M. Tillmann-Healy. "Interactive Interviewing: Talking about Emotional Experience." In *Reflexivity and Voice*, ed. Rosanna Hertz, 119–149. Thousand Oaks, Calif.: Sage, 1997.

Ellison, Julie, and Timothy K. Eatman. *Scholarship in Public: Knowledge Creation and Tenure Policy in the Engaged University*. Syracuse, N.Y.: Imagining America, 2008.

EL Shabazz, Takuna Maulana. *"Black I Am!" Cajun/Creole I Am Not!* Lafayette, La.: Saba Enterprise, 2012.

Ethridge, Robbie. *From Chicaza to Chickasaw: The European Invasion and the Transformation of the Mississippian World, 1540–1715.* Chapel Hill: University of North Carolina Press, 2010.

———. "The Making of a Militaristic Slaving Society." In *Indian Slavery in Colonial America,* ed. Alan Gallay, 251–276. Lincoln: University of Nebraska Press, 2009.

Eubanks, W. Ralph. "'Manufactured Ideas of History': Patriotic Education Fund in the Playbook of Totalitarian Leaders." *Mississippi Free Press,* December 9, 2020, https://www.mississippifreepress.org/7422/manufactured-ideas-of-history-reeves-patriotic-education-fund-in-the-playbook-of-totalitarian-leaders.

Falck, Susan T. *Remembering Dixie: The Battle to Control Historical Memory in Natchez, Mississippi, 1865–1941.* Jackson: University Press of Mississippi, 2019.

Fenderson, Jonathan B., and Candace Katungi. "'Committed to Institution Building': James Turner and the History of Africana Studies at Cornell University, an Interview." *Journal of African American Studies* 16, no. 1 (March 2012): 121–167.

Ferree, Lyda K. "Holly Springs 77th Pilgrimage Home and Heritage Festival." *Jackson Sun,* March 28, 2015, http://www.jacksonsun.com/story/life/2015/03/27/holly springs-th-pilgrimagehome-heritage-festival/70550594.

Festival International de Louisiane. "What Is Festival International de Louisiane?" https://festivalinternational.org.

Foster, B. Brian. *I Don't Like the Blues: Race, Place, and the Backbeat of Black Life.* Chapel Hill: University of North Carolina Press, 2020.

Foster, Elissa. *Communicating at the End of Life.* Mahwah, N.J.: Lawrence Erlbaum, 2006.

Gallas, Kristin L., and James DeWolf, eds. *Interpreting Slavery at Museums and Historic Sites.* New York: Rowman and Littlefield, 2015.

Ganucheau, Adam, Bobby Harrison, and Geoff Pender. "After Waffling for Years, Gov. Tate Reeves Signs Bill to Change State Flag." *Mississippi Today,* June 30, 2020, https://mississippitoday.org/2020/06/30/after-waffling-for-years-gov-tate-reeves-signs-bill-to-change-state-flag.

Gates, Jimmie E. "Confederate Group Loses Fight over Ole Miss' Civil War Monuments Changes." *Clarion Ledger,* September 5, 2018, https://www.clarionledger.com/story/news/2018/09/05/confederate-groups-cant-stop-ole-miss-renaming-monuments/1194419002.

Giancarlo, Alexandra. "'Don't Call Me a Cajun!' Race and Representation in Louisiana's Acadiana Region." *Journal of Cultural Geography,* July 23, 2018, doi:10.1080/08873631.2018.1500088.

Gibson, Tammy. "We Grew Up Together." *The Slave Dwelling Project* (blog), April 23, 2016, https://slavedwellingproject.org/we-grew-up-together.

Gonsoulin, Aaron. "UL Officials, Students Silent on Secret Committee." *Vermilion*, March 26, 2019, https://www.thevermilion.com/news/ul-officials-students-silent-on-secret-committee/article_6cec3496-4f6a-11e9-9d6a-67d6a678d19f.html.

Grinberg, Emanuella. "These States Are Observing Confederate Memorial Day This Month." *CNN*, April 23, 2018, https://www.cnn.com/2018/04/23/us/confederate-memorial-day-trnd/index.html.

Hale, Charles R., ed. *Engaging Contradictions: Theory, Politics, and Methods of Activist Scholarship.* Berkeley: University of California Press, 2008.

Hales, Rob, Dianne Dredge, Tazim Jamal, and Freya Higgins-Desbiolles. "Academic Activism in Tourism Studies: Critical Narratives from Four Researchers." *Tourism Analysis* 23, no. 2 (2008): 189–199, doi.org/10.3727/1083542 18X15210313504544.

Harden, Kimberly, and Tai Harden-Moore. "Moving from Ally to Accomplice: How Far Are You Willing to Go to Disrupt Racism in the Workplace?" *Diverse: Issues in Higher Education*, March 4, 2019, https://diverseeducation.com/article/138623.

Hawkins, Shirley. "10 Things to Know about Dr. James Turner, Africana Studies Pioneer at Cornell University." July 13, 2019, https://africana.cornell.edu/news/10-things-know-about-dr-james-turner-africana-studies-pioneer-cornell-university.

Herman, Bernard L. "Slave and Servant Housing in Charleston, 1770–1820." *Historical Archaeology* 33, no. 3 (1999): 88–101.

Hoelscher, Steven. "Making Place, Making Race." *Annals of the Association of American Geographers* 93, no. 3 (September 2003): 657–686.

Jabali, Malaika. "Plantation Weddings Are Wrong: Why Is It So Hard for White Americans to Admit That?" *Guardian*, December 11, 2019, https://www.theguardian.com/commentisfree/2019/dec/11/plantation-weddings-are-wrong-why-is-it-so-hard-for-white-americans-to-admit-that.

Jackson, Antoinette T. *Speaking for the Enslaved: Heritage Interpretation at Antebellum Plantation Sites.* Walnut Creek, Calif.: Left Coast Press, 2012.

Jaschik, Scott. "The Black Academic's Guide to Winning Tenure—Without Losing Your Soul." Interview with Kerry Ann Rockquemore. *Inside Higher Education*, August 8, 2008, https://www.insidehighered.com/news/2008/08/08/black-academics-guide-winning-tenure-without-losing-your-soul.

Jones, Daniel W. "Chancellor Dan Jones Inauguration Speech." *Olemiss: University of Mississippi News*, April 9, 2010, https://news.olemiss.edu/djonesinaugspeech.

Joyner, Charles. "Furling That Banner: The Rise and Fall of the Confederate Flag in South Carolina, 1961–2000." *State*, July 9, 2015, https://www.thestate.com/opinion/op-ed/article26889922.html.

———. "Furling That Banner: The Rise and Fall of the Confederate Flag in South Carolina, 1961–2000." In *Citizen-Scholar: Essays in Honor of Walter Edgar*, ed. Robert H. Brinkmeyer with the assistance of Evan A. Kutzler, 21–33. Columbia: University of South Carolina Press, 2016.

Kestenbaum, Sam. "Contested Legacy of Dr. Ben, a Father of African Studies." *New York Times*, March 27, 2015, https://www.nytimes.com/2015/03/29/nyregion/contested-legacy-of-dr-ben-a-father-of-african-studies.html?auth=login-email&login=email.

Kiegelmann, Mechthild. "Ethik." In *Handbuch Qualitative Forschung in der Psychologie*, ed. Günter Mey and Katja Mruck, 382–394. Wiesbaden: VS Verlag/Springer, 2010.

Kimball, Catherine D. "State v. Dorsey." September 7, 2011, https://caselaw.findlaw.com/la-supreme-court/1579482.html.

King, Stephen A. *I'm Feeling the Blues Right Now: Blues Tourism and the Mississippi Delta*. Jackson: University Press of Mississippi, 2011.

King, Stephen A., and Roger Davis Gatchet. "Marking the Past: Civil Rights Tourism and the Mississippi Freedom Trail." *Southern Communication Journal* 83, no. 2 (2018): 103–118, doi.org/10.1080/1041794X.2017.1404124.

Klein, Ross A. "Breaking Loose from the Ivory Tower: The Challenges for Academic Researchers with an Activist Agenda in Tourism." Paper presented at the International Critical Tourism Studies Conference V, Sarajevo, Bosnia and Herzegovina, June 25–28, 2013.

Knecht, Phillip. "Boling-Gatewood House." *Hill Country History* (blog), August 13, 2015, https://hillcountryhistory.org/2015/08/13/holly-springs-boling-gatewood-house-1860.

———. "Crump Place." *Hill Country History* (blog), August 30, 2016, https://hillcountryhistory.org/2016/08/30/holly-springs-crump-place-1837.

———. "Herndon." *Hill Country History* (blog), April 8, 2015, https://hillcountryhistory.org/2015/04/08/holly-springs-herndon-1845.

———. "Hugh Craft House (1851)." *Hill Country History* (blog), May 30, 2015, https://hillcountryhistory.org/2015/05/30/holly-springs-hugh-craft-house-1851.

———. "Walter Place." *Hill Country History* (blog), March 29, 2015, https://hillcountryhistory.org/2015/03/29/holly-springs-walter-place-1859-b.

———. "Yellow Fever Martyrs Church and Museum (1841)." *Hill Country History*

(blog), May 23, 2015, https://hillcountryhistory.org/2015/05/23/holly-springs
-yellow-fever-church-1840.

Knight, Michael Muhammad. *The Five Percenters: Islam, Hip Hop and the Gods of New York*. Oxford: Oneworld, 2007.

Kruse, Beth R., Rhondalyn K. Peairs, Jodi Skipper, and Shennette Garrett-Scott. "Remembering Ida, Ida Remembering: Ida B. Wells-Barnett and Black Political Culture in Reconstruction-Era Mississippi." *Southern Cultures: The Women's Issue* 26, no. 3 (Fall 2020): 20–41, doi: 10.1353/scu.2020.0038.

Lawson, Elizabeth. "George Washington Albright." *Daily Worker*, June 18, 1937, http://msgw.org/slaves/albright-xslave.htm.

Legg, John R. "A Romantic Union? Thoughts on Plantation Weddings from a Photographer/Historian." *The NCPH Blog*, February 24, 2020, https://ncph.org/history-at-work/plantation-weddings.

Leggs, Brent. "Expanding the American Story, Clip 3." YouTube, filmed November 18, 2019, at the New York Historical Society, Brookline, https://www.youtube.com/watch?v=u9w5n8486TQ&list=PLAzqpHuQ_QsNx2M9iXpCjg64paDc4cWEj&index=3%3Frel%3Do.

———. "Out of Crisis, an Opportunity." *National Trust for Historic Preservation*, June 11, 2020, https://savingplaces.org/stories/an-opportunity-in-crisis#.X993-NhKg2w.

Lipsitz, George. "Breaking the Chains and Steering the Ship." In *Engaging Contradictions: Theory, Politics, and Methods of Activist Scholarship*, ed. Charles R. Hale, 88–112. Berkeley: University of California Press, 2008.

———. *The Possessive Investment in Whiteness*. Philadelphia: Temple University Press, 1998.

Liu, Michelle. "Dubbed a '21st Century Billy Graham Crusade on Steroids,' Revival Aims to Unite Mississippians." *Mississippi Today*, April 25, 2019, https://mississippitoday.org/2019/04/25/dubbed-a-21st-century-billy-graham-crusade-on-steroids-revival-aims-to-unite-mississippians.

Lloyd, Stephen. "Sacrilisation of Secular Pilgrimages as Archetypal Transformational Journeys: Advancing Theory through Emic and Etic Interpretations." *International Journal of Tourism Anthropology* 4, no. 1 (2015): 25–45, https://doi-org.umiss.idm.oclc.org/10.1504/IJTA.2015.067643.

"Local People Enjoy Garden Pilgrimage." *Lexington Advertiser*, May 4, 1939, https://chroniclingamerica.loc.gov/lccn/sn84024271/1939-05-04/ed-1/seq-5.

Luongo, Michael T. "Despite Everything, People Still Have Weddings at 'Plantation' Sites." *New York Times*, October 17, 2020, https://www.nytimes.com

/2020/10/17/style/despite-everything-people-still-have-weddings-at-plantation
-sites.html.

Maguire, Robert E. "Hustling to Survive: Social and Economic Change in a South
Louisiana Black Creole Community." PhD dissertation, McGill University, 1987.

Mallory, Willie H. *The Strawberry Story: When I Can Read My Title Clear*. Bloom-
ington, Ind.: Xlibris, 2008.

Manning, Patrick. *The African Diaspora: A History through Culture*. New York:
Columbia University Press, 2010.

Marvasti, Amir. "Being Middle Eastern American: Identity Negotiation in the
Context of the War on Terror." *Symbolic Interaction* 28, no. 4 (2006): 525–547.

Marx, Mary Frances. "Hiram Rhodes Revels." In *The Mississippi Encyclopedia*, ed.
Ted Ownby and Charles Reagan Wilson. Jackson: University Press of Mississippi, 2017. Article updated April 15, 2018, http://mississippiencyclopedia.org/
entries/hiram-thoades-revels.

Mary Turner Project. "Remembering Mary Turner." http://www.maryturner.org.

McAlexander, Hubert H. *A Southern Tapestry: Marshall County, Mississippi,
1835–2000*. Virginia Beach, Va.: Donning Company Publishers, 2000.

———. *Strawberry Plains Audubon Center: Four Centuries of a Mississippi Landscape*. Jackson: University Press of Mississippi, 2008.

McAlexander/Marshall County Collection, Finley-Davis Letters, M/MCCA box 9,
location BB-14, 19.1. University of Mississippi Libraries, Department of Archives
and Special Collections, Oxford, Mississippi.

McArthur, Danny. "Leona Harris: Director of Ida B. Wells Museum." *Tupelo Daily
Journal*, December 10, 2019, https://www.djournal.com/news/leona-harris
-director-of-ida-b-wells-museum/article_0540a0ec-819c-5c1f-ad4c-86eb31f9fb
f9.htm.

McGill, Joseph, Jr. "Back of the Big House: Slave Dwelling Project a Stop on Holly
Springs, MS Pilgrimage Tour." *Lowcountry Africana* (blog), April 30, 2012,
http://www.lowcountryafricana.com/back-of-the-big-house-slave-dwelling
-project-a-stop-on-holly-springs-ms-pilgrimage-tour-tour.

———. "We Grew Up Together." *The Slave Dwelling Project* (blog), April 23, 2016,
http://slavedwellingproject.org/we-grew-up-together.

McLeod, Alisea Charmain. "Living Detroit (on the Edge of Disorder): Time and
Space in the Twentieth Century." PhD dissertation, University of Michigan,
1998.

McLeod, Alisea Williams. "Student Digital Research and Writing on Slavery." In
Web Writing: Why and How for Liberal Arts Teaching and Learning, ed. Jack

Dougherty and Tennyson O'Donnell. Ann Arbor: University of Michigan Press, 2016.

McMillen, Neil R. "Feature Story: WPA Slave Narratives." *Mississippi History Now: An Online Publication of the Mississippi Historical Society*, February 2005, http://mshistorynow.mdah.state.ms.us/articles/64.

Miles, Tiya. *Tales from the Haunted South: Dark Tourism and Memories of Slavery from the Civil War Era*. Chapel Hill: University of North Carolina Press, 2015.

Mills, Gary B. *The Forgotten People: Cane River's Creoles of Color*. Baton Rouge: Louisiana State University Press, 1977.

Mississippi Blues Trail. "Mississippi Blues Trail Selection Criteria." http://msblues trail.org/pdfs/MBT_marker_criteria%202018.pdf.

Mississippi Development Authority. "Fiscal Year 2018 Annual Report." December 2018, https://mississippi.org/manage/wp-content/uploads/18-1053-MDA -AnnualReport2018-web.pdf.

———. "Mississippi—Find Your True South." YouTube, 2013, https://www.you tube.com/watch?v=CIdH68Do5uc.

Mississippi Encyclopedia Staff. "Pontotoc County." In *The Mississippi Encyclopedia*, ed. Ted Ownby and Charles Reagan Wilson. Jackson: University Press of Mississippi, 2017.

Mississippi State Government. "Agencies: Visit Mississippi Tourism." https://www .ms.gov/Agencies/visit-mississippi-tourism.

Mitchell, Jerry. "Ole Miss Reflects on the 50 Years since Integration." *Clarion Ledger*, October 1, 2012, https://www.usatoday.com/story/news/nation/2012/09 /30/mississippi-meredith-integration/1602783.

Mitchell, Tania D. "Traditional vs. Critical Service-Learning: Engaging the Literature to Differentiate Two Models." *Michigan Journal of Community Service Learning* 14, no. 2 (Spring 2008): 50–65.

Moore, John Hebron. *The Emergence of the Cotton Kingdom in the Old Southwest: Mississippi, 1770–1860*. Baton Rouge: Louisiana State University Press, 1988.

Newhall, David S. "Chickasaw-European Relations." In *The Mississippi Encyclopedia*, ed. Ted Ownby and Charles Reagan Wilson. Jackson: University Press of Mississippi, 2017.

———. "Chickasaw-U.S. Relations." In *The Mississippi Encyclopedia*, ed. Ted Ownby and Charles Reagan Wilson. Jackson: University Press of Mississippi, 2017.

———. "Chickasaw War." In *The Mississippi Encyclopedia*, ed. Ted Ownby and Charles Reagan Wilson. Jackson: University Press of Mississippi, 2017.

Nicholas, Chani. "Horoscopes for the Full Moon in Aquarius." August 3, 2020, https://mailchi.mp/chaninicholas/new-moon-cancer-908694?e=468ba37829.

Nogués-Pedregal, Antonio Miguel. "Anthropological Contributions to Tourism Studies." *Annals of Tourism Research* 75 (March 2019): 227–237.

Norwood, Ashley. "Mississippi Edition." Interview with Chelius Carter. *Mississippi Public Broadcasting Online*, April 19, 2018, http://mississippiedition.mpbonline.org/episodes/5d892b58673eacfd68155519.

O'Brien, Greg. "Chickasaws: The Unconquerable People." *Mississippi History Now: An Online Publication of the Mississippi Historical Society*, May 2003, http://mshistorynow.mdah.state.ms.us/articles/8/chickasaws-the-unconquerable-people.

Oliver, Sylvester, Jr. "African-Americans in 19th Century Holly Springs." *Holly Springs South Reporter*, March 8, 2007, http://archive.southreporter.com/2007/wk10/sylvester_oliver.html.

O'Meara, KerryAnn. "Encouraging Multiple Forms of Scholarship in Faculty Reward Systems: Have Academic Cultures Really Changed?" *New Directions for Institutional Research*, no. 129 (Spring 2006): 77–95.

"On the Calendar." *Washington Evening Star*, April 13, 1940, https://chroniclingamerica.loc.gov/lccn/sn83045462/1940-04-13/ed-1/seq-12.

Organization of American Historians. "Historical Associations Issue Recommendations about Rewarding Public History Work for Promotion and Tenure." April 8, 2010, https://www.oah.org/insights/archive/historical-associations-issue-recommendations-about-rewarding-public-history-work-for-promotion-and-tenure.

Osler, Jonathan, ed. "Opportunities for White People in the Fight for Racial Justice." https://www.whiteaccomplices.org/your-white-communities.

Ownby, Ted, and Charles Reagan Wilson, eds. *The Mississippi Encyclopedia*. Jackson: University Press of Mississippi, 2017. Published online 2018, https://southernstudies.olemiss.edu/publications/mississippi-encyclopedia.

Pate, James P. "George (Chooshemataha), Levi (Itawamba Mingo), and William (Tootemastubbe) Colbert." In *The Mississippi Encyclopedia*, ed. Ted Ownby and Charles Reagan Wilson. Jackson: University Press of Mississippi, 2017. Updated April 13, 2018, https://mississippiencyclopedia.org/entries/george-levi-and-william-colbert.

"Paved Route to Picturesque Spring Pilgrimages." *Durant News*, February 29, 1940, https://chroniclingamerica.loc.gov/lccn/sn87065228/1940-02-29/ed-1/seq-5.

Perdue, Theda. *"Mixed Blood" Indians: Racial Construction in the Early South*. Athens: University of Georgia Press, 2005.

Pérez-Peña, Richard. "Woman Linked to 1955 Emmett Till Murder Tells Historian Her Claims Were False." *New York Times*, January 27, 2017, https://www.ny times.com/2017/01/27/us/emmett-till-lynching-carolyn-bryant-donham.html.

Pinho, Patricia. "African-American Roots Tourism in Brazil." *Latin American Perspectives* 35, no. 3 (May 2008): 70–86.

Pittman, Ashton. "Gov. Bryant Declares April 'Unity Month,' Not 'Confederate Heritage Month.'" *Jackson Free Press*, April 23, 2019, http://www.jacksonfree press.com/news/2019/apr/23/gov-bryant-declares-april-unity-month-not -confeder.

———. "Tate Reeves Spoke at Event Where 'Yankees' Were Compared to 'Nazis.'" *Jackson Free Press*, February 13, 2019, https://www.jacksonfreepress.com/news /2019/feb/13/tate-reeves-spoke-event-where-yankees-were-compare.

Preserve Arkansas. "Behind the Big House." https://preservearkansas.org/what-we -do/education/behind-the-big-house.

Radishofski, Kathryn. "Last (Un)fair Deal Goin' Down: A Case Study on the Racial Ideologies and Projects Advanced by the Blues Tourism Industry in Clarksdale, Mississippi." Master's thesis, University of Mississippi, 2013.

———. "Last (Un)fair Deal Goin' Down: Blues Tourism and Racial Politics in Clarksdale, Mississippi." In *Navigating Souths: Transdisciplinary Explorations of a U.S. Region*, ed. Michele Grigsby Coffey and Jodi Skipper, 214–226. Athens: University of Georgia Press, 2017.

Reeves, Tate. "FY22 Executive Budget Recommendation." https://mcusercontent .com/08cb3e52aa1308600f84d49ea/files/526c69c0-c141-46ce-b22e-2856c7a1b8 61/FY2022_Governor_Tate_Reeves_EBR.pdf.

Representing Enslavement in Public: Louisiana's Past in the Present. "About." https://representingenslavement.com.

Robinson, Zandria F. "Riots and Rumors of Riots: Lessons from the University of Mississippi." New South Negress, October 15, 2013, https://newsouthnegress .com/lessonslearned.

Rockquemore, Kerry Ann, and Tracey Laszloffy. *The Black Academic's Guide to Winning Tenure—Without Losing Your Soul.* Boulder, Colo.: Lynne Rienner, 2008.

Rogers, Justin. "Constructing and Crossing Color Lines: Race and Religion in the Southern Confluence, 1810–1865." PhD dissertation, University of Mississippi, 2019.

Ronai, Carol R. "Multiple Reflections of Child Sex Abuse." *Journal of Contemporary Ethnography* 23, no. 4 (1995): 395–426.

———. "My Mother Is Mentally Retarded." In *Composing Ethnography: Alternative*

Forms of Qualitative Writing, ed. Carolyn Ellis and Arthur P. Bochner, 109–131. Walnut Creek, Calif.: AltaMira Press, 1996.

Rosen, Joel Nathan. "Mound Bayou." In *The Mississippi Encyclopedia*, ed. Ted Ownby and Charles Reagan Wilson. Jackson: University Press of Mississippi, 2017.

Sather-Wagstaff, Joy. "Heritage and Memory." In *The Palgrave Handbook of Contemporary Heritage Research*, ed. Emma Waterton and Steve Watson, 191–204. London: Palgrave Macmillan, 2015.

Severson, Kim. "New Museums to Shine a Spotlight on Civil Rights Era." *New York Times*, February 19, 2012, https://www.nytimes.com/2012/02/20/us/african-american-museums-rising-to-recognize-civil-rights.html.

Shackel, Paul A. *Memory in Black and White: Race, Commemoration, and the Post-Bellum Landscape.* Walnut Creek, Calif.: AltaMira Press, 2003.

Skipper, Jodi. "Community Development through Reconciliation Tourism: The Behind the Big House Program in Holly Springs, Mississippi." *Community Development* 47, no. 4 (2016): 514–529, doi.org/10.1080/15575330.2016.1146783.

———. "Hidden in Plain Sight: Contested Histories and Urban Slavery in Mississippi." In *Challenging History: Race, Equity, and the Practice of Public History*, ed. Leah Worthington, Rachel Clare Donaldson, and John W. White, 73–92. Columbia: University of South Carolina Press, 2021.

Skipper, Jodi, and Suzanne R. Davidson. "The Big House as Home: Roots Tourism and Slavery in the U.S." *International Journal of Tourism Anthropology* 6, no. 4 (2018): 390–410, doi: 10.1504/IJTA.2018.096372.

Skipper, Jodi, Kathryn Green, and Rico D. Chapman. "Public History, Diversity, and Higher Education: Three Case Studies on the African American Past." In *Navigating Souths: Transdisciplinary Explorations of a U.S. Region*, ed. Michele Grigsby Coffey and Jodi Skipper, 101–122. Athens: University of Georgia Press, 2017.

Skipper, Jodi, and James M. Thomas. "Plantation Tours." *Contexts: Sociology for the Public* 19, no. 2 (Spring 2020): 64–67, doi.org/10.1177/1536504220920199.

Small, Stephen. "Still Back of the Big House: Slave Cabins and Slavery in Southern Heritage Tourism." *Tourism Geographies: An International Journal of Tourism Space, Place and Environment* 15, no. 3 (2013): 405–423.

Smith, Barbara. "Doing Research on Black American Women." *Radical Teacher*, no. 3 (1976): 25–27.

Smith, Chesley Thorne. *Childhood in Holly Springs: A Memoir.* Lafayette, Calif.: Thomas Berryhill Press, 1996.

Smith, Laurajane. *Uses of Heritage.* London: Routledge, 2006.

Southern Claims Commission Approved Claims. "Cato Govan." December 20, 1865, Claim 3394, National Archives.

Southern Foodways Alliance. "Smith Fellows." https://www.southernfoodways .org/award-categories/smith-symposium-fellows/#:~:text=In%202014%2C%20 the%20SFA%20selected,southern%20region%20and%20its%20foodways.

Spry, Tami. "Performing Autoethnography: An Embodied Methodological Praxis." *Qualitative Inquiry* 7, no. 6 (December 2001): 706–732.

Staggs, Sean. "Confederate Flag Removed from Caddo Courthouse Overnight." *KSLANews12*, November 4, 2011, https://www.ksla.com/story/15959929/ confederate-flag-already-gone-from-caddo-courthouse.

Stewart, Cailyn Petrona. "The Mule of the World: The Strong Black Woman and the Woes of Being 'Independent.'" *Knots: An Undergraduate Journal of Disability Studies* 3 (2017): 31–39, https://jps.library.utoronto.ca/index.php/knots/ article/view/29187/21755.

St. Louis Convention and Visitors Commission. "Explore St. Louis." https://explorestlouis.com.

Supreme Court of the United States. "Docket No. 11-8470." https://www.supreme court.gov/search.aspx?filename=/docketfiles/11-8470.htm.

Swain, Martha, and Roger D. Tate, Jr. "Great Depression." In *The Mississippi Encyclopedia*, ed. Ted Ownby and Charles Reagan Wilson. Jackson: University Press of Mississippi, 2017.

Swearer Center at Brown University. "The Carnegie Foundation for the Advancement of Teaching, 2020 Classification Carnegie Elective Community Engagement Classification, First-Time Classification Documentation Framework." January 22, 2018, https://www.brown.edu/academics/college/swearer/2020 -carnegie-classification-cycle-launches-swearer-center-jan-22.

Tell, Dave. *Remembering Emmett Till.* Chicago: University of Chicago Press, 2019.

Thomas, Lynell L. *Desire and Disaster in New Orleans: Tourism, Race, and Historical Memory.* Durham, N.C.: Duke University Press, 2014.

Thomas, Rhondda Robinson. *Call My Name, Clemson: Documenting the Black Experience in an American University Community.* Iowa City: University of Iowa Press, 2020.

Thompson, Netty Fant. "Lizzie Fant Brown." In *The American Slave: A Composite Autobiography*, supplement, series 1, vol. 6, Mississippi Narratives, part 1, Contributions in Afro-American and African Studies, no. 35, ed. George P. Rawick, Jan Hillegas, and Ken Lawrence, 257–261. Westport, Conn.: Greenwood Press, 1978.

———. "Belle Caruthers." In *The American Slave: A Composite Autobiography*, supplement, series 1, vol. 7, Mississippi Narratives, part 2, Contributions in Afro-American and African Studies, no. 35, ed. George P. Rawick, Jan Hillegas, and Ken Lawrence, 364–368. Westport, Conn.: Greenwood Press, 1978.

———. "Liza McGhee." In *The American Slave: A Composite Autobiography*, supplement, series 1, vol. 9, Mississippi Narratives, part 4, Contributions in Afro-American and African Studies, no. 35, ed. George P. Rawick, Jan Hillegas, and Ken Lawrence, 1402–1404. Westport, Conn.: Greenwood Press, 1977.

———. "Alice Shaw." In *The American Slave: A Composite Autobiography*, supplement, series 1, vol. 10, Mississippi Narratives, part 5, Contributions in Afro-American and African Studies, no. 35, ed. George P. Rawick, Jan Hillegas, and Ken Lawrence, 1920–1924. Westport, Conn.: Greenwood Press, 1977.

Tillmann, Lisa M. "Body and Bulimia Revisited: Reflections on 'A Secret Life.'" *Journal of Applied Communication Research* 37, no. 1 (2009): 98–112.

Tillmann-Healy, Lisa M. *Between Gay and Straight: Understanding Friendship across Sexual Orientation*. Walnut Creek, Calif.: AltaMira Press, 2001.

Timothy, Dallen J., and Stephen W. Boyd. "Heritage Tourism in the 21st Century: Valued Traditions and New Perspectives." *Journal of Heritage Tourism* 1, no. 1 (2006): 1–16.

Travel South USA. "Showcase History: Celebrating 38 Years of Travel South Showcase." https://industry.travelsouthusa.com/travel-south-showcase/showcase-history.

Trouillot, Michel Rolph. *Silencing the Past: Power and the Production of History*. Boston: Beacon Press, 1995.

Twitty, Michael W. *The Cooking Gene: A Journey through African American Culinary History in the Old South*. New York: Amistad, 2017.

———. "An Open Letter to Paula Deen." *Afroculinaria*, June 25, 2013, https://afroculinaria.com/2013/06/25/an-open-letter-to-paula-deen.

United States Census Bureau. "QuickFacts: Claremont City, California." https://www.census.gov/quickfacts/claremontcitycalifornia.

United States National Archives and Records Administration. "Southern Claims Commission Records." Military Records, https://www.archives.gov/research/military/civil-war/southern-claims-commission.

University of Mississippi. "Community and Service." https://olemiss.edu/community.html.

———. "UM/2020 Strategic Plan." https://hesrm.olemiss.edu/wp-content/uploads/sites/3/2015/02/2.01.02_UM2020_Final_Print.pdf.

Visit Mississippi Travel Blog. "Find Your True South in Mississippi." January 6,

2011, http://visitmississippi.blogspot.com/2011/01/find-your-true-south-in
-mississippi.html.

Vlach, John Michael. *Back of the Big House: The Architecture of Plantation Slavery.* Chapel Hill: University of North Carolina Press, 1993.

Wade, Lisa. "Sociological Images: The Ragin' Cajuns." *Society Pages,* January 14, 2010, https://thesocietypages.org/socimages/2010/01/14/the-ragin-cajuns.

Walter, Ronald A. "Robert R. Church Sr." In *The Tennessee Encyclopedia of History and Culture.* Knoxville: Tennessee Historical Society, 2017.

Washburn, Jeffrey D. "Chickasaw Gender Roles and Slavery during the Plan for Civilization." U.S. Studies Online, November 2, 2015, https://usso.uk/chickasaw -gender-roles-and-slavery-during-the-plan-for-civilization.

———. "Directing Their Own Change." *Native South* 13 (2020): 94–119.

———. "Labor in the Field Is Much Changed: The Chickasaws and the Civiliza- tion Plan, 1790–1837." PhD dissertation, University of Mississippi, 2020. Under embargo until August 31, 2022.

Watson, Sue. "New Group Focuses on Healing Wounds of History." *Holly Springs South Reporter,* October 17, 2013.

Wells, Carlie Kollath. "Barbour: Mississippi Is 'Birthplace of America's Music.'" *Tupelo Daily Journal,* May 13, 2009, https://www.djournal.com/news/business/ barbour-mississippi-is-birthplace-of-america-s-music/article_3e497a1f-84bc-5e 26-92cb-c3136146d9e8.html.

Wendt, LeeAnne J. "Understanding Strawberry Plains through Landscape Archae- ology." Master's thesis, University of Mississippi, 2014.

Whitfield, Stephen J. "Emmett Till." In *The Mississippi Encyclopedia,* ed. Ted Ownby and Charles Reagan Wilson. Jackson: University Press of Mississippi, 2017.

Wickham, Kathleen Woodruff. "William Raspberry." In *The Mississippi Encyclo- pedia,* ed. Ted Ownby and Charles Reagan Wilson. Jackson: University Press of Mississippi, 2017. Article updated April 17, 2018, http://mississippiencyclopedia .org/entries/william-raspberry.

Wilder, Craig Steven. *Ebony and Ivy: Race, Slavery, and the Troubled History of America's Universities.* New York: Bloomsbury, 2013.

Wilson, Charles Reagan. "The Religion of the Lost Cause: Ritual and Organization of the Southern Civil Religion, 1865–1920." *Journal of Southern History* 46, no. 2 (1980): 219–238.

Yamamura, Erica K., and Kent Koth. *Place-Based Community Engagement in Higher Education: A Strategy to Transform Universities and Communities.* Ster- ling, Va.: Stylus Publishing, 2018.

Yellow Fever Martyrs Church and Museum. "The Church Episcopalian Beginnings." https://yellowfevermartyrs.com/church.

Yiga, Eugene. "How the Black Travel Movement Is Gaining Momentum." *CNN Travel*, August 4, 2019, https://edition.cnn.com/travel/article/black-travel -movement/index.html?utm_sq=g5oefsr3t7.

Zivi, Karen D. "Reflections on Integrating Service Learning into the Curriculum." In *Experiencing Citizenship: Concepts and Models for Service-Learning in Political Science*, ed. Richard M. Battistoni and William E. Hudson, 49–67. Sterling, Va.: Stylus Publishing, 1997.

Zucchino, David. *Wilmington's Lie: The Murderous Coup of 1898 and the Rise of White Supremacy*. New York: Atlantic Monthly Press, 2020.

Index

Abrams, Jasmine, 131
academic service, 127–28, 131–33, 135, 139, 152–53. *See also* service-learning
Acadiana, 2
activism, 3, 9, 110, 127, 139; anthropological, 1, 129, 140; antiracist, 82; anti-lynching, 102, 175n60; civil rights, 55, 102, 175n60; grassroots heritage, 47, 103; scholarly, 129–30, 135–36, 153
Africa, 4, 58, 89, 107, 111, 112, 170n5; libation ceremonies, 101, 106–07; and food, 70–75, 120; West, 31–32, 72, 73, 99. *See also* pan-Africanism
African American Islamic Institute, 35
African Americans, 4, 89, 96, 111, 147–48, 179, 182n47; and blues tourism, 25; and heritage tourism, 11, 28–39, 63–64, 75, 88, 103–06, 116; and Jewish communities, 138; and racism, 85, 159–60; representations of, 97, 101; and slavery, 22, 55, 72, 91, 147; students, 67–68. *See also* African American Cultural Heritage Action Fund; African American Islamic Institute; College of Charleston Avery Research Center for African American History and Culture; Marshall County African American Living History Association; National Trust for Historic Preservation; Smithsonian National Museum of African American History and Culture
African Burial Ground project, 10
African diaspora, 2–3, 58, 82; and anthropology, 7; courses on, 62, 64, 66–70, 153; and food, 70–75, 120; and Mississippi, 28
African Heritage Studies Association, 182n43, 183n54
African Studies Association, 183n54

African/Africana studies, 182n41, 182n43, 183n54
Afrocentrism, 4–5, 82, 107, 182n41
Aiken, William, 115
Aiken-Rhett House, 115
Albright, George Washington, 103
Alcorn University, 148
Alderman, Derek, 11, 19
Amen, Ra Un Nefer, 107
American Anthropological Association, 140; Anthropology of Tourism Interest Group, 172n13
American Blues Scene, 26
American Civil Liberties Union (ACLU), xvi–xvii
American Civil War Center at Historic Tredegar, 143
American Missionary Association, 59
"American Way," 18–19
Ames Plantation Heritage Festival, 104
Amistad Defense Committee, 59
ancestor veneration, 107
Ancestry.com, 98
Anderson, Jeramey, 16
Annie's Home Cooking, 69, 104
anthropology, 62, 107, 150–51; activist, 1, 129, 140; four-fields approach, 7; public, 80; students of, 32, 64–66, 118–19; of tourism, 20, 40, 140, 172nn12–13; university departments, 5, 11, 127, 130–33, 146
anti-racism, 27, 139
apartheid, 1, 4. *See also* racial segregation
Arbery, Ahmaud Marquez, 18
archaeology, 114, 119, 131, 133, 153; archaeozoology, 66; excavations, 6, 9–10, 65, 97, 114, 129–30, 146; historical, 7, 20, 23, 65, 97; plantation, 5–6; public, 7, 11, 21, 46,

Kellogg Foundation, 118–19
Kelly, Abe, 41
Kemetic Institute, 106
Kikuyu language, 106
King, Martin Luther, Jr., 19, 135
King, Stephen, 25, 27, 40, 81, 171n11
Kirkwood National Golf Club, 117
Kiswahili language, 106
Koth, Kent, 74
Ku Klux Klan (KKK), 29, 86
Kumba, Guelel, 31

Labode, Modupe, 150
Lafayette County, MS, 57, 147–48, 166
Lafayette Oxford Community Archive and
    Legacy group (LOCAL), 147–48
Laszloffy, Tracey, 132–33
Leggs, Brent, 159
Leonard, Sarah, 100
Lesueur, Chester, 116
libation ceremonies, 101, 103, 105–07, 118–19
Library of Congress, 41, 61
Lincoln, Abraham, 42
Lindsay, Madge, 93
Lost Cause southern mythology, 12, 158
Louisiana, 2, 10, 22, 96, 124, 131, 147, 149, 158,
    170n3; Acadiana, 2; Lafayette, 1, 3–4, 57,
    81–82, 169n3; Natchitoches Parish, 5; New
    Orleans, 9, 23, 27, 44, 179n52; St. Martin
    Parish, 5. See also *State of Louisiana v.
    Felton D. Dorsey*
Louisiana Association of Criminal Defense
    Lawyers, 169n4
Louisiana Supreme Court, 169n4
Louisville, KY, 18
Lounsbury, Carl, 146
Lucas, Annie R. Moffitt, 69, 104
lynching, 7–8, 25, 89–90, 102, 108, 175n60; of
    Emmett Till, 19, 23, 29, 57, 100, 160, 172n20

Magnolias, 62–64, 67–68, 178n28
Maguire, Robert, 4–5
Mallory, Willie, 61
Manning, Patrick, 73
Mardi Gras, 23
Marrinan, Rochelle, 5

Marsh, Allison, 150
Marshall, Matt, 26
Marshall County, MS, 61, 73, 96–98, 108,
    116–17; race in, 86, 88; slavery in, 36,
    40–43, 55, 74, 92, 103–05; tourism in, 38,
    40–41. *See also* Marshall County African
    American Living History Association;
    Marshall County Board of Supervisors;
    Marshall County Democratic Executive
    Committee; Marshall County Genealog-
    ical Society; Marshall County Library;
    Preserve Marshall County and Holly
    Springs, Inc.
Marshall County African American Living
    History Association, 103–04
Marshall County Board of Supervisors, 111
Marshall County Democratic Executive
    Committee, 111
Marshall County Genealogical Society, 97
Marshall County Library, 98
Marshall County School District, 63
Martin, Trayvon, 57
Martinique, 2
Maryland, 120; Baltimore, 4, 145, 150
Maryland Historical Society, 120
material culture, 5, 11, 114, 130, 136, 160
Maxwell, Morgan, 131
Mayan culture, 65
McCarroll Place, 45, 61–63, 178n28
McCorkle, Sam, 51
McCrosky, Marjorie, 37
McEwen, Annie, 148
McEwen, Earnest, Jr., 148
McGhee, Fred, 9, 21, 129
McGhee, Liza, 41–42
McGill, Joseph "Joe," Jr., 36, 55–56, 59, 61–62,
    69–71, 75–76, 79, 117, 145–46. *See also*
    Slave Cabin/Dwelling Project
McLeod, Alisea Williams, 65, 86–87, 94–99,
    116, 119–23
McLeod Plantation, 158
Medgar Evers House, 35
Medu Neter language, 106
Melrose Estate, 19, 114
Memphis Free Speech, 102
mentorship, 131, 133–35

North Carolina, 92, 100; Polk County, 160
nostalgia, 19, 27, 37, 40, 58, 78, 85, 90, 118

Obama, Barack, 86, 141
O'Connell Spanish mission site, 5
Okolona, MS, 96
Oliver, Sylvester, 103, 105, 181n30
O'Neal, Jim, 25–26
oral history, 20, 57, 59–60
Oren Dunn City Museum, 56
outbuildings, 44
Ownby, Ted, 143
Oxford, MS, 15, 29, 31–32, 36, 50, 56, 58,
    69–70, 90, 139; historic sites in, 166;
    race in, 24, 134–35, 146, 147–48. *See also*
    Lafayette Oxford Community Archive
    and Legacy group (LOCAL); University of
    Mississippi

pan-Africanism, 107
Panic of 1857, 50
Parents for Public Schools: Parents' Leader-
    ship Institute, 57
Patriotic Education Fund, 18
Patton, Alco "Al," 123
PBS, 23, 99
PBS Scientific American Frontiers: "Unearth-
    ing Secret America," 23
Peairs, Rhondalyn, 31, 50, 57, 80, 100, 148;
    Making History Last workshop, 56
Person, David, 45, 112–13, 148; and Gracing
    the Table, 65, 85–94, 99–101, 104–05, 116,
    119, 122–23, 167
Petty, Mrs., 89–90, 113
Phoenix, AZ, 160
pilgrimage tourism, 58, 112; in Holly Springs,
    37–42, 44–45, 54–57, 60–64, 74, 77, 81, 87,
    92–93, 116–18; in Natchez, 37–40, 124,
    174n55
plantations, 20, 23, 32, 68, 72, 92–93, 98, 108,
    157; histories of, 43–44; and museums, 22;
    plantation archaeology, 5–6; plantation
    songs, 39; postplantation societies, 5; as
    tourist sites, 22, 35, 39–40, 58–62, 75, 104,
    158, 178n28
Pocahontas, MS, 29

Poland, 89
police violence, 18, 157, 159
Polk Place, 62, 178n28
Pope, Michell, 131
possessive investment in whiteness, 144
postplantation societies, 5
Preservation South Carolina, 36
Preserve Arkansas, 46
Preserve Marshall County and Holly
    Springs, Inc., 36, 54–55, 63, 70, 74, 76, 88,
    117, 149
Presley, Elvis, 23
Pride, Charlie, 35
Prince Among Slaves, 99
Project in Interpreting the Texas Past, 8, 130
public anthropology, 80
public archaeology, 7, 11, 21, 46, 97, 129–30,
    136, 140, 151
public engagement, 76, 149, 150–52.
    See also community engage-
    ment; community-based research;
    service-learning
public history, 7, 11, 21, 23, 82, 115, 150; and
    Behind the Big House, 64, 67, 74, 87. *See
    also* National Council on Public History;
    Transforming Public History from
    Charleston to the Atlantic World confer-
    ence; University of Louisiana at Lafayette
public humanities, 150–52
public scholarship, 127–54

racial battle fatigue, 145
racial reconciliation, 5, 15, 82, 180n2; and
    Behind the Big House, 69, 77–78, 119; and
    blues tourism, 24–25, 28; and civil right
    tourism, 100; and Gracing the Table, 65,
    85–124. *See also* William Winter Institute
    for Racial Reconciliation
racial segregation, 1, 3, 10, 22, 27, 53, 108–09,
    165. *See also* apartheid; Jim Crow
racialization, 7
racism, 3, 70, 82, 102, 108–10; and academia,
    131–49; antiracism, 7, 94, 139; and blues
    tourism, 25–27; and Confederate symbol-
    ism, 6, 16, 35, 36, 85–86, 142–45, 159–60,
    166, 169n4; internalized, 1–2; and racial